INSIGHT GUIDES

Created and Directed by Hans Höfer

aRGENTINA

Project Editor: Deirdre Ball
Editorial Director: Brian Bell

Houghton Mifflin

APA PUBLICATIONS

The one thing you can be sure of with Argentina is that one person's generalisation is unlikely to match another's. Buenos Aires has been variously described as the Paris of South America, or a "most civilized anthill" (Paul Theroux). Argentina is a nation gripped by psychoses, says writer John Gunther; more like Australia than Peru, wrote J. H. Ferguson.

Even local authors acknowledge its diversity. "Our entire country is imported; everyone here is really from somewhere else," said Jorge Luis Borges. The local saying used to run that "an Argentine is an Italian who speaks Spanish, thinks he's French, but would like to be English" – although these days the latter no longer applies.

Such a destination lends itself to the approach taken by the 190-title *Insight Guides* series, created in 1970 by **Hans Höfer**, founder of Apa Publications and still the company's driving force. Each book encourages the reader to celebrate the essence of the place rather than try to tailor it to their expectations and is edited in the belief that, without insight into a people's character and culture, travel can narrow the mind rather than broaden it.

Insight Guide: Argentina is carefully structured: the first section covers the nation's history, and then analyzes its culture in a series of magazine-style essays. The main Places section provides a run-down on the things worth seeing and doing. Finally, a listings section contains useful addresses, telephone numbers and opening times.

Höfer

The original edition of this book was the first foray for Apa into the South American continent. Many titles have been added since then, and this book has been extensively revised.

The original project editor, **Deirdre Ball**, was working in Buenos Aires as a freelance writer and teacher of English. Raised in Beirut and educated at Yale University, Ball has lived and worked as an editor and journalist in Montana and Cairo, and now lives in São Paulo, Brazil. She assembled a team of outstanding Argentine writers and photographers.

Ball reserved for herself the chapters on geography (From Jungles to Glaciers), people (In Search of a National Identity), the west (Cuyo) and gauchos (Orphans of the Pampas).

The Prehistory chapter was written by the Argentine archaeologist **Elena Decima**. Decima has worked on digs throughout South and Central America, including the Tunel site on Tierra del Fuego. She also wrote the chapter on the Córdoba.

Argentina's long and complicated history after the arrival of the Spanish was covered by **Philip Benson**, who has taught history in East Jerusalem, Cairo and Buenos Aires. Since completing a Masters at Brown University, he has been teaching in São Paulo. He also compiled the chapter of travelers' accounts of Argentina.

Tony Perrottet brought his deft journalistic touch to the contemporary history piece. Raised and educated in Australia, Perrottet has worked as a stringer for various Australian, British and US newspapers, and he went on to manage Apa's other titles on the South American continent.

The daunting task of detailing Buenos Aires in the Places section was undertaken by **Patricia Pittman** who has been involved in Latin American affairs since her student days at Yale University. She first went to Argentina in 1982 on a one-year grant to work with a human rights organization and now works there as a consultant and writer.

The pieces on the tango and the economy were written by journalist **Judith Evans**. Evans received a Masters

Benson

Pittman

Ball

Foster

Kirbus

in history from the University of California at Berkeley, and has worked in Buenos Aires as a correspondent off and on since 1972.

Buenos Aires-based food and wine critic **Dereck Foster** wrote the pieces on dining out and wine. Foster has been a columnist for the *Buenos Aires Herald*. His published books include *The Argentines, how they live and work*, and *The Wines of Argentina.*

Journalist, explorer and publisher **Federico Kirbus** wrote the chapters on the Atlantic Coast and the Northwest. He operates the *Adventurismo* tour company and writes travel articles.

Another contributor whose articles are based on long years in the field is **Maurice Rumboll** (wildlife and the Northeast). Educated in Argentina, England and Scotland, he worked for many years in the Argentine national park service.

Goodall

P. Jones

The chapter on Patagonia was written by Bariloche-based authors, **Hans Schulz, Carol Jones** and **Edith Jones.** Schulz is an anthropologist who manages Polvani Tours. Carol Jones' family moved to Patagonia from Texas in the 19th century.

The piece on the Welsh was written by **Parry Jones**, a Welshman who lives in Bucks County, Pennsylvania.

The article on Tierra del Fuego was written by **Rae Natalie Prosser Goodall** who moved to Argentina in 1963, after receiving degrees from Kent State University (Ohio) in education and biology. She is a researcher in Ushuaia, specializing in marine mammals, and has also completed several studies of the flora and fauna of the islands.

The sports editor of the *Buenos Aires Herald*, **Eric Weil**, was the co-author of the Sports feature. Co-author **Doug Cress**, a journalist based in Los Angeles, worked for many years at *The Washington Post.*

The grueling task of compiling the Travel Tips was accomplished by **Hazel McCleary**, who worked for several years at Cosmopolitan Tours based in Buenos Aires.

Nearly a quarter of the photos were contributed by **The Photoworks**, which is directed by the photographer **Alex Ocampo**. The co-founder of The Photoworks, the late **Roberto Bunge** is represented and remembered with many fine, and often rare, photos.

Nearly all of the archival material and many of the Buenos Aires photos were shot by **Fiora Bemporad**, a professional working in Buenos Aires.

More photos, including most of the delightful wildlife shots, were taken by **Roberto Cinti** and **Carlos Passera**, at the **Photohunters** agency. **Focus**, an agency founded by **Marcelo Brodsky**, was the source for many shots by a group of up-and-coming professionals.

Jorge Schulte contributed photos of the northwest. Other Argentine photographers included are **Eduardo Gil, Pablov Cottescus, Arlette Neyens, Gabriel Bendersky** and **Ricardo Trabucco** (who are all based in Bariloche) and **Natalie** and **Thomas Goodall** (Ushuaia). The work of New York photographers **Don Boroughs** and **Joe Hooper** are also represented.

T his latest extensive update of the book is the work of contributors co-ordinated by **Andrew Eames** at Insight's London office. **Bonnie Tucker**, travel and news editor for the *Buenos Aires Herald*, revised the essays and some Places chapters. **Rachel Raney**, freelance television producer, looked after selected Places chapters, inclucing the all-important section on Buenos Aires. **Natalie Goodall** revised Tierra del Fuego and Patagonia, the latter with the input of **Claudio Campagna**.

New pictures for this edition came from Buenos Aires-based **Eduardo Gil**.

Rumboll

Weil

Raney

CONTENTS

Preceding pages: portrait of tango singer Carlos Gardel; a gaucho chats to his *china* in an early 19th-century painting.

WELCOME TO ARGENTINA

Some of Argentina's characteristics are world-famous, while its other charms have gone unheralded. Everyone knows it is the home of the tango, but almost no one is aware that the highest peak in the Americas, Aconcagua, lies on its western border; Argentine beef is world-renowned, but few have heard about the rare glacial formations of the Lake District; and while the name Tierra del Fuego is familiar to most, not many know that Ushuaia, on its lower shore, is the southernmost town in the world.

Beyond the sophisticated metropolis of Buenos Aires, rough-riding gauchos, and the wide open spaces of Patagonia and the pampas, Argentina will astonish the visitor with fine wines, jungle waterfalls, colonial cities and penguin colonies. One can create a vacation here with activities as diverse as horseback trekking in the Andes and gambling in a seaside casino. There are polo matches, ski tournaments, German Oktoberfests and Welsh Eisteddfods.

While certain attractions in Argentina have long been appreciated by select groups, such as climbers in search of a challenge and ornithologists pursuing filled-out life lists, the country has gone virtually undiscovered by the traveling world at large. Argentina is enough off the beaten track that one can romp on the resort beaches surrounded only by Argentines, and it is possible, on a lucky day, to have a national park all to oneself.

As the visitor goes about enjoying the refinements of Buenos Aires or the natural beauties of the interior, he or she should make a point of meeting Argentines along the way. An afternoon spent chatting with a bunch of spirited *porteños* in a café, or talking horses with a seasoned gaucho in Patagonia, will help one to appreciate the Argentines' unique culture, of which they are justifiably proud.

Preceding pages: the Patagonia express; the Moreno Glacier, Glaciers National Park; Iguazú Falls; late afternoon on the Pampa; Mount Fitz Roy in Santa Cruz. Left, couple dancing the tango.

Subtropical forests: The isolated northeast reaches of Argentina is referred to as Mesopotamia, as most of it lies between the Paraná and Uruguay Rivers. The whole area is crosscut by rivers and streams, and a great deal of the land here is marshy and low. The region receives a lot of rainfall.

The southern sector, with its swamps and low, rolling hills, has an economy supported by sheep farming, horse breeding and cattle raising. This is one of the major wool-producing areas of the country.

Towards the north, the climate becomes subtropical and very humid. The economy here is based on agriculture, with the principal crops being *yerba mate* (a form of tea)

feet) through the lush subtropical forest.

The hunting ground: The north-central part of Argentina is called the Chaco. It is the southern sector of the Gran Chaco, which extends into Bolivia, Paraguay and Brazil, and which borders on the north with Brazil's Mato Grosso region. In the local dialect, *chaco* means "hunting ground," and across this wide and largely undeveloped region there are many forms of wildlife that would justify the name.

The area is covered by flat jungle plains and the drier chaqueña savanna, and the climate ranges from the tropical to the subtropical. The Chaco lies within the Río de la Plata river basin, and although it is dry much

and various types of fruit. Enormous tracts of the virgin forest have been lost to a lumber business that has become increasingly important to the Argentine economy.

Towards the northern tip of Misiones, a plateau of sandstone and basalt rises from the lowlands. The landscape here is characterized by a rough relief combined with fast-running rivers. Along Argentina's northern border with Brazil sits the magnificent Iguazú Falls, which has more than 275 separate cascades dropping over 60 meters (200

of the year, the summer rains always cause extensive flooding.

The forests of the area contain high quality hard woods, and lumbering has become a major industry. In the cleared areas of the forest, cotton is grown and there is some ranching. One of the region's most important economic activities is the harvesting of the quebracho tree. This tree produces a resin used in the tanning of leather, and fine leathers are a major by-product of the cattle industry in Argentina.

High desert: Going west from the Chaco, one reaches the plateau region of the northwest, where the bordering Andes create an

Left, a rainbow over the Pampa. **Above**, going upriver in Mesopotamia.

arid or semi-arid environment over much of the terrain. Here the elevation rises steadily until it reaches the altiplano (high plateau) on Argentina's northern border with Bolivia. Along this stretch, the Andes are divided into two parallel *cordilleras* (ranges), the Salta-Jueña to the west and the Sierra Subandinas to the east.

The Puna is a dry cold desert that stretches over the Andes, north from the province of Catamarca towards Bolivia and covers part of northern Chile as well. Here the population, largely of mestizo stock, raises goats, sheep and llamas.

Further to the east, the climate across much of the provinces of Tucumán, Salta

and Jujuy is mountain tropical, with mild winters. Along with cattle ranching, there are vineyards, olive and citrus groves, and tobacco and sugar cane plantations. Vegetable farms lie in the valleys and piedmonts.

Grapes and oil: The central western section of Argentina, comprising the provinces of San Juan, Mendoza and San Luis is known as the Cuyo. The Andes here become a single towering range, with many peaks over 6,600 meters (21,780 feet). West of the city of Mendoza lies Aconcagua, at 6,980 meters (23,034 feet) the highest peak in the Western Hemisphere. Just south of Aconagua is the Uspsallata Pass, the *Camino de los Andes*,

which at its highest point of 3,800 meters (12,540 feet), crosses over into Chile.

Fingers of desert extend eastward from the glacial mountains down into the plains. Much of the land here is dry and wind-eroded, and dotted with scrub vegetation. Rivers nourished by the melting snows of the Andes cut through the desert.

It is these rivers which, with the help of extensive irrigation, allow for large scale agriculture in the region. The Cuyo is the heart of Argentina's wine country; the arid climate, sandy soil, and year-round sunshine makes this ideal for viticulture. Citrus fruits are also grown.

The Cuyo area is blessed with mineral wealth. Copper, lead and uranium are mined, and oil discovered here and in Patagonia has made Argentina nearly self-sufficient in that vital resource.

Open steppe: South of the Rio Colorado, covering more than a quarter of Argentina, is Patagonia, where a series of dry plateaus drop from the Andes towards the rugged cliffs of the Atlantic coast. The Patagonian Andes are lower than those to the north, and are dotted with lakes, meadows, and glaciers. Many of the slopes are forested.

The central steppes are battered by sharp winds, and towards the south these winds become nearly constant. The terrain has been eroded by these winds as well as by rivers and glaciers.

In the low, wide river valleys of northern Patagonia, fruit and vegetable farming is made possible with irrigation. Towards the south, the rivers run through deep, flat-bottomed canyons. Although there is rainfall throughout most of the year, the climate is cold and doesn't allow for much vegetation. The plains are covered by grasses, shrubs and a few hardy trees. Sheep raising is the major economic activity.

To the south, between the Strait of Magellan and the Beagle Channel, lies Tierra del Fuego. The climate here is subantarctic, despite its name, and although that sounds rather intimidating, it could be worse, given the latitude. The nearness of the Atlantic and the Pacific waters helps to moderate the temperatures somewhat, and some parts of the island are quite green.

Left, giant cardones cactus of the Northwest. **Right**, Cerro Torre, in Glacier National Park.

area received the influences that diffused from Bolivia (during the peak of the Tiahuanaco empire) and Peru (especially during the expansion of the Inca empire, which incorporated northwestern Argentina within its great realm).

The early 16th century found the natives of the northwest living in architecturally simple stone houses, in towns with populations that might have reached 3,000 people in some cases, making this area the most densely populated.

Many of the towns were walled, located on hilltops for defense purposes, and had their own ceremonial buildings. Intensive agriculture and irrigation was practised every-

The Central Mountains and the region around Santiago del Estero was a less developed area. Small villages existed in this region, in some cases with semi-subterranean houses. Though agriculture was practised, hunting and gathering still played an important role. Ceramics were made but were rather crude, and little to no metal was worked in the area. Many of the metal pieces were imported from the Northwest.

Fish and nomads: Life in the northeastern region of Argentina had many of the characteristics of that in the Central Mountains except that the presence of two major rivers, the Paraná and the Uruguay, added a new dimension in the Northeastern economies:

where and domestic animals, mostly camelids like the llama and alpaca, were widely used by the people.

Most of the arts had reached a high level of development by the 16th century; good ceramics, wood carvings, excellent metalworking (mostly consisting of copper and bronze pieces) and stone sculptures have been found, relics of the different groups living in the area. Tribes and confederations of tribes were the units of political organization.

Preceding pages: the Cueva de las Manos, in Santa Cruz. **Left**, ruins of a Quilmes Indian settlement, Tucumán. **Above**, ancient stone tools.

fishing. Though pottery was known, metallurgy seems to have been absent. Unfortunately this is one of the less archaeologically studied areas.

The last region, which encompasses the southern half of the country from southern Santa Fe and Córdoba to the southernmost islands, had very little to no architecture. Many of the groups here were nomadic and erected temporary settlements with simple houses of branches or hides.

Almost no agriculture was practised, with hunting (both on land and at sea) and gathering playing important roles. Pottery was either not known or, when practised, very crude. Metalworking was unknown until the Chilean Araucanian migrations. Most of the tools were of stone or bone and in both mediums they reached a highly developed technology. In Patagonia it is estimated that some of these roaming bands had, at times, up to 150 members.

Dating difficulties: Archaeologists have been able to confirm and expand backwards most of the information collected by the first visitors. What is the story of each region and how did they develop to the various stages that the Spaniards encountered?

Though there are many archaeological sites throughout the country, the dating of many of them has still not been satisfactorily settled and only a few can be ascribed to the end of the Pleistocene and beginning of the Holocene, around 10,000 to 9,000 BC.

Many archaeologists call the earliest-known cultural tradition the hunting tradition or the hunting and gathering tradition. As the names suggest, these early groups roaming the country were hunter-gatherers living from the hunting of big game and the collection of plants, seeds and fruits. Many of the animals hunted and eaten are now extinct. Many of the early sites are either rock shelters or caves.

Colorful caves: The Fells and Pailli Aike caves, located on the southern tip of the continent, contain horse, guanaco (llama) and ground sloth bones, together with those of humans. In southern Chile the Eberhardt cave has remains of Mylodon and Onohippidon. The Los Toldos site, in Santa Cruz, is a group of caves containing horse bones.

All of these sites have stone tools which include points, scrapers, and knives; some of them have bone tools and Eberhardt has worked hides. The sites represent seasonal occupations within a pattern of nomadism that followed the food resources.

The Los Toldos caves have walls and ceilings covered with paintings, mostly of hands, done in what is called negative technique (the hand is placed on the wall and the paint applied around it). Because some of the stone artifacts from the early levels have paint remains, it is thought that the cave paintings also correspond to the early levels, i.e. circa 9,000 BC.

Stone points: The hunting tradition survived for several thousand years, throughout the country, and until the European contact in some areas. These manifestations appear in the different regions in the form of archaeological sites which have certain common characteristics: absence of ceramics and metal, no clear sign of the practice of agriculture (though by 2,500 BC, some milling stones are present in some of the places), and the presence of stone and bone tools and objects for personal decoration.

Both the stone and bone tools exhibit change through time. One of the most useful tools for gauging change is the stone point, as its development reflects technological advances, functional changes, specialization in hunting, and discovery of new and better raw materials.

Sea hunters: As mentioned earlier, development was uneven throughout the country and certain areas, within the Patagonia and Tierra del Fuego zones, never moved beyond the hunting tradition stage. The Tunel site, on the Beagle Channel, on the southern coast of Tierra del Fuego, testifies to that. After a first occupation, oriented on guanaco hunting, the inhabitants (either the same or different groups) converted to a sea-oriented economy. For 6,000 years – until their full contact with the Europeans in the late 1800s – their economy and way of life remained mostly within a sea-based hunting and gathering pattern, complemented by guanaco (llama) hunting and seed and fruit collection. The lack of revolutionary changes does not reflect primitiveness or cultural backwardness but a successful and, with time, comfortable adaptation to the local environment by people who knew the resources and exploited them.

Agriculture arrives: In other areas of the country the hunting tradition gave way eventually to agriculture. The transformation was from a pattern of collecting fruits, seeds and leaves when and where they could be found (nomadism of course being a consequence of this regime) to an organized pattern of planting, tending and collecting the fruits within a more restricted area, usually under

sedentary patterns of settlement.

Within the New World, Mexico and the Andean area were the centers of domestication of wild plants. The vegetables and fruits that with time became the main staples of all the pre-Columbian societies and later of the European settlements – maize, potatoes, squash, beans, peppers – appear in either Meso-America or the Andean area by approximately 5,000 BC.

Standing stones: The advent of agriculture is often closely followed by the development

Left and above, decorated menhirs found in the Province of Tucumán.

of ceramic skills. It is possible that the harvesting of crops and the new phenomenon of surplus food was an incentive for the making of containers which could hold and store seeds and fruits. Although pottery appeared in the New World during the 4th millenium BC, it is not seen in Argentina's archaeological record until circa 500 BC.

This period of transition between hunting and collecting patterns and sedentary agriculture is called either incipient agriculture or Early Ceramic (when ceramic is present). The Ceramic Period is usually subdivided into Early, Intermediate and Late, according to the different styles that succeeded each other in the different areas. One should remember once again that most of the ceramic cultures occurred in the northern half of what is now Argentina.

To the Early Ceramic Period, which extended from around 500 BC to AD 600, belong several cultures which occupied an arch extending from the center of Jujuy to the eastern part of San Juan. One of the early complexes is the Tafí culture of Tucumán, which is noted for its stone sculptures. Some of these beautiful carved monoliths (some of which reach 3 meters/10 feet in height) have stylized human faces.

The people of the area lived in settlements formed by groups of houses arranged around a patio. Their diet included *quinoa* (an Andean cereal), potatoes and possibly maize, and they practised llama herding. Mounds have been found, which were used either for burials or as platforms for special structures.

Another extraordinary example of excellent stone sculpture is found at the site of the Alamito culture, on the Tucumán–Catamarca border. The statues here (both of women and men) reached an unusual level of development, with an almost abstract style both powerful and expressive.

In contrast to these stone-oriented cultures there is Condorhuasi, a culture in which ceramic art reached levels of expression not known in any other groups. Strange figures, often with both animal and human characteristics, sit and crawl, with globular bodies and legs, painted in white and red, cream and red or black and red combinations.

Corn and tweezers: The Middle Ceramic Period, dating from AD 650 to 850, witnessed the development and continuation of the advances made by preceding cultures, the existence of full agricultural communities and llama and alpaca herding.

Architecture was still not impressive, at times just clay walls, probably with straw or wood roofs. Ceramic art continued to be very developed, but stone work declined. Metalworking was by then highly developed, with the making of bronze and copper axes, needles, tweezers, bracelets and disks with complicated designs. The distinct differences in the quantity of artifacts found in the graves is a clear indication that by now social stratification existed. The lack of monumental works or clear examples of organized labor points to a still simple political organization.

The Aguada complex (mostly from Catamarca and La Rioja) is a good representative of this period.

Inca invasion: The Late Ceramic Period, from AD 850 to 1480, witnessed some changes. The settlements became larger, some in defensible locations, and thick walls made of round stones are found in many of these sites. Llama and alpaca herding was practised on a large scale. Roads, cemeteries, irrigation works and what were probably ceremonial centers appeared.

The ceramic urn (used for the burial of children) is one of the markers of the period. These vessels (between 40 and 60 cm/16–24 inches in height) often have painted human faces showing what could be tear marks. Other markers for this period are beautiful metal disks or breastplates with human head and snake motifs on them.

Finally, in AD 1480, the Inca armies arrived and conquered what was to become the Northwest region of Argentina. Remains of Inca roads, *tambos* (places of rest, supply and storage), and forts or *pucarás* can be found in the region. The Incas introduced their styles and artistic values and many of the pieces of this period are just local reproductions of original Inca pieces.

Hands and feet: A last word should be dedicated to the cave and rock paintings and decorations. Examples of this form of art are now being found throughout the country, but it is in Patagonia where it has been most thoroughly studied. Within this area several styles have been recognized. One of them is the style of the painted hands, which is present in many caves, some of them with hundreds of hand representations. The painting is done with the negative technique, and the depictions are mostly of adult left hands. An excellent example of this type of painting is found at the Cave of the Painted Hands in Santa Cruz.

Another style is the naturalist style or scenes style. It often depicts whole scenes related to dancing ceremonies and the hunting and corralling of guanacos. Along the Upper Pinturas River, in Santa Cruz, several such paintings can be found on the walls of the gullies.

Footprint paintings constitute another style, and the geometric design style completes the range of motifs.

As can be seen, the Spaniards found, upon their arrival, a mosaic of cultural developments ranging from groups which were still practising a hunting and gathering mode of subsistence to others that were moving to the threshold of civilization.

The story of the area's uneven cultural development goes back to approximately 10,600 BC and still has not been completely revealed. However, the continuing work of archaeologists is slowly but surely filling the gaps in our understanding of the prehistory of Argentina.

Left, well-worn grinding stone. **Right**, petroglyph, thought to depict the devil, at Talampaya.

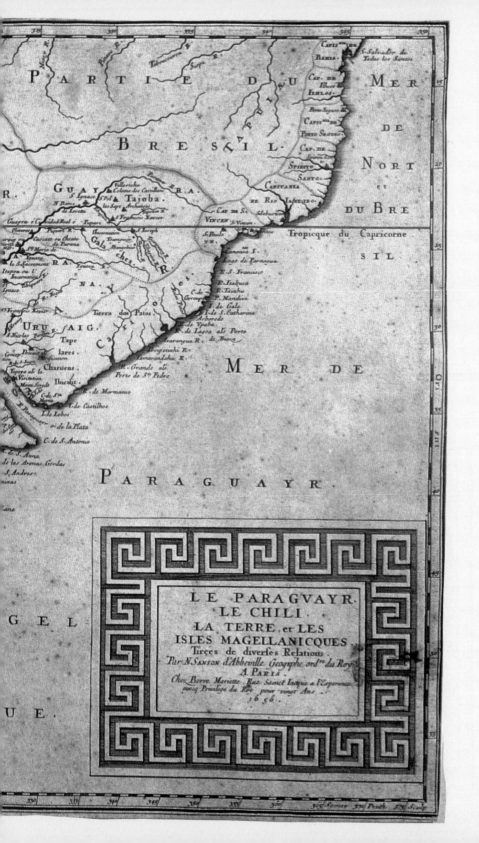

TIEMBVS

Cap 13.

Parana fluuius

B. Speranza

Corp: Chr

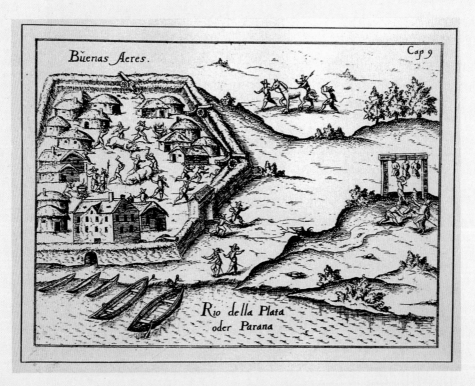

Buenas Aeres.

Cap 9

Rio della Plata
oder Parana

CAUDILLOS, TYRANTS AND DEMAGOGUES

The history of Argentina has been written in blood, from the earliest days under the colonial administration of the Spaniards until very recently. There have been periodic outbursts of democratic rule in the past, but the tradition of representative government does not run deep in the people of this remote South American nation.

Paradoxically, Argentina has assisted in the liberation of minds and souls throughout the countries of Latin America, exerting intellectual power and military force on behalf of other Latin peoples during the course of its history.

Admirable achievements and depressing lowpoints have marked the development of the Argentine nation as it has struggled to liberate itself first from a distant master and then from the cruel and selfish local potentates, the *caudillos*.

Heroic actions such as San Martín's crossing of the Andes, and the liberation of workers from a status similar to serfdom have, unfortunately, been overshadowed by an ultra-nationalistic conceit that borders on hubris and has proved time and again to be self-defeating.

The conflict between Buenos Aires and the interior, a problem that persists to this day, has also been a major obstacle in the development of the nation.

The first explorers: From a European perspective, the first half of the 16th century was a period of intense exploration on behalf of the Portuguese and Spanish Crowns. Not quite 10 years after Columbus' first voyage to the new world, Amerigo Vespucci was probing the eastern shores of South America. Today, many credit him with the discovery of the Río de la Plata, although standard Argentine accounts cite Juan de Solís as the first European to sail these waters.

Solís reached the Río de la Plata estuary in 1516 and named the river Mar Dulce or Sweet Sea. Not long after, while Solís was

leading a small party ashore, he was killed by Charrua tribesmen along with all but one of the sailors accompanying him. After killing the Spaniards, the natives proceeded to eat them in full view of the remains of the crew on board ship.

In 1520, Ferdinand Magellan, on his voyage to the Pacific, was the next explorer to reach what is now Argentina. Then came Sebastian Cabot. Sailing under the Spanish flag, and drawn by rumors of a mountain of silver, he was the next to venture into the Río

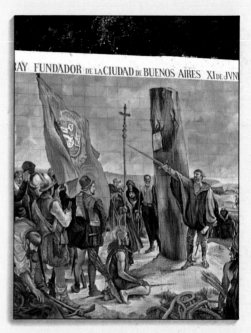

de la Plata region in 1526. His three-year search proved fruitless, but he at least gained credit for having established the first settlement, although it was later abandoned.

The Spanish nobleman Pedro de Mendoza led a very large expedition to the area, also drawn by reports of great wealth in the region. On February 3, 1536, he founded Santa Maria de los Buenos Aires. The natives were at first helpful and fed the Spaniards, but then they turned furiously against them. As one of Mendoza's soldiers wrote, "The Indians attacked our city of Buenos Aires with great force... There were around 23,000 of them... While some of them were

Preceding pages: 17th-century map of the Southern Cone. Left top, Paraná river culture, and bottom, the early, difficult years of the settlement at Buenos Aires. Right, mural depicting the resettlement of Buenos Aires.

attacking us, others were shooting burning arrows at our houses, so that we wouldn't have time to see to both problems and save our houses... In this attack they burned four large ships." The natives finally retreated under the fire of Spanish artillery.

Mendoza and his men never did locate any great mineral wealth and eventually left Buenos Aires for the more hospitable Asunción, in Paraguay.

A second group of Spaniards, this time approaching overland from Chile, Peru and Upper Peru (today's Bolivia), was more successful in founding lasting settlements. The northwest towns of Santiago del Estero, Catamarca, Mendoza, Tucumán, Córdoba, Salta, La Rioja and Jujuy were all founded in the second half of the 16th century, with Santiago del Estero being the oldest continuously settled outpost (it was founded in 1551) in Argentina.

For all of the following century and most of the 18th, the northwest was the center of most activity in Argentina. This was mostly due to protectionism on the part of the king of Spain, who in 1554 prohibited traffic on the Río de la Plata. Manufactured goods from Spain and enslaved Africans were shipped in a South American triangular trade via Panama and then Peru. The king's ruling was of great benefit to the Spanish colonial cities of Lima and Mexico City but kept the Río de la Plata estuary isolated and commercially backward.

Northwest/Central supremacy: While Argentina was part of the Peruvian viceroyalty until 1776, two areas of the colony became important centers. Tucumán developed into a successful agricultural region, supplying wheat, corn, cotton, tobacco and livestock to neighboring Upper Peru. Somewhat later, Córdoba attained status as a center of learning, with the establishment of the Jesuit university in 1613.

Córdoba also prospered economically, owing to its central location and fertile lands. By contrast, Buenos Aires, which had been refounded in 1580, was a small town that relied on smuggling for its income. Because all manufactured goods had to come the long route from Spain via Panama, their prices were very high, and this led to the cheaper contraband traffic.

Shift from west to east: The decline of the Andean mining industries, coupled with growing calls for direct transatlantic trade, finally persuaded the Spanish Crown to establish the new viceroyalty of Río de la Plata, which established its administrative center at Buenos Aires.

With a new viceroyalty, which included Uruguay, Paraguay and parts of Upper Peru and the Argentine, Spain hoped to exert greater control over a region which was growing in importance. Buenos Aires experienced an explosion in population, as the city increased its numbers from 2,200 in 1726 to well over 33,000 by 1778. Upwards of a quarter of this rapidly growing population was Afro-Argentine and still held in bondage. Many others were of mixed Indian and Spanish parentage, a consequence of the Spanish men suffering a paucity of Spanish women in the viceroyalty.

Another important appearance in the demographic picture was the rise of the gaucho which came with the large ranches in the latter half of the 18th century. The gaucho represented a culture very different from that of the perfumed and groomed inhabitants of Buenos Aires.

The growing importance of the viceroyalty of the Río de la Plata did not go unnoticed in Europe. The Franco-Hispanic alliance during the Napoleonic Wars (1804–15) resulted in a loosening of Argentina's ties with the motherland, when Spain's fleet was destroyed by the English navy. The Spanish colonies in Latin America were open for English attention.

The British invade: In 1806 and again the following year, the British invaded Buenos Aires. During the first invasion, the inept Spanish viceroy fled to Montevideo, across the Río de la Plata, taking with him many of his troops. The retaking of the city was left to Santiago de Liniers, who organized the remaining Spanish troops and the local inhabitants, including one battalion of blacks. The British were quickly routed but were to return soon afterwards.

After seizing Montevideo, the British attempted the recapture of Buenos Aires with an army of 10,000. They were met by Liniers and his men, and by women pelting them with roof tiles and pouring boiling oil on them from above. The city's streets were turned into what the British later called "pathways of death". The English commander of the expedition promptly evacuated his troops.

Beyond the immediate consequences of repelling the invaders, a number of very important effects stemmed from the confrontations with the British.

Pride in the colony was a natural outcome of having defeated a large and well-trained army with a mostly local militia.

Tensions arose between the *criollos* (Argentine-born colonists) and the Spanish troops, who realized they could not be of any assistance to the Crown in the troubled Iberian Peninsula.

The creation of a rudimentary provisional government also helped to foster an independent-minded local elite. Thoughts of a booming economy without the strictures and wards the creation of a new nation based on a reordering of colonial society. Naturally enough, the old order – the rich merchants, the *estancieros* (large landowners), members of the clergy and, indeed, the whole colonial administrative structure – was violently opposed to any tampering with its status in the country.

A house divided: This lack of unity made the realization of an independent nation much more of a tortured process than the criollo intellectuals could have imagined. Indeed, a civil war was in the making following what the Argentines call the May Revolution. On May 25, 1810, an autonomous government was set up in Buenos Aires. This date is

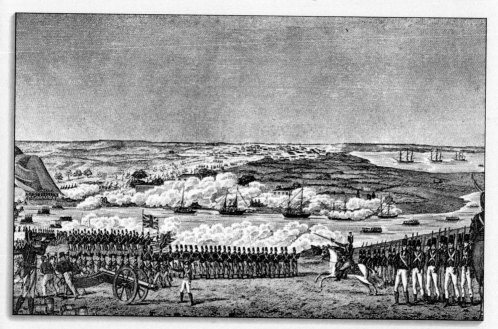

regulations of a Crown that could not even protect the colony began to enter the minds of the *criollos*.

Independence steps: Napoleon Bonaparte's invasion of Spain in 1808 provided the final push for a rupture in relations; a *cabildo abierto* (open town council) in Buenos Aires deposed the Spanish viceroy and created a revolutionary junta to rule in his stead.

Bernardino Rivadavia, Manuel Belgrano and Mariano Moreno were three *criollo* intellectuals, inspired by European liberal thought, who channelled their energies to-

Above, the first British invasion, 1806.

celebrated in Argentina as the nation's day of independence, although a formal declaration was not made until 1816.

These early years were not easy; the people of the viceroyalty were split along regional, class and political lines. The Unitarios, or Unitarians, were intent upon having a strong central government which would be based in offices in Buenos Aires. Meanwhile, the Federales, or Federalists, hoped to establish a loose confederation of autonomous provinces.

A confusing series of juntas, triumvirates and assemblies rose and fell, as one group would have the upper hand for a brief period only to lose the advantage to another. Whatever unity the viceroyalty had was soon shattered, as Uruguay, Paraguay and Bolivia went their separate ways. The eight original jurisdictions of the viceroyalty dwindled to three, and these three then fragmented into seven provinces.

Before this loose group of provinces further disintegrated, a congress was called to maintain whatever unity was left. On July 9, 1816, the congress at Tucumán formally declared independence under the blue and white banner of the United Provinces of South America.

Enter José de San Martín: The task of ridding the continent of Spanish armies remained.

to keep their forces intact. It was at this time, in 1822, that San Martín met the other great liberator of South America, Simón Bolívar, at Guayaquil. What actually was discussed at this meeting is not known and has kept historians speculating ever since. The upshot, though, was San Martín's retirement from battle, leaving the remaining honors to be garnered by Bolívar.

Of José de San Martín and his motivations, Basil Hall, a contemporary of San Martín's, had this to say: "There was little, at first sight, in his appearance to engage attention; but when he rose up and began to speak, his great superiority over every other person I had seen in South America was sufficiently

José de San Martín was to execute one of the boldest moves of the South American wars of liberation. Gathering a large army, San Martín crossed the icy Andes at Mendoza in 21 days and met and defeated a Spanish army at Chacabuco in Chile (1817). He again engaged the Spaniards, this time at Maipú (1818), where he ended the Spanish menace to Chile once and for all.

San Martín's next move was no less audacious than his crossing of the Andes. He amassed a fleet of mostly English and American ships to convoy his army the 2,400 km (1,500 miles) to Lima. The Spanish army evacuated the city without fighting, wishing

apparent… General San Martín is a tall, erect, well-proportioned, handsome man, with a large aquiline nose, thick black hair, and immense bushy whiskers extending from ear to ear under the chin; his complexion is deep olive, and his eye, which is large, prominent and piercing, jet black; his whole appearance being highly military… I have never seen any person, the enchantment of whose address was more irresistible… The contest in Peru, he said, was not of an ordinary

Left, the Latin-American liberator, San Martín.
Above, the formal declaration of independence on July 9, 1816, in Tucumán.

description – not a war of conquest and glory, but entirely of opinion; it was a war of new and liberal principles against prejudice, bigotry and tyranny."

San Martín was elevated to a position of sainthood by the Argentines but this only happened posthumously. Today, every town in Argentina has a street named after him and every classroom a portrait of the general crossing the Andes on a gallant white horse. However, it was a different story when he returned to Buenos Aires in 1823 from his campaigns on behalf of Argentina. He received no acknowledgment for the services he rendered his country. Soon afterwards San Martín left for France, where he was to die in obscurity.

Continued disorder: The period from independence to the commencement of the dictatorship of Juan Manuel de Rosas in 1829 were difficult years for the United Provinces of the Río de la Plata (the earlier and grander name of the United Provinces of South America had to be dropped with the fragmentation of the original grouping of provinces). Bernardino Rivadavia, a man of great vision, valiantly but vainly attempted to shape the country's future.

Rivadavia was interested in establishing a constitution for the nation, forming a strong central government, dividing up the land in more equitable shares, and attracting immigrants to settle in the United Provinces. His plans were quickly sidetracked, however, by *caudillos* in the interior, who were none too anxious to surrender any of their power, and the draining Cisplatine War (1825–28) with Brazil over the status of Uruguay. When Rivadavia resigned from the presidency of the United Provinces in 1827 and went into exile, there remained little to show for his years of effort. The region remained as anarchic as ever.

Caudillo and tyrant: One of Latin American history's most intriguing, if blood-thirsty, figures must be Juan Manuel de Rosas, who ruled much of Argentina as his personal domain for over 20 years. In his quest for power, Rosas forged a coalition of rough gauchos, wealthy landowners and others who represented the Federalist cause, and this combination proved a formidable one for many years. Above all else, Rosas is remembered for the terror to which he and his followers subjected the new nation.

Although born in Buenos Aires in 1793, Rosas was a product of the open pampa. It was here on his family's *estancia* that he learned to ride and fight and toss the *boleadoras* (three stones attached to connected thongs) with a skill that equalled any of the gauchos he kept company with, gaining their respect and later their support.

Rosas became wealthy in his own right at an early age. By his mid-twenties, he owned thousands of acres of land and was a successful businessman, having helped to establish one of the first meat-salting plants in his province. He chose well when he married Maria de la Encarnación Escurra, the daughter of another rich family. She would later prove invaluable to Rosas' ascent to power, plotting and organizing in a subtle and effective way on her husband's behalf.

In order to stem the rising tide of anarchy that followed the exile of Rivadavia, Rosas was asked to become the governor of the province of Buenos Aires in 1829. Rosas, a powerful *caudillo* and experienced military man, seemed the perfect individual to restore order and stability.

The major problem with the Federalists was that there was little unity among the various factions. Federalists in the provinces demanded autonomy and an equal footing with Buenos Aires, while those espousing the Federalist cause in Argentina's major city were not willing to surrender their premier position.

As governor with extraordinary powers, in 1831 Rosas signed the Federal Pact which tied together the provinces of Buenos Aires, Entre Ríos, Santa Fe and Corrientes.

The opposition to Rosas, the Unitarian League, was dealt a severe blow when its leader, José Maria Paz, was unhorsed by a Federalist soldier wielding *boleadoras*. Paz was taken prisoner and jailed by Rosas. By 1832 the Unitarians had suffered a number of reverses on the battlefield and, for the moment, did not pose a deep threat to the Federalists.

When Rosas' first term as governor ended in 1832, he refused to accept another stint in office because the council of provincial representatives was unwilling to allow him to maintain his virtually unlimited authority.

Darwin and Rosas: In the midst of this struggle, Rosas did not absent himself from combat. He took command of the campaign against the native Argentine tribes in the south, and earned himself even more dubious glory by wiping out thousands.

It was during this Desert Campaign of 1833–34 that the British naturalist Charles Darwin was entertained by Rosas. Of his meeting, Darwin wrote: "General Rosas is a man of extraordinary character; he has at present a most predominant influence in this country and may probably end up by being its ruler… He is moreover a perfect gaucho: his feats of horsemanship are very notorious. He will fall from a doorway upon an unbroken colt, as it rushes out of the Corral, and will defy the worst efforts of the animal. He wears the Gaucho dress and is said to have

called upon Lord Ponsonby in it, saying at the time he thought the costume of the country the proper and therefore the most respectful dress. By these means he obtained an unbounded popularity in the Camp, and in consequence despotic power. A man a short time since murdered another; being arrested and questioned he answered, 'the man spoke disrespectfully of General Rosas and I killed him,' in one week's time the murderer was at liberty. In conversation he is enthusiastic, sensible and very grave. His gravity is carried to a high pitch."

Though Rosas was campaigning in the south, he was not out of contact with events in Buenos Aires. His wife waged a "dirty war" to have her husband reinstated as governor, forming the Sociedad Popular Restauradora and its terror-wing, the *mazorca*. Through the Sociedad Popular Restauradora, Doña Encarnación hampered the efforts to rule effectively of the three governors who followed Rosas.

The junta finally acquiesced to Rosas' demands in 1835; he was to have all the power deemed necessary to defend the national cause of the Federalists without restrictions. Rosas then assumed his post as Restorer of the Laws and governor in a regal ceremony on April 13, 1835.

Rosas now had the means to institute the most personal of regimes. The red color of the Federalists became the distinguishing factor in dress. Women wore scarlet dresses and men red badges that proclaimed "Federation or Death." Decorating in blue, the hated color of the "savage Unitarians," could be cause enough for imprisonment or execution, so deep ran the paranoid streak of the Rosistas (followers of Rosas).

The horror: While Rosas did not create the brutal methods of repression that so characterized his regime, he did give a certain order and system to them in making himself supreme dictator. Generally speaking, Rosas' victims were not massacred wholesale but rather executed on an individual basis. Long lists of suspected Unitarians and what property they possessed were drawn up by Rosas' effective spy network, the police, the military and justices of the peace.

The methods of silencing opponents ranged from exile to imprisonment to execution. The favored manner of despatching them was throat-cutting, reflecting the traditions of the gauchos. W. H. Hudson, naturalist and chronicler of the pampas, wrote that the Argentines "loved to kill a man not with a bullet but in a manner to make them know and feel that they were really and truly killing." Another method of killing was lancing; two executioners, standing on either side of the prisoner, would plunge lances into the body simultaneously.

Throat-cutting, lancing, castration and the carving out of tongues were acceptable means at the disposal of the violent *caudillos* but it was only under Rosas that these methods were institutionalized. The actual number of those who perished remains unclear, but estimates range in the thousands. Whatever the correct number, Rosas created and maintained a climate of fear for over 20 years.

With Rosas at the helm, the Argentine state did not prosper. Rosas meddled in the affairs of neighboring Uruguay often, expending scarce resources in the process, but he was never able to conquer its capital, Montevideo.

Extreme xenophobia on Rosas' part also kept the country from attracting much needed immigrants and foreign capital. Indeed, during two periods, the first from 1838 to 1840 when French troops occupied a customs house on the River Plate, and then during the 1845–47 Anglo-French blockade of the river, the finances of Buenos Aires suffered severely. Rosas' treatment of European nationals, his extreme paranoia, and the inevitable consequences did nothing to help the growth of the nation.

In response to the atmosphere of terror and lack of freedom, Argentines organized in secret, and some in exile, to overthrow Rosas. These intellectuals, whose ranks included such luminaries as Bartolomé Mitre, Juan Bautista Alberdi and Domingo Faustino Sarmiento, provided the rhetoric which galvanized the opposition.

A quick end: Justo José de Urquiza, a *caudillo* who had long supported Rosas, turned against the Restorer and organized an army that soon included thousands of volunteers, and even many Uruguayans and Brazilians. On February 3, 1852 Urquiza's army engaged Rosas' demoralized and rebellion-weary troops at Caseros, near Buenos Aires. "The battle," as Mitre later wrote, "was won before it was fought." A new age in Argentina's history had begun, with Urquiza intent on consolidating the nation as one unit and not a collection of semi-independent provinces; progress in all areas came quickly.

State foundations: The period from Rosas' downfall to 1880 was a time of organizing the nation-state and establishing the institutions required to run it. The major conflict of this period was an old one: the status of Buenos Aires in relation to the interior. This issue was finally settled in 1880 by federalizing the city and making it something like the District of Columbia in the United States.

Urquiza's first task was to draw up a constitution for Argentina. A constitutional convention was held in the city of Santa Fe and this meeting produced a document modeled on the Constitution of the United States. Among its provisos were the establishment of a bicameral legislature, an executive chosen by an electoral college, and an independent judiciary.

The Argentine constitution was accepted by the convention on May 1, 1853. Not surprisingly, Urquiza was chosen as the first president. During his tenure, he established a national bank, built schools and improved transportation in the republic. What plagued Urquiza and the development of the nation

Soldado de Rosas - Buenos Aires
Monvoisin - Oleo - 1842

was the uncertain role of Buenos Aires. Until 1862 there were, in fact, two Argentinas, one based in the wealthy port city of Buenos Aires and the other in the interior with its capital at Paraná. A congress met in Buenos Aires in 1862 and it was decided that Buenos Aires would become the capital city of both the republic and the province.

Bartolomé Mitre, an historian and former governor of the province of Buenos Aires became the next president. While the task of creating a national infrastructure was of great importance to Mitre, he found himself distracted by the Paraguayan War (1865–70) in which it took five years of bloody fighting

Left, the tyrant Juan Manuel de Rosas. **Right**, a Rosas soldier in Federalist colors.

THE CASE OF
THE AFRO-ARGENTINES

Argentina's greatest puzzle is the vanished Afro-Argentines. Historians throughout the years have offered diverse explanations. Ordinary citizens are ready with stories that range from the plausible to the ludicrous.

Argentines of African heritage existed in large numbers – comprising 30 percent of the Buenos Aires population for almost 40 years (1778–1815). Slaves were first brought to Argentina in the 16th century by their Spanish owners. Due to the peculiar trading arrangements with the Spanish Crown, most slaves were imported to Buenos Aires via Panama and Peru and then overland from Chile, thereby greatly increasing their price. Tens of thousands of Africans were shipped via the conventional routes but some were brought in illegally, directly to Buenos Aires or from Brazil.

Argentine slaves were generally domestic servants but also filled the growing need for artisans in the labor-short colony. While the degree of their labor differed greatly from that of plantation workers in Brazil and the United States, they suffered similarly. Families were torn apart, gruesome punishments awaited runaways and blacks' status in society was kept low, through law and custom, even after emancipation.

In the post-independence era, the move to free slaves was fitful at best; the road to freedom was a long one, Argentine history textbook accounts notwithstanding. While the majority of slaves had gained their liberty by 1827 (through military service, the largesse of friendly masters or by purchasing their own freedom), some remained in bondage until 1861. One early 1800s law stipulated that the children of slaves would be free upon birth, though their mothers would remain slaves. However, it was not unusual for slaveowners to spirit their pregnant slaves to Uruguay, where slavery was still legal, and then bring both mother and child back to Argentina as slaves.

The North American professor George Reid Andrews has done much research to uncover the fate of the blacks in his important work, *The Afro-Argentines of Buenos Aires, 1800–1900*. He offers no definitive conclusions, but he has explored in depth some of the more likely theories.

Reid Andrews researches four strong possibilities. A great percentage of Afro-Argentine males served in the army, organized into their own battalions. Many of them might have perished in the incessant warfare during and after independence. Miscegenation, or the mixing of races, is an explanation that many ascribe to. This might also seem sensible given the degree to which the black community was swamped by the hundreds of thousands of European immigrants who reached Argentina after the mid-1800s. The great yellow fever epidemic of 1871 and the general ill health and horrendous living conditions of the blacks is also cited as a possible factor. Finally, Reid Andrews explores the decline of the slave trade (outlawed in 1813) and its impact on a community that would not have its numbers refreshed with new shipments of human chattel.

Census figures for the city of Buenos Aires from 1836 to 1887 point to a steep decline in the

numbers and percentages of blacks, from a figure of 14,906 or 26 percent of the total population to 8,005 or 1.8 percent.

The contributions blacks made to Argentine society have, for the most part, been written out of the records. After the early 19th century, Afro-Argentines to all intents and purposes disappeared or were intentionally made to vanish. One must sift through prints and photographs of the late 1800s to discover that this group, although in decline, remained a part of the greater community. In these representations we might see blacks working as gauchos or as street vendors or artisans in Buenos Aires. ∎

for the triple alliance of Brazil, Uruguay and Argentina to subdue the Paraguayan dictator Francisco Solano López. The conflict placed extreme financial burdens on the young republic and its citizens, but Argentina did receive a large chunk of territory (the provinces of Formosa, Chaco and Misiones) for its efforts.

Mitre was succeeded by Domingo Faustino Sarmiento whose role in promoting education in Argentina has taken on mythic proportions. It was during Sarmiento's administration (1868–74) that Argentina made enormous strides in development. Hundreds of thousands of immigrants poured into the city of Buenos Aires, railroads were built,

the hands of such non-*porteños* as Sarmiento, Avellaneda and Julio Roca led a revolt against the government. It took three months to crush this rebellion.

As Avellaneda's minister of war, Roca headed a series of expeditions against the natives of Patagonia in the infamous Conquest of the Desert which was concluded by 1879. Many thousands of square miles were opened up for settlement and exploration after this war of genocidal proportions.

Golden age: In 1880, Argentina entered its golden age which lasted until the outbreak of World War I. An enormous number of European immigrants arrived, while exports to Europe soared. The latter was made possi-

and the use of barbed-wire fencing spread, thereby controlling the open range. Sarmiento continually stressed the need to push for a removal of the "barbaric" elements within Argentine society, namely the *caudillos* and the gauchos. Groups such as these had kept Argentina from advancing at a faster rate, Sarmiento believed.

Following Sarmiento came President Nicolás Avellaneda whose inauguration in October, 1874 almost didn't happen. Mitre, fearing a decline in Buenos Aires' prestige at

Left, Afro-Argentine street vendor, 1844. **Above**, Indians captured during the Desert Campaign.

ble, in part, by technological advances which permitted ships to carry refrigerated beef to the Old World. There was a corresponding growth in the intellectual field, as well. Newspapers were founded, political parties sprang up, writers were published and a world-class opera house, the Teatro Colón, opened in Buenos Aires.

This is not to say that all was well in Argentina. Politics remained closed to most Argentines; a few had taken it upon themselves to run the country. The middle class, supporting the new political party, the Radical Civic Union, pressed for entry into what had been a government run by a small group of conservative families. Workers also became politicized and were attracted to the Socialist Party and the anarchists. Strikes hit turn-of-the-century Argentina and labor unrest grew. The workers found themselves expendable as the country struggled to pay back international loans and as imports began to exceed exports.

One of the worst periods of governmental repressions occurred in 1919. In what was called the *Semana Trágica* (Tragic Week), troops opened fire on strikers and many lives were lost. The Radical Civic Union governed Argentina from 1916 until 1930. Hipólito Yrigoyen served as president for all but six of those years.

blatant dishonesty and fickle policies that triggered the military's coup d'état in 1943. The significance of the intervention this time around cannot be underestimated for it was during this regime that Juan Perón emerged to lead his nation.

A demagogue's demagogue: Although Juan Domingo Perón served as president for only 11 of the past 50 years, his shadow has been long. Even today, more than 20 years after his death in 1974, the man and his ideology are strongly influential. He elicits the most powerful of responses from the citizenry: complete adoration or utter revulsion. In his name, governments have fallen, terrorist acts have been committed and workers organized.

With the coming of the Great Depression, the military swept Yrigoyen from office. With this move, a new element entered modern Argentina's political body. The pattern was to be followed all too frequently over the next half century.

The Radicals staged a comeback with the ascension of Roberto Ortiz in the fraudulent elections of 1937. Ironically, Ortiz then set about restoring voter confidence by annulling the corrupt elections that followed. Ortiz died in office and was succeeded by Vice-President Ramón Castillo, who reversed his predecessor's campaign to cleanse the political system of corruption. It was this man's

His greatest achievement was to harness the energy of the Argentine laborer. Through the workers Perón established a political party that is still a force to be reckoned with, and only recently has abandoned its pro-labor stance.

Perón's background certainly indicated no pro-labor tendencies. He attended a military college and rose through the ranks as a career officer. While stationed in Italy in 1939 as a military observer, he was impressed by the nationalism of the fascists. The state's intervention in Italy's economy he also thought logical. On his return to Argentina, Perón involved himself deeply in the secret military organization, the GOU (*Grupo Obra de Unificación* or Unification Task Force), which was composed of Young Turks bent on remodeling Argentina's political system along the lines of those in Germany and Italy.

The GOU overthrew Castillo on June 4, 1943. Perón was given the post of Secretary of the Labor and Social Welfare Ministry from which he was to build his power base. His labor reforms – job security, child labor laws, and pensions among them – were immensely popular with the working class. Furthermore, Perón tied union and non-union members together through the national welfare system, a move that assured him control over and allegiance from most workers.

rectly that his moment on the national stage had arrived. In the presidential elections of 1946, Perón won with a majority of 54 percent. The clumsy US intervention in these elections, operating through its ambassador to Buenos Aires, ironically contributed to electing the man described by Washington as a fascist.

In the years immediately following World War II, Argentina was wealthy and seemed to be a nation on the move. The country possessed a healthy surplus in its treasury, workers' salaries increased greatly, and industrialization proceeded apace. Although storm clouds were gathering on the economic horizon, nobody seemed to notice: this

The military became uneasy with Perón's growing power and arrested him. This led to a series of demonstrations, capped by a gigantic display in the Plaza de Mayo by the *descamisados* (shirtless ones or poor workers). Perón's consort, Eva Duarte, and labor leaders were behind these actions, rallying support for the imprisoned Perón. Within weeks he was free. He would soon marry Eva to legitimize their relationship in the eyes of the voters and the church. Perón sensed cor-

Left, the masses turn out for Loyalty Day, 1946. **Above**, Perón and Evita appear on the balcony of the Casa Rosada.

was a golden age when every family could eat fine steak twice a day, and it is little wonder that Argentina re-elected Perón to a second term in 1951 with a massive 67 percent majority.

Severe droughts and a decrease in the international prices of grain led to a 50 percent increase in Argentina's trade deficit. Eva Perón's death shortly after her husband's second inauguration left him without one of his most successful organizers and contributed to the malaise the nation was experiencing. Without Eva, Perón seemed to lose his willpower and left many decisions to be made by his increasingly radical acolytes.

Also, the president's affair with a 13-year-old did not sit well with the more traditionally minded Argentines.

Middle-class revolt: A triumvirate of middle-class forces gathered to push Perón from office in 1955. Students resented the total Peronist control over their institutions, while the church hierarchy felt threatened by Perón's secular views regarding education, divorce and prostitution.

The armed forces, having been removed from the center of attention, were convinced that they would see their power diminished. A church-sponsored demonstration drew 100,000 to the center of Buenos Aires, and was soon followed by the rebellious airforce's bombing of the Casa Rosada and the Plaza de Mayo. The army struck back against the dissident airforce while Peronist mobs burned churches.

Events were rolling out of control for Perón as the navy then rebelled, joined by some army units in the interior. Perón spared his country enormous bloodshed by not making good his promise to arm the workers and instead fleeing to Paraguay.

The interregnum that was to follow, before Perón's triumphant return, lasted 18 years. During this period, Argentina would suffer nine leaders, none of whom succeeded in taming the economic demons that tormented the country's health.

It would be difficult to describe these years in a positive light. The military constantly meddled in politics, overthrowing elected presidents and installing generals when it was felt that the professional politicians were not guiding the country correctly. Perón's followers were alternately persecuted or allowed to organize and run for office.

Perón's influence continued to be felt although he was in exile. No group, not the military nor the other political parties such as the UCRP (People's Radical Civic Union) and the UCRI (Intransigent Radical Civic Union), could totally ignore the strongman or his workers' party.

Arturo Frondizi was the first president to be freely elected after Perón, in February 1958, and his tenure was marked by a state of seige, an economic downturn and many (35) coup attempts. What brought Frondizi down was his decision to allow Peronists to participate in the congressional elections of 1962. Frondizi's attempts to accommodate the Per-onists disturbed the Argentine military; they ordered him to annul the election results and when he refused to declare all Peronist wins illegal, the army stepped in.

Arturo Illia did not fare much better when he won the presidential elections in 1963. While the economy was stronger than under Frondizi's administration, inflation remained oppressively high. Illia's minority government stood little chance of survival; the military was apprehensive over the president's inability to hold back the increasingly popular Peronist party, then called the Popular Union.

The next in line to try his hand at governing Argentina was General Juan Carlos Onganía, leader of the 1966 coup against Illia. Onganía ushered in an extremely repressive era; political parties were banned, Congress was dissolved and demonstrations were outlawed. The economic situation reached new lows. Foreign ownership of companies hit 59 percent in 1969, as workers' real income slumped sharply.

The Cordobazo (Córdoba coup) of 1969 precipitated Onganía's departure from government. Argentina's second largest city was the focus of anti-government activity among a new alliance of students, workers and businessmen, all of whom had been badly hurt by Onganía's policies. For two days Córdoba became a war zone, as soldiers battled with demonstrators. Over 100 were killed or wounded in the street-fighting.

Onganía was ousted by General Lanusse and representatives of the other branches of the military. An obscure general assumed the presidency, lasting only nine months in office. Lanusse himself then took charge and prepared the nation for a return to civilian elections which were to be held in 1973.

Continued interferences and repression by the military spawned the growth of a number of guerrilla groups in Argentina, chief among them the Montoneros and the People's Revolutionary Army (ERP). The use of torture and murder by Lanusse led to a new cycle of violence in which both sides were engaged. Over 2,000 political prisoners languished in jail, reflecting the very broad subversion laws Lanusse decreed.

In this climate, the presidential election of 1973 took place. Perón chose Héctor Cámpora to run as his proxy as the head of the Peronist Justicialist Party. On a familiar platform of national reconstruction, Cámpora won just under half of the vote. The Peronists had come back strongly and the time to end their leader's exile had arrived.

Round two: Perón's return to Argentina did not have auspicious beginnings. Two million were on hand at the international airport to greet the aging man they thought could restore order to the economy and dignity to the working class. Riots among different groups of demonstrators and security police at the airport turned into pitched battles that left hundreds dead.

Héctor Cámpora resigned from office and in the new presidential elections Perón easily emerged as victor. Following past form, his

except her husband's name. Her government was marked by ultra conservatism, corruption and repression.

Additionally, Isabel came to rely for advice on one of Argentina's most bizarre and sinister figures, the ex-police corporal José López Rega. This Rasputin-like character wielded great power and founded the infamous right-wing terrorist group, the Alianza Argentina Anticomunista. Reportedly, under Lopéz Rega's influence, Isabel even took to employing astrological divination as a means to determine national policy.

Isabel Perón's inability to come to grips with Argentina's chronic economic problems, as well as her failure to curb rising

wife, Isabel, was given political power, in this case as vice-president. The president's initial efforts at national reconciliation appeared to work but again the economy began to unravel and with it the fragile unity Perón had achieved.

The sudden death of Juan Domingo Perón on July 1, 1974 brought Isabel to the supreme position in the land, but her administration was an unmitigated disaster. She was no Evita and she had little to offer Argentina

Above, **left, President Onganía confers with General Lanusse, 1967, and right, Perón's third wife, Isabel.**

terrorism, led the military to intervene yet again. In a move that was widely expected and hoped for, they removed the last Perón from the Casa Rosada on March 24, 1976.

The Proceso: Although the military had never proved itself any more able to solve the nation's problems, there seemed to be a different attitude with this band of uniformed men steering the nation. Each of the four successive juntas made a point of coordinating efforts among the various branches of the armed forces. The first junta tried to lend legitimacy to its leadership by amending the constitution. This amendment, the Statute for the National Reorganization Process, called for the ruling junta to shoulder responsibility of both executive and legislative functions of the state. From this amendment the period of military rule from 1977–83 has come to be known as the Proceso.

General Videla was chosen as the first president and he attacked the problem of left-wing guerrilla action through a campaign dubbed the "dirty war." It was while office was held by Videla that the majority of the *desaparecidos* (disappeared) vanished. Anyone suspected of anti-government activity, and this was loosely interpreted by the military, could be made to disappear.

Nuns, priests, schoolchildren and whole families were kidnapped, raped, tortured and

had staged a protest against rising bus fares.

The whole campaign was conducted secretly, abductions often occurring at night. It was in this dirty war that the military lost all claims to represent the civilized and often touted European standard of conduct which Argentines believe they uphold.

Attempts by university professors and students to gain greater control over their institutions were regarded as subversive, and so the universities were gutted. The heavy hand of censorship of the media also fell across the country.

International condemnation, the pleas of human rights groups and the efforts of the mothers of the disappeared – the Mothers of

then murdered by a nefarious coalition of the military, police and right-wing death squads acting in the name of Christianity and democracy. Estimates of the numbers of *desaparecidos* (also known as the NNs or no names) range from 10,000 to 40,000 people, of whom only the tiniest fraction had actually been involved in any kind of terrorist activities.

The military had, in fact, set about "cleansing" Argentine society of any left-wing influence, whether real or imagined, by eliminating union leaders, intellectuals and student radicals – even, in a famous case, executing a group of high school students who

the Plaza de Mayo who have marched every Thursday since the late 1970s, demanding to know what became of their missing children – did not alleviate the problem of state-sponsored terrorism.

Videla was succeeded by General Viola who was then forced from office and replaced by General Galtieri. In economic matters, the military fared no better than it had in politics. The foreign debt soared to $45 billion while the inflation rate went from bad to worse, unemployment increased and the peso was constantly devalued. It was in this climate that General Galtieri and his junta chose to try something new.

The Malvinas conflict: It was ironic that the Argentine military, having won its dirty war against its own people, was forced from power attempting to achieve what it had been trained to do, namely, fight in a conventional conflict. General Galtieri hoped to divert his people's attention from the worsening domestic situation through the traditional method of turning their eyes to foreign matters, in this case the British-occupied Malvinas (Falkland) Islands.

The ensuing South Atlantic War was a brief but bloody engagement begun on April 2, 1982, with the Argentine invasion of the islands and ending with their surrender at Port Stanley on June 14.

The disputed Malvinas or Falkland archipelago appeared the perfect target for Galtieri: the islands lay more than 13,000 km (8,000 miles) from Great Britain and their tiny population was heavily outnumbered by sheep. However, Galtieri and the other military commanders did not consider the possibility that Britain would actually fight to retain her claims to the islands. This major miscalculation was one of many that the Argentine junta was to make during the

following weeks. Technically, tactically and politically Argentina's rulers blundered badly. The conscripted army was ill-prepared for battle against trained professionals and did not put up much of a fight, while the navy stayed in port after a British submarine sank the cruiser *General Belgrano* on May 2. Only the brilliant and courageous performance of the Argentine air force prevented the country's honor from becoming completely tarnished.

Although, initially, most Argentines were wildly enthusiastic in their support of the military's adventurism, their euphoria soon collapsed. The people were soon to realize that their government had consistently fabricated stories of success in the field and that rather than having achieved a glorious repossession of islands which all Argentines feel are theirs, the country was made to suffer a humiliating blow.

General Galtieri resigned three days after the Argentine surrender and was replaced a week later by the retired general, Reynaldo Bignone. Bignone's attempts to curb inflation failed as the rate rocketed to 433 percent in 1983. Additionally, the junta was under increased pressure to lift the seige on democracy and hold elections for a civilian government; massive demonstrations at the Plaza de Mayo helped to force the government to honor its promises.

The military, knowing its days in power were numbered, sought to protect itself from anticipated criminal prosecution for human rights abuses by issuing its own study, *The Final Document of the Military Junta on the War Against Subversion and Terrorism.* This white paper praised the efforts of the armed forces in combating and defeating terrorism and denied any involvement by the administration in the barbaric actions undertaken during the dirty war. As an extra protective measure, the government proclaimed a general amnesty for all those involved in the "extralegal" efforts to crush the opposition.

The election campaign of 1983 was full of surprises. Many analysts expected a Peronist return to power or possibly a coalition government. A majority of voters, however, selected Raúl Alfonsín and his Radical Party to lead the nation out of years of repression and economic distress. Alfonsín was sworn in as president on December 10, one day after the military junta dissolved itself.

EVITA

Although Maria Eva Duarte de Perón, known throughout the world as Evita, lived in the limelight only very briefly, her impact on Argentine politics was enormous and continues today, more than four decades after her death.

Evita was venerated by the Argentine working class, mocked by the *grandes dames* of Buenos Aires society, and misunderstood by the military establishment. Through all of this she came to symbolize a wealthy Argentina, full of pride and with great expectations immediately following the Second World War.

Her meteoric rise from her beginnings as a poor villager in the backwaters of the interior to a status as one of the most intriguing, engaging, and powerful figures in a male-dominated culture is a tale worth retelling because it is unique.

Evita was born in the squalid village of Los Toldos in 1919, one of five illegitimate children her mother bore to Juan Duarte. After her father's death, the family moved to the northwestern provincial town of Junín, under the patronage of another of her mother's benefactors.

It was in Junín, at the age of 14, that she became determined to be an actress, and when she was given the opportunity to flee the dusty town, she grabbed it. Evita ran off to Buenos Aires, the cultural mecca of Latin America, in the company of a young tango singer.

As an aspiring 15-year-old actress, Evita faced almost insurmountable odds in landing jobs in the theater. She led a miserable existence, often falling ill and never having much to eat. Her opportunities took a dramatic leap forward when a rich manufacturer fell for her and provided her with her own radio show. Shortly thereafter, Evita's voice became a regular feature on the airwaves of Radio Argentina and Radio El Mundo.

Evita's energy was boundless; her work pace became frenetic and she made powerful friends. Her lack of acting talent and sophistication did not seem to hinder her ability to attract some very important people to her cause. Among her admirers were the president of Argentina and, more importantly, the Minister of Communications, Colonel Imbert, who controlled all radio stations in the country.

Evita met Colonel Juan Domingo Perón, the reputed power behind the new military government, at a fund-raising event for victims of the devastating 1944 San Juan earthquake, in which thousands died. She wasted no time in catching the widowed colonel and later left the fund-raiser on his arm.

Though exactly half Perón's 48 years, Evita, at numerous turns, assisted her husband's rise to power in ways that were beyond the imagination of even the most astute politicians. When Perón became Minister of Labor and Welfare, Evita convinced him that his real power base should be the previously ignored masses of laborers living in the horrible *villas miseria* (slums) that still ring the capital city.

A stream of pronouncements issued forth from the ministry instituting minimum wages, better living conditions, salary increases and protection from employers. The working class, for the first time in Argentina's history, began to see some of the profits of its labor.

Additionally, and most brilliantly, Perón empowered and shepherded the giant Confederación General del Trabajo (CGT or General Confederation of Labor), which embraced many of the trade unions. In the process, recalcitrant labor leaders were picked up by the police and sent to prisons in Patagonia.

It was not long before Evita called Perón's constituency – the *descamisados*, the shirtless ones – to his aid. An army coup was on the point of success when Evita called all her chips in. Upwards of 200,000 *descamisados* entered the capital city and demanded that Perón be their president. The colonel accepted the mandate of the Argentine people.

Evita, now married to Perón, cemented her ties with the workers by establishing the Social Aid Foundation. Through this charity, scores of hospitals and hundreds of schools were built, nurses trained, and money dispensed to the poor. Evita also furthered the cause of women's rights and suffrage and formed the first women's political party, the Peronista Feminist Party.

Although a cult was developing around her personality, she would always tell the people in her countless speeches that all credit should go to her husband and that she would gladly sacrifice her life for him, as they should sacrifice theirs. Perhaps Evita's finest personal and political moment came

years in the past. Family and friends were placed in high positions well above their levels of competence.

The people's heroine was dying by 1952, a victim of uterine cancer, but she kept up her intense work schedule. At her last speech, on May Day, her husband had to hold her up as she spoke to the *descamisados*. Evita's death on July 26, 1952 brought the whole of Argentina to a standstill. Her body was embalmed, and at her wake thousands paid their last respects.

In 1955, Evita's corpse disappeared, stolen by the military after they had deposed Juan Perón. It was carried to Germany and then Italy, where it was interred for 16 years under another name. After negotiations, it was finally returned to her husband

with her long tour of Europe, during which she met Franco, the dictator of Spain, Pope Pius XII, and the Italian and French foreign ministers.

She absolutely dazzled post-war Europe with her jewels and elegant gowns. Her rags-to-riches story was told and retold in the press, and she was even on the cover of *Time* magazine.

On the negative side, Evita would brook no criticism of her husband. Newspapers were closed, careers destroyed, and opponents jailed on trumped-up charges. She could be extremely vindictive, never forgetting an insult, even if it lay

Left, the glamorous First Lady. **Above**, the Peróns with their pet poodles.

in Spain. Evita's long odyssey came to an end when Juan Perón died in Argentina in 1974. Her coffin was brought from Spain and lay in state next to that of the one she had said she would die for.

Even though efforts to have her canonized in Rome met with polite refusal, Evita still holds near-saint status in Argentina. Graffiti proclaiming *Evita Vive!* (Evita lives!) can be seen everywhere. At the Duarte family crypt in the Recoleta Cemetery, devotees still leave flowers and a continual guard is kept to prevent vandalism.

Her epitaph, made famous by the Andrew Lloyd Webber–Tim Rice musical *Evita*, reads: "Don't cry for me Argentina, I remain quite near to you." It still rings true, decades after her early death. ■

them, he may be tortured and killed, but it is very improbable that he should happen to find them on the road; however, they are so cunning, and ride so quick, and the country is so uninhabited, that it is impossible to gain any information."

Along with the violence one might have encountered in the wild-west style atmosphere, there were natural hazards to be overcome along the way. Darwin soon experienced the trials of the terrain. "Changing horses for the last time, we again began wading through the mud. My animal fell, and I was well soused in black mire – a very disagreeable accident, when one does not possess a change of clothes."

sort of problem. The American Katherine S. Drier described what she had to contend with in Buenos Aires in 1918. "Before leaving for Buenos Aires everybody in New York told me that the Plaza Hotel was the only hotel in Buenos Aires, and that of course I would make it my headquarters during my sojourn there. But my information had been given me by men, and neither they nor I expected to find that the Plaza did not take women unaccompanied by their husbands or supposed husbands. Not even sisters accompanied by their brothers, or wives whose husbands have to travel, or widows, are made welcome. Much less respectable maiden ladies!"

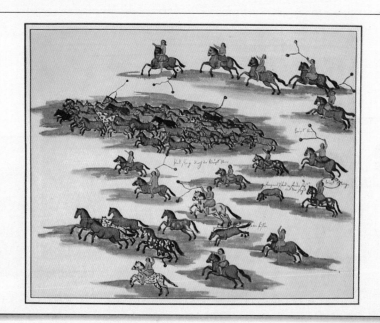

Darwin also noted that the wild animals of the pampas could prove problematic. "It is very difficult to drive animals across the plains; for if in the night a puma, or even a fox, approaches, nothing can prevent the horses dispersing in every direction; and a storm will have the same effect. A short time since, an officer left Buenos Aires with five hundred horses, and when he arrived at the army he had under twenty."

A woman traveling alone faced another

Left, rampant Spaniards on the hunt in Puerto Deseado, 1586. **Above**, boleadora-wielding pampean Indians.

Tehuelche and Puelche: The native Americans were of constant interest to the traveler of the 1800s, although by the 1870s they were becoming rarer and rarer as the campaigns to conclude the "Indian problem" reached their peak. One intrepid individual, the Jesuit Thomas Falkner, spent almost 20 years living among the Puelche and Tehuelche tribes of southern Argentina, from the 1730s until the religious order was expelled from the country. His account, *A Description of Patagonia*, was used as a guide by Darwin a century later.

Meeting an Indian could be a highpoint of a journey, as Lady Florence Dixie related in her *Across Patagonia* (1881). "We had not gone far when we saw a rider coming slowly towards us, and in a few minutes we found ourselves in the presence of a real Patagonia Indian. We reined in our horses when he got close to us, to have a good look at him, and he doing the same, for a few minutes we stared at him to our hearts' content, receiving in return as minute and careful a scrutiny from him."

Of the Indians themselves, many travelers remarked on their positive characteristics, especially of the doomed Tehuelche. Julius Beerbohm, who wrote *Wanderings in Patagonia or Life Among the Ostrich-Hunters* (1879), had much to say about the original

One of Galloping Head's fondest wishes was to be able to spend time with the native South American. "His profession is war, his food simple, and his body is in that state of health and vigor that he can rise naked from the plain on which he has slept, and proudly look upon his image which the white frost has marked out upon the grass without inconvenience. What can we 'men in buckran' say to this?"

Country life: The gauchos (Argentine cowboys) were often perceived as being as wild as the Indians, and just as interesting. Additionally, the gauchos and others living in the countryside were noted for their hospitality. Colonel King writes that, "whether in health

inhabitants of Argentina. "The Tehuelches are on the whole rather good-looking than otherwise, and the usual expression of their faces is bright and friendly. Their foreheads are rather low but not receding, their noses aquiline, their mouths large and coarse, but their teeth are extremely regular and dazzlingly white... in general intelligence, gentleness of temper, chastity of conduct, and conscientious behavior in their social and domestic relations, they are immeasurably superior not only to the other South American indigenous tribes, but also, all their disadvantages being taken into consideration, to the general run of civilized white men."

or sickness, the traveler is always welcome to their houses and boards, and they would as soon as think of charging for a cup of water, as for a meal of victual or a night's lodging."

Darwin, too, was greatly struck by their manners. "The gauchos, or countrymen, are very superior to those who reside in the towns. The gaucho is invariably most obliging, polite, and hospitable. I did not meet with even one instance of rudeness or inhospitality." And once, when Darwin inquired whether there was enough food for him to have a meal, he was told, "We have meat for the dogs in our country, and therefore do not grudge it to a Christian."

But traveling in the countryside was generally not a very comfortable affair. Galloping Head presents a none too appealing description of his night's accommodations. "We arrived an hour after sunset – fortified post – scrambling in the dark for the kitchen – cook unwilling – correo (the courier) gave us his dinner – huts of wild-looking people – three women and girls almost naked ('They be so wild as the donkey,' said one of the Cornish party, smiling; he then very gravely added, 'and there be one thing, sir, that I do observe, which is, that the farther we do go, the wilder things do get!') – our hut – old man immovable – Maria or Mariquita's figure – little mongrel boy – three or four other

following: "One of the least nasty is to kill and cut open two puppies and bind them on each side of a broken limb. Little hairless dogs are in great request to sleep at the feet of invalids."

Many travelers were impressed by the skills the gauchos demonstrated as they worked their horses, threw *bolas* to fell cassowaries – the South American ostrich – or lassoed cattle. Darwin mentioned a sight to which he was witness. "In the course of the day I was amused by the dexterity with which a gaucho forced a restive horse to swim a river. He stripped off his clothes, and jumping on its back rode into the river till it was out of its depth; then slipping off over

persons. Roof supported in the center by crooked poles – holes in roof and walls – walls of mud, cracked and rent... Floor, the earth – eight hungry peons, by moonlight standing with their knives in their hands over a sheep they were going to kill, and looking on their prey like relentless tigers."

In the country, far from doctors and hospitals, the people often relied on an assortment of folk medicine. Darwin was appalled at the remedies and only felt able to mention the

Left, Indian settlement by the Sierra de la Ventana. **Above**, Darwin's research vessel, the *HMS Beagle*.

the crupper, he caught hold of the tail, and as often as the horse turned around, the man frightened it back by splashing water in its face. As soon as the horse touched bottom on the other side, the man pulled himself on, and was firmly seated, bridle in hand, before the horse gained the bank. A naked man on a naked horse is a fine spectacle; I had no idea how well the two animals suited each other. The tail of a horse is a very useful appendage."

Earth and sky: The size of the country and the rough paths made the traveler's trip a very long one, indeed. E.E. Vidal, an early 19th-century traveler, quotes the unnamed author of *Letters from Paraguay,* who describes his trip from Buenos Aires to Mendoza, at the foot of the Andes, as taking 22 days in a large cart drawn by oxen. "We set off every afternoon about two, and sometimes three hours before sunset, and did not halt till about an hour after sunrise."

Having a sufficient supply of water was one of the obstacles the writer faced in his journey. "We were obliged to halt in a spot, where even the grass seemed to have been burned to the very roots, and nothing was presented to the eye but barrenness and desolation...We had but one small jar of water left, our thirst seemed to increase every moment."

Nature intervened as a thunderstorm struck the camp. "'Look at the oxen; they smell water.' We all eagerly turned to the poor panting animals, and saw them stretch their heads to the west, and snuff the air, as if they would be certain of obtaining drink could they but raise themselves into the atmosphere. At that moment not a cloud was to be seen, nor a breath of air felt; but in a few minutes the cattle began to move about as if mad, or possessed by some invisible spirit, snuffing the air with most violent eagerness, and gathering closer and closer to each other; and before we could form any rational conjecture as to what could occasion their simultaneous motion, the most tremendous storm of thunder, lightning, and rain I ever witnessed in my life came on. The rain fell in perpendicular streams, as if all the fountains of heaven had suddenly broken loose."

Many travelers commented on the seemingly endless flat pampas. W.J. Holland, an American scientist on an expedition to Argentina in 1912, described the scene from his train compartment. "I have crossed the prairies of Minnesota and the Dakotas, of Kansas and Nebraska, of Manitoba and Alberta; I have traveled over the steppes of Russia; but in none of them have I seen such absolutely level lands as those which lie between Rosario and Irigoyen. The horizon is that of the ocean; an upturned clod attracts attention; a hut looks like a house; a tree looms up like a hill."

Food and politics: The customs of the Argentines, whether of city folk, gauchos, or Indians, have always been cause for comment. Thomas Turner, describing one well-known and wealthy family at supper in the 1880s had this to say: "Of the domestic habits of the Argentines, their manners at table, *en famille*, it is impossible to give an attractive description. Their manners at table are ultra-Bohemian. They read the papers, shout vehemently at each other, sprawl their limbs under and over the table, half swallow their knives, spit with true Yankee freedom on the carpeted floor, gesticulate and bend across the table in the heat of argument, smoke cigarettes between the courses, and even while a course of which some of them do not partake is serving – a soothing habit which stimulates expectoration and provokes discussion – use the same knife and fork for every course – fish, entree, or joint, in a word, the studied deportment of the street is, in the house, exchanged for the coarse manners of the tap-room."

Turner was also shocked at the way politics dominated discussions, something that still is prevalent. "Although forbidden subjects are discussed by both sexes with zest and freedom, the staple topic of conversation is politics. Everybody talks politics... Even children talk politics, and discuss the merits of this, that or other statesmen with parrot-like freedom of opinion and soundness of judgment."

Many of the travelers' accounts are tinged with racism and the deep-seated assumption that the writers' own cultures were nearly always superior to that of the Argentines. Comments abound such as, "Most of the corruption which exists in public life is due to the participation of foreigners therein; Italians chiefly," or "the Argentine is not old enough yet to have developed the sense of humor," or, "I was becoming accustomed to the polite airs of this town that prints literature mad with Yankeephobia to snarl and bite all over SA against North America whose Monroe Doctrine, money, mentality and morality have been Argentina's help in the past and is her only hope in the future." These attitudes can be found in many firsthand descriptions of Argentina.

At the same time, the wanderers and explorers have passed on the country's lore, which might otherwise have been lost to us. Their tales are sometimes unintentionally amusing to today's reader but they are almost always fascinating and illuminating.

Right, a 19th-century gentleman farmer.

Alfonsín's presidency brought about early triumphs – the trial and imprisonment of the military juntas for human rights violations during the "dirty war;" the settlement of a long-standing border dispute with Chile over the Beagle Channel; divorce and shared paternal control laws. Unfortunately, these were soon forgotten as the economic problems left as a legacy by the military came home to roost – a soaring foreign debt, rising unemployment, and rampant inflation. Inflation quickly rose to over 1,000 percent annually. Argentines became resigned to seeing food prices and bus fares go up daily.

Alfonsín eventually accepted the advice of the International Monetary Fund (IMF) to stimulate the economy. The massive bureaucracy continued to devour state funds, industry stagnated, and inflation again became part of Argentine life.

Meanwhile, human rights lawyers were attempting to bring to trial those who had carried out the kidnappings, torture and murders of the "dirty war." But, hundreds of middle- and lower-ranking military officers were found to be involved, and they responded to the pressure by touching off a series of army mutinies that obliged Alfonsín to end further trials altogether.

From Peronism to Menemism: The deepening economic crisis of the late 1980s allowed the Justicialist (Peronist) party to claw its

and created a new currency (the austral) by lopping three zeros off the value of the old peso, freezing prices and wages, and making some cuts in government spending.

Instead of a storm of protest, most Argentines initially accepted the plan. The government was surprised at its own audacity in virtually ending inflation by decree.

Unfortunately, the Radical Party was uncertain of what to do next. They reinstated the plan with various modifications, but failed

Preceding pages, a political meeting at Buenos Aires Cathedral. **Left**, newsstand in Buenos Aires. **Above**, local chapter of the Radical Party.

way back from the shock of losing the 1983 general elections – the first defeat in the party's history. In mid-1989, the party's flamboyant candidate Carlos Menem – a one-time truck driver who entered the union movement to become governor of La Rioja Province – won the presidential elections by a landslide after making wage increases his main campaign proposal.

At that point, inflation was running at 200 percent a month, the new austral currency was splintering and food riots were rocking the country. Alfonsín decided to resign and hand over the presidential sash to Menem several months before his term was over.

Once in power, Menem's "man of the people" look changed in accordance with a stunning conservative about-face that shattered the populist Peronist policies he had set forth while on the campaign trail.

Bolstered by economist Domingo Cavallo – who first held the Foreign Affairs portfolio and later reigned as Economy Minister (and was the man who nationalized the privately held foreign debt toward the end of the military dictatorship) – the new president's Third World convictions were replaced by free market First World policies.

In a remarkably short time, Menem's picturesque long hair and sideburns were shortened to acceptable First World lengths and

devaluation with a steady erosion of wage-earners' buying power.

Nevertheless, bank interest rates remained high, and when the domestic market was suddenly opened to imports, more than 10,000 businesses went under.

Both deficit-ridden and profitable state-run utilities were sold off in record time, without first establishing regulatory agencies to stop monopolistic practices, or setting up an adequate social security network and retraining system for tens of thousands of workers who were suddenly left jobless.

Cost-cutting measures to make the country's products more competitive on international markets centered almost entirely on

his Third World ponchos were left for special occasions in the interior. Argentina left the Non-Aligned Movement and took up what one wag wryly termed "carnal relations" with the United States.

Convinced that free market economic stability and quick privatization of state enterprises were the only way to woo foreign investment and obtain money to pay the country's crushing foreign debt, the Menem-Cavallo duo replaced the austral with the peso, which was pegged to the dollar. Inflation was brought under control, albeit through the artifice of a dollar–peso convertibility that had the effect of replacing currency

reducing labor costs. Spanish- and Chilean-style labor flexibility measures which are known to produce unemployment were brought to bear on workers. New labor legislation officially did away with job security, wages were lowered and working conditions were pushed back to pre-Peronist times.

The power of labor unions has been drastically undermined; the general strikes that made Alfonsín's administration difficult have been notably lacking during Menem's latter-day Peronist government.

So too has the power of the military. After

Above, President Carlos Menem.

Economically, Peronism left a contradictory heritage that continues to weigh on efforts to modernize, rationalize and streamline the productive apparatus to this day. Under strong protection from imports, local manufacturing grew but remained inefficient, costly, uncompetitive and unable to provide sustained growth. At the same time, continued dependence on imported raw materials and capital goods, vulnerability to agricultural price cycles and the burden of a state sector designed to provide high levels of employment and social welfare, led to a series of balance of payments crises, beginning in the late 1950s.

Perón's return to power and subsequent

tized in record time, imports of all types flooded in, new labor legislation made it possible to cut payrolls and pay lower salaries, and the federal government freed itself of many social welfare obligations by passing control of hospitals and schools to provinces and cities and privatizing pension funds.

Unfortunately, interest rates remained high and much of the foreign capital attracted by these policies was not oriented toward production; deposits and capital fled Argentina as well as other Latin American countries when Mexico devalued its currency at the end of 1994, cutting short a three-year growth trend. Many small industries and businesses closed and tax collections dropped. Unem-

efforts to revive the 1940s economic model deepened the crisis, which, coupled with a militant labor offensive and an urban guerrilla campaign, threatened to create chaos.

Since 1983, Argentina has once again enjoyed civilian democratic government. The Menem administration, elected in May 1989 and re-elected in 1995, installed a dollarized free market economy aimed at achieving economic stability, attracting investment and paying the country's crushing foreign debt (*see page 70*). State enterprises were priva-

ployment, already fuelled by privatizations and private sector cutbacks, quickly shot up to around 20 percent, more than double the historic average.

Industrial exports have increased, but the goods involved are not labor-intensive, and they are being exported because the shrinkage of the domestic market has made them available to growing Mercosur (Southern Cone common market) demand, which has turned out to be one of the saviors of the Argentine economy.

In Argentina as elsewhere, it has become clear that economic growth does not necessarily create jobs.

Left, slum-dwellers. Above, the Mothers of the Plaza de Mayo campaign for human rights.

Walking in Buenos Aires, visitors with untrained ears might think they are hearing an awful lot of Italian. From the look of some of the streets they might at first think they are in Europe. Both these illusions are created by Argentina's mixed social heritage.

Who are the Argentines? Trying to define the national character can be difficult. Ask an Argentine, and one is likely to get an agonized response. Many are very quick to confess to a national identity crisis; "We don't know if we're Europeans or Latin Americans," they tell you.

Jokes abound about the confused Argentine psyche. One line has it that an Argentine is an Italian who speaks Spanish, lives in a French house and thinks he is British. Another holds that the Mexicans descended from the Aztecs, the Peruvians descended from the Incas, and the Argentines descended from boats.

All of this uncertainty arises because Argentina is a nation of immigrants. Other countries have a similar cultural mix, but the dynamics were different here. The melting pot effect that took place in the United States, over a long period of time, did not really happen here. Too many people arrived in Argentina in too short a time, and the country is still trying to work things out.

In the beginning, things were much simpler. The original inhabitants of Argentina were divided into many distinct tribes, but their numbers were few. The first European settlers, in the 16th century, were almost all Spanish, as were those arriving over the next 300 years. A minority population of *mestizos* (mixed Indian and Hispanic stock) developed early. A large number of enslaved Africans were brought in, and *mulattos* (mixed black and white stock) and Indian/black mixtures were added. But that was as complicated as things got.

The 19th century saw severe changes in the ethnic make-up of Argentina. Through a concerted effort, the vast majority of the Indian population was wiped out by the

Argentine army, thus freeing land for Europeans. Also, after the abolition of slavery, the black population faded from view (*see "The Case of the Afro-Argentines," page 46*).

New hands: These changes coincided with massive immigration from Europe. Inspired by European liberalism, Argentina sought to develop its economy and fill out as a nation, so immigration was encouraged by government policy. Argentina was seen as a land of opportunity, and the Europeans came in droves. Between 1857 and 1939, over 3½

million laborers were added to the population. They were predominantly Italian (45 percent) and Spanish (30 percent), but others came from France, Poland, Russia, Switzerland, Wales, Denmark, Germany, England and elsewhere. In the early 20th century, there were arrivals from Syria and Armenia.

By 1914, the population was 30 percent foreign-born, and in some of the larger cities, the foreigners outnumbered the natives. These new hands were put to work filling positions in the expanding agricultural industry, in cattle-raising and processing, and in the developing economies of the cities.

With the Depression, there was a halt to

Preceding pages: *porteño* family in the park. **Left,** everyone likes to talk. **Right,** a child of the Northwest.

the influx. After World War II, more people started to come in, but they were mostly from surrounding countries, where work was often hard to find.

Recession is slowing the influx of immigrants from bordering countries that marked the early 1990s. Workers from bordering Bolivia and Paraguay, who have Argentine-based relatives with whom to stay, are sticking it out, but Peruvians, who lack this support structure, are leaving in droves. Meanwhile, as rural economies continue to falter, domestic migrations to the cities by those looking for work continue.

Argentina's urban economies have been unable to accommodate the increasing population demands, and *villas miseria* (shanty towns) have grown outside larger industrial areas. Although Argentines as a whole enjoy a fairly high standard of living, conditions in the slums continue to worsen, and the situation will have to be addressed by those seeking to govern the country as a whole.

Distinguishing angst: All these comings and goings have created the great Argentine identity crisis. Nonetheless, while people continue to proclaim their lack of a cultural identity, the live their lives in a uniquely Argentine way. It is, in part, this malaise which distinguishes Argentines from their neighbors. The Peruvians and Brazilians don't spend too much time on this sort of soul-searching. The Argentines are still trying to figure out if they're European or Latin American, and they are famous in Latin America for not yet making up their minds.

The demographics have stabilized somewhat in recent years. The current population is around 33 million. Of these, nearly 11 million live in the federal capital – Greater Buenos Aires. Over 80 percent of the total is urban. Roughly 85 percent are of European descent; the remainder are divided among small groups of Indians, those of *mestizo* stock, and members of small non-European immigrant groups, such as Arabs and Asians.

The official language is Spanish, but it is spoken by many with a zesty Italian lilt. The accent is often hard for visitors to understand, but the ear soon becomes accustomed. Dialects vary around the country.

Although there has been a fair amount of intermarriage of nationalities, many groups in Argentina have kept themselves distinct. Some communities have, over the years, strived for ethnic purity. Examples include the small Welsh enclaves in Patagonia, and the German and Eastern European villages in the north. Many communities maintain their own social services, such as hospitals, schools, and athletic clubs. Newspapers come out in a variety of languages.

Mother England: One relatively small but tight community is Anglo-Argentine. To a large extent, British capital built the Argentine railway and banking systems in the second half of the 19th century. British money also helped develop the cattle industry, with modern methods of refrigeration, packaging, and transportation. British cattle were imported to upgrade the national stock. Some

Englishmen bought gigantic tracts of land in the south to raise sheep, and for a time, southern Patagonia seemed an extension of the British Empire.

The first British settlers came to administer the building of the industrial infrastructure, and their services helped to make Argentina one of the world's ten richest countries by the start of the 20th century. That position has been lost, but the Anglo-Argentine pride in their contribution to the nation still holds.

Today, the community remains cliquish. Their children are educated in schools modeled after the British system, with names like

St Andrew's and St George's, and full time rugby coaches are hired from England. Polo and cricket are played at weekends on the manicured lawns of the exclusive Hurlingham Club outside Buenos Aires. However, the Anglo-Argentines do feel their loyalties lie with Argentina, and the war with Mother England over the Malvinas (Falkland) Islands placed a heavy social burden upon them to demonstrate this.

Tribal ways: There are not many pure Indians left in Argentina, but small pockets remain, mostly in the far north and south. Exact populations are disputed, but estimates suggest 100,000–600,000. Figures are confused by blurred ethnic identities.

Araucano-Mapuches and the Tehuelche were the major groups of Patagonia and the pampas although there are very few pure-blooded descendents left today. Settlers committed genocide at the turn of the century against the indigenous groups of Tierra del Fuego, the Yamana and Ona.

City versus country: There is one clear distinction one should make when talking about Argentines, and that is the one between *porteños* (residents of Buenos Aires) and the rest of the population. This schism is as old as Argentina, and the difference is insisted upon by both sides of the division. *Porteños* say, only half in jest, they are the only Argentines worth a mention. Isn't Buenos

Reservations were created by the government for certain groups, but the land was largely barren, and poverty is severe. Few of the tribes still practice traditional lifestyles, but certain ceremonial elements have been maintained. Some still speak their native dialects as first or second languages. Quechua is still spoken in the northwest, where the Colla are the largest Indian group. Chiriguan, Choroti, Wichi, Mocovi and Toba are spoken in the Chaco area; the Chiriguan are the principal tribe of Mesopotamia. The

Left and above, immigrants from Russia and Holland in the early 1930s.

Aires the seat of the nation's culture, heritage, etc? With pity and resentment, the rest of the population seems resigned to this egocentric designation. Those of the interior have their own ways of doing things, and they don't need the *porteños* to help them. A brief, informal survey shows the perceptions of both sides. The *porteños* think they are sophisticated, glamorous and cultured and the country folk are unsophisticated, ugly, superstitious and ignorant. Those of the interior believe themselves to be humble, commonsensical, and more in touch with the land, and consider the *porteños* aggressive, pretentious, highly-strung and ignorant.

Much of this can be explained as the standard conflict between city dwellers and country folk. But here, one city is pitted against the rest of the country. There are other cities in Argentina, but none could be considered a major cosmopolitan center. Occasionally, inhabitants of the interior will venture to the Big City, but after a few days of movies, bright lights and crowded streets they are more than ready for the clean air and quiet of their home terrain.

Porteños, on the other hand, rarely venture into the rest of their country. Many middle-class families have small weekend houses on the outskirts of Buenos Aires, and upper-class families have their *estancias* or

through all Argentines. This often exhibits itself in the warmth of personal contacts and a high degree of tactility. During conversation, people are always touching each other lightly on the arm or slapping each other on the back. The intimate and colloquial *vos*, rather than the formal *usted*, is used to address nearly everyone. Greetings and goodbyes involve a lot of hugging and kissing. Kisses on the cheek are in order whenever one is introduced, except under highly formal business circumstances. Women kiss women, and women kiss men. Only men don't kiss men until a friendship develops.

Families here tend to be closely knit. It is not unusual for young people to live at home

"camps" to visit, and there are the occasional ski trips out west for the comfortably-off, but that's about the extent of the adventuring.

Tactile-defensives beware: Geographical factionalism aside, there are some qualities which all Argentines could be said to share: their relaxed approach to life and time frames. If it doesn't get done today, it will surely get done tomorrow. When waiting for an Argentine to keep an appointment, whether for a cup of coffee or an important business meeting, allowance should be made for benign tardiness. It's a way of life.

There is a sentimental streak, captured in the melancholy strains of the tango, that runs

until they get married, and even then they may only move a few blocks away. Students do not often move out when they enter university, as they often attend schools in their home towns. Argentines view as heartless the practice, in other cultures, of shipping kids off to college at the tender age of 18.

Families are always extended, and children often have cousins as their best friends. This closeness frequently carries into adulthood. Weekend gatherings of the clan for an *asado* (barbecue) keep everyone in touch.

Creatures of fads and habit: Argentines still tend to be conservative: they don't much like to try new things but are, paradoxically, very susceptible to fads. Finally convinced that white meat is healthier than red, they have doubled their consumption of chicken in recent years at the expense of traditional beefsteaks. Beef consumption is still higher than in most countries (48 kilos/105 lbs per year per capita), but the days of grilled beef twice a day are long gone.

Fish, however, still fails to tempt them: consumption fails to reach two digits per capita. Nevertheless, scanty servings of bland "health food" are in far greater vogue than the taste bud adventures offered by Buenos Aires' few ethnic restaurants, thanks to the daily bombardment of the media and their advertisers, whose products are promoted

Drinking habits are similarly conservative. For all the wine that is produced here, consumption is in measured amounts. Beer is increasingly popular, and is now seen as more than a means to cutting summer thirst. Much of the aforementioned steak (and a growing number of hamburgers) gets washed down with economy-size bottles of soda pop or mineral water.

One doesn't see much dancing on table tops here, and it is because of this widespread reserved behavior that a trip to the La Boca district of Buenos Aires is so much fun. Here one can see Argentines cutting loose. High-spirited crowds mix with the sailors in port, in a free-for-all of dancing, drinking

by gymnasium-formed, invariably young models. In times of recession, price is also a consideration.

The increase in receptiveness to fads is largely due to ever-longer hours in front of TV sets. Cable networks in particular are expanding now people have less money to spend and dedicate most of their free time to watching television and doing at-home tasks, rather than enjoying weekend excursions and socializing with friends.

Far left, Araucanian woman, and **left**, fertility dance of the Chirimuskis. **Above**, leather chic from Le Fauve.

and general spectacle-making. But this is not the norm. In general, Argentines hate to draw attention to themselves. Loud and unusual behavior in public is sternly looked down upon.

Even when it comes to vacations, Argentines are creatures of habit. Although their country has a variety of destinations nearly unparalleled, year after year people will return to the same resort for their summer holidays. Foreigners, even on a short visit, will often see more of this country than a native will in a lifetime.

Listening to accounts of the adventures to be had out there, an Argentine will sigh and say that, yes, maybe next year he'll go to see the whales at the Valdés Peninsula, or the glaciers of Lago Argentino, but one way or the other he probably won't make it. The government has started a major campaign, with the theme *Primero lo nuestro* (Our own places first), to encourage Argentines to see their own country. One of the motives of this campaign is to keep hold of the money of those who can afford to go elsewhere.

Strong opinions: There are a couple of topics on which Argentines conduct heated public debate, where making an emotional display is no embarrassment; one is sport and the other is politics. Soccer, or football, is the big national sport, and team allegiances are

Argentines are aware of the issues at both national and global levels, but they reserve their passion for the former, especially when it comes to summing up their own personal economic situation.

More than a decade of democracy has all but obliterated memory of life under a dictatorship. The political renaissance of the Alfonsín years gradually slipped into disenchantment with politics and politicians during the Menem years.

During that first decade of long-awaited democracy Argentines saw their country first deeply involved with the Non-Aligned Movement under Alfonsín, and then so closely aligned with the United States by Menem

strong. At a fairly early age, most Argentines must decide where those allegiances lie. Matches draw large crowds, and the enthusiasm of fan support has gotten increasingly out of hand in recent years.

Argentines are a highly opinionated bunch, and one subject on which anyone will have strong opinions is politics. The population is one of the most highly politicized in South America. Anyone will readily tell you what political party he belongs to and why, what party he voted for in the last election and why (these matters are sometimes separated for reasons of expediency), and what the main issues are.

that one wag spoke of the country's "carnal relations" with Uncle Sam.

Voting is mandatory, and if the law were rescinded, it is anybody's guess whether people would stop voting altogether, or vote only to "punish" officials who feel no responsibility toward their electorate.

There is a broad range of political parties in Argentina, including many regional and provincial ones. They range from the ultra conservative to the ultra left, and seem, ideologically, to form a full circle rather than a linear progression; the two extremes start to look a lot alike on certain issues. There are severe splits even within single parties, the most notable being within the Justicialist (Peronist) Party. Most parties have youth branches, which offer younger members a chance to get involved. This makes for some colorful names, perhaps the best being Intransigent Youth.

It doesn't matter what a person's party membership is, people will often end up explaining their persuasion in relation to Peronism. The effect of this party's ideologies has been so pervasive that it has become the basis for putting everything else in perspective. You may love them or you may hate them, but where you stand is to be explained through them.

Evita Duarte Perón holds a special place in

feminist, and many today take strength from her example.

Observed rites: The 1994 constitutional reforms continue to guarantee religious freedom, but Catholicism is no longer the state religion, nor does the President have to be a Catholic. Nominally, about 90 percent of the population is Catholic, but strict faith does not seem to have a firm grip on the national psyche. The church is kept in its role as an institution, and its teachings seem more an incentive for periodic observances than a model for day to day living.

Annual pilgrimages to holy sites such as Luján draw thousands of participants, and special occasions like papal visits can bring

Argentine political thinking. Even those who do not agree with the precepts of Peronism as a whole give her credit for initiating several large steps forward in national policy. Feminists hold her in very high esteem, pointing out that she was behind her husband's moves to give women the vote, to protect the rights of women workers, and to legalize divorce (this last was held invalid, soon after her husband's fall in 1955, and the right to divorce was only reinstated in 1987). Evita is viewed by many as the original Argentine

Left, a meeting of generations. **Above**, two faces of *porteño* youth.

the country to a near standstill. However, weekly attendance at mass is a much less pressing matter for many.

The influence of the church has been lessening over a long period. Towards the end of the 19th century, schools and the rites of burial and marriage were secularized. But elements of the faith continue to play a role: the legalization of divorce has been an extremely divisive issue for years, although introduced by Péron and recognized until his fall from power. In 1987, after repeated votes and hard debate in Congress, divorce was legalized, but many unmarried couples who have been living in a *de facto* state of marriage with second or third partners, feel that the process of legal disentanglement from original contracts is too complicated and costly to be bothered with.

There is a standing law that all children in Argentina must be registered upon birth with Christian names. This can present problems for immigrants wishing to maintain an ethnic heritage from the mother country. If the proposed name has a Spanish translation, this must be used, at least for official purposes. The stringency of the application is up to the presiding judge; if he doesn't mind that the desired name isn't one of a verifiable saint, then it can squeeze by. Once the new name is on the books, it is open for use by

religion. Pilgrimages are made and offerings brought to local shrines revering unofficial saints. Miracles are averred to have taken place in all sorts of out of the way spots.

A quasi-religious cult of devotion has grown up around the person of Evita Perón. Flowers are placed before her tomb daily. In the northwest region of the country, festivals such as the annual carnival can be seen to contain certain elements which are not Christian in origin.

Villa Freud: Once almost popular enough to qualify as a secular religion of sorts, psychoanalysis is fast losing ground to psychology, which costs patients less in terms of time and money. A small group of local

others to follow. The list of usable names is reportedly much longer in Buenos Aires than elsewhere.

Riding around on city buses, a visitor may periodically see his fellow passengers make the sign of the cross; this means a church has been passed. In some sections of town, this may happen every few blocks. One gothic secular structure in Buenos Aires, which looks for all the world to be a church, invariably gets a misguided devotional response from out-of-towners.

The further one goes from Buenos Aires, the more you will see versions of Catholicism taking on the characteristics of folk

pioneers who were devotedly reading the works of Freud, got a boost from European-trained practitioners who came over in the 1930s and 1940s. Thereafter, psychoanalysis became increasingly popular, to the point that Buenos Aires is still said to have more psychoanalysts per capita than the state of New York. One sector of the Palermo district is even nicknamed Villa Freud in recognition of its heavily analysed population.

Explanations for this phenomenon usually center around the much discussed national identity crisis. Analysis has helped to lessen anxieties, real or imagined, about not belonging to a greater whole. Also, as the standard of living has slipped, and other problems have come to plague the nation, many people have come to feel more disoriented than ever.

The study and practice of psychology was heavily suppressed during the years of the *Proceso*. Military authorities viewed the field as somehow subversive, and books on the subject were even removed from public and private shelves. University departments were either drastically reduced or closed down altogether. Psychology enjoyed a strong resurgence with the return to democracy in 1983, and ended up displacing psychoanalysis for largely economic reasons. Private health schemes include both specialties, but

of the work force, 15 percent more than in 1980. One third of Argentine households are supported by female breadwinners.

More women than men now attend university, comprising 53 percent of student bodies. Forty-five percent of political party militants are women, but a law that they must occupy 30 percent of party electoral lists is rarely complied with. In general, women have yet to have a say that corresponds to their numbers in most walks of life. Only 12 percent of female employees hold top managerial jobs in big companies.

Nowadays, women receive more comprehension and support from their husbands or boyfriends at home than they do at the office.

sessions are usually limited because long treatments are not considered necessary or desirable. The days when wealthy patients made monthly deposits in their analyst's foreign bank account are definitely over. And as the number of practicing psychologists is fast overtaking the number of clients able to pay for even a short treatment, it is no longer the vogue subject for university study.

Family democracy: Argentine family life has also undergone a striking metamorphosis. Women now comprise nearly 40 percent

Left, the *après-ski* set at Bariloche. **Above**, Argentine rocker Charly Garcia.

Recent social attitude surveys show that more than 80 percent of Argentine men and women now accept that household chores should be shared, that couples have a right to exercise family planning, and that women have the right to choose a career over marriage and family. Those most open to family democracy are upper- and middle-class people under 35.

Tea ceremony: Young visitors to Argentina will often ask where they can meet Argentines of their age. A coffee house wouldn't be a bad place to start. Here and in bookstores, young intellectuals congregate to discuss politics and art. There are also many small clubs that feature local bands playing everything from punk rock to jazz. The *sí* portion of the *Clarín* daily paper which comes out on Friday, has a complete listing of events. Popular rock groups include Soda Stereo, the Charly García Band, Los Redonditos de Ricota, Los Ratones Paranoicos, Divididos and Las Pelotas.

One of the best ways to get a feel for the youth of Argentina today is to get invited to someone's house. Small gatherings in tiny apartments are a favorite form of entertainment and relaxation. Party goers will begin the evening chatting about studies, rock groups, and sports, and end up dancing to loud music, accompanied by gallons of beer

or soda pop. If they are well-enough heeled, the party may move on to one of the city's many youth-oriented discos, which begin to swing around 3am.

Today's young people are not interested in the politics and protest songs that once fascinated their parents. Most feel that they have no power over the formation of government policy, and only 10 percent belong to a political party.

Of the political singers who were once very popular at all levels of society, only Argentine communist Mercedes Sosa, one of Latin America's biggest stars, still commands a following of sorts among young

people. Her concerts have been packing people in for several decades.

Only people raised in the interior of the country, and the big-city counter-culture exponents of the previous generation, seem inclined to take the time necessary to indulge in the camaraderie of passing around *mate* – a strong herbal tea served in a hollow gourd and sipped through a communal straw.

This Argentine version of a tea ceremony has a magical way of increasing the feeling of camaraderie in a small group. The visitor should beware; ignorance of the finer points of the ritual will inevitably make for much scrutiny and merriment on the part of practiced hands. Nowadays, most Argentines prepare *mate* from bags, like other teas.

The history of Argentine counter-culture in recent years has had its own twists and turns. Argentina experienced a hippie period which paralleled that in the rest of the world, but its development was cut short by the arrival of the military regimes in the 1970s. During the *Proceso*, it was too dangerous to appear overtly leftist. Now that democracy has returned, many seem to be picking up the thread. This is even true for many who were too young to remember the original movement. Hair is getting longer on many young men; beads, beards, and a love and peace attitude are reminiscent of earlier times.

Sidewalk poetry: Women who don't take kindly to being accosted on the streets may have a rough time of it here. Verbally passing judgment on women in the street is practically the male national sport, elevated, some say, to an art form, otherwise known as *piropo*. This is not a matter of a few crude words thrown over the shoulder in passing; poetry, albeit hasty and primitive, is supposed to be involved.

The subject is not really expected to take the man up on his implied interest. Most of these *calle* Casanovas probably wouldn't know what to do with an aggressively positive response. The man's ego is satisfied through this simple exercise, and he figures it hasn't done the target any harm.

There are, of course, men who are out looking for more, but that is beyond the confines of the game of *piropo*, and with time one learns to distinguish the two.

Left, a moment's uncertainty. **Right**, a butcher takes a breather.

and in 1917 Victor Records captured the young voice of Carlos Gardel singing *Mi Noche Triste* (*My Sad Night*). It was, in many ways, the end of one era and the beginning of another.

Carlos Gardel was the tango's first international superstar. This career shows the most important developments of the genre in its golden era. Despite the debate among aficionados, it seems most likely that Gardel was born in Uruguay, the tango's other home base, sometime around 1881.

What transformed Gardel into a star, as they transformed the tango into music with a far wider appeal, were recordings, radio, and the new talking, moving pictures. Gardel

around the old Central Market. In 1984 the municipality renamed the local subway stop in honour of Gardel.

The tango's ebbs and flows in popularity were always tied to politics and the broader social condition of Argentina. In the late 1930s it dipped, only to hit a new peak under the Peronist governments of 1945 and 1955, when, with a heightened nationalism and increased worker earnings, driven by Perón's focus on trade unionism, new clubs and dance halls boomed.

Towards the end of the 1950s the tango had entered a crisis, in part because its keenest followers suffered political defeats, in part because of the onslaught of new forms

went to France in 1929, where he made films at Joinville, and in 1934 he signed a contract with Paramount, for which studio he was to make five films.

By the time of his death in a plane crash in Colombia in 1935, Gardel had become the personification of the tango. When the boat bearing his body arrived in the port of Buenos Aires, hundreds of thousands gathered to say goodbye to the *"pibe de Abasto"* (kid from Abasto) the neighborhood which is

Far left, *tanguistas* **perform at a street fair, and left**, tango lives on in dance halls. **Above**, it takes two and a lot of passion.

of music, mainly rock, and in part because the great names of tango were disappearing from the scene.

New names have appeared, with new ideas about how to rescue and revive the tango, creating controversy, at times acrimonious, between defenders of the old guard and promoters of the new.

Unquestionably, the most important of the neo-*tanguistas* was Astor Piazzola, whose training as a classical musician and experience as a jazz performer helped him produce a series of daring experiments in musical fusions that won acclaim both in the United States and Europe.

The gaucho stands as one of the best-known cultural symbols of Argentina. This rough, tough, free-riding horseman of the pampa, a proud cousin of the North American cowboy, is maintained in Argentine culture as the perfect embodiment of *argentinidad*, the very essence of the national character. He has been elevated to the level of myth, celebrated in both song and prose, and well endowed with the virtues of strength, bravery and honor.

However, as with all elements of national history, the gaucho and his culture continue to be hotly debated topics among the Argentines.

Some say the gaucho disappeared as an identifiable social character in the late 19th century. Others will argue that, although his world has undergone radical changes in the last few centuries, the gaucho still survives in Argentina. However, while there are still people scattered throughout the country who call themselves gauchos, their lives bear a limited resemblance to the lives of their forebears.

Pampean orphans: Gaucho life had its beginnings on the pampa, the vast grasslands of the east-central Southern Cone some time in the 18th century. There is some dispute as to the exact location, but a favored theory gives the gauchos their origin on the so-called East Bank, in the territory that is today called Uruguay.

As to the origin of the name gaucho, there are again many theories which trace the word to everything from Arabic and Basque, to French and Portuguese. The most likely answer, however, is that the word has joint roots in the native Indian dialects of Quechua and Araucanian, a derivation of their word for orphan. It is not hard to imagine how a word meaning orphan evolved into a term for these solitary figures, as they were neither loved nor ruled by anyone.

The first gauchos were mostly *mestizos*, of mixed Spanish and native American stock. As with the North American cowboy, some also had varied amounts of African blood, a legacy of the slave trade.

Hides and tallow: Cattle and horses that had escaped from early Spanish settlements in the 16th century had, over the centuries, proliferated into enormous free-roaming herds, and it was this wild, unclaimed abundance that was the basis for the development of the gaucho subculture. The horses were caught and tamed, and then used to capture the cattle.

Beef at that time did not have any great commercial value; there was more meat than the tiny population of Argentina could consume, and methods to export it had not yet been developed. This surplus led to waste on a grand scale; any excess meat was simply thrown away.

The primary value of the cattle was in the hides and tallow they provided, which were non-perishable exportable items. The first gauchos made their living by selling these in exchange for tobacco, rum and *mate*; gauchos were said to be so addicted to this stimulating tea that they would rather have gone without their beef. Their existence was fairly humble, with few needs. Most did not possess much beyond a horse, a saddle, a poncho and a knife.

The work was not terribly rigorous, and early travelers' accounts of the gauchos portray them as savage and uncouth vagabonds. They were left with plenty of extra time on their hands, and much of this was spent drinking and gambling.

This unwise combination of activities often led to a third favorite pastime: the knife fight. The violent lifestyle of the gaucho was looked upon with horror and disdain by the city folk, but the animosity was mutual. The gauchos had nothing but scorn for what they saw as the fettered and refined ways of the *porteños*.

Skilled horsemanship: The primary reputation of the gaucho, however, was that of a horseman, and this was well deserved. It was said that when a gaucho was without his horse he was without legs.

Almost all his daily chores, from bathing to hunting were conducted from atop his steed. The first gauchos hunted with lassoes

Preceding pages: a gentleman gaucho displays his wealth. **Left,** gauchos of Salta with their stiff leather *guardamontes*.

and *boleadoras*, both of which they borrowed from Indian culture. The *boleadoras* consisted of three stones or metal balls attached to the ends of connected thongs. Thrown with phenomenal accuracy by the gauchos, this flying weapon would trip the legs of the fleeing prey.

Charles Darwin, in his descriptions of Argentine life in the 1830s, has an amusing account of his own attempt to throw the *boleadoras*. He ended up catching nothing more than himself, as one thong caught on a bush, and the other wound around his horse's legs. As one might imagine, this ineptitude was the source of much chiding and laughter from the attendant gauchos.

skills in everyday survival is the practice of *pialar*. In this challenge, a man would ride through a gauntlet of his lasso-wielding comrades, who would try to trip up the feet of his mount. The object of the exercise was for the unseated man to land on his feet with reins firmly in hand. This kind of control was often necessary on the open plain, where hidden animal burrows presented a constant danger underfoot.

As outsiders bent on enforcing order in the countryside sought to control the lives and activities of the gauchos, these competitions came under increasing restrictions. Organized and contained rodeos became the forum for the showing off of skills.

The great emphasis placed on equestrian skills inevitably led to competition. Strength, speed and courage were highly prized, and the chance to demonstrate these came often.

In one event, the *sortija*, a horseman would ride full tilt with a lance in his hand to catch a tiny ring dangling from a crossbar. Another test of both timing and daring, the *maroma*, would call for a man to drop from a corral gate as a herd of wild horses was driven out beneath him. Tremendous strength was needed to land on a horse's bare back, bring it under control and return with it to the gate.

A good illustration of how these competitions were born of the necessity to develop

Ranch hands: Profound change came to the gauchos' way of life as increasing portions of the pampa came under private ownership. Beginning in the late 18th century, large land grants were made to powerful men from Buenos Aires, often as a form of political patronage.

The gauchos, with their anarchistic ways, were seen as a hindrance to the development of the land. Increasing restrictions were put on their lives, in order to bring them to heel and to put them at the service of the new landowners.

It was not only the land which came under private ownership, but the cattle and horses that were found on them as well, making them inaccessible to the free riders.

The gauchos were suddenly put in the position of being trespassers and cattle thieves. This made their situation similar to that of the remaining tribes of plains Indians. The shaky reputations of the gauchos grew worse. When they got into trouble in one area, they simply rode on to another, and little by little they were found further from the settled areas.

New order: With such an obvious conflict of interests, there had to be a resolution, and it was, predictably enough, in favor of the landowners. The open prairie lands were fenced off, and the disenfranchised gauchos

pean markets opened up, an ever-increasing amount of land was turned over to agriculture, and the gaucho work ethic ensured that the business of planting and harvesting was all done by the immigrants.

When barbed wire fencing was put up, fewer hands were needed to maintain the herds. Combined with the increase in agriculture, this led to even harder times for the gauchos and animosity grew between them and the employable newcomers. Many of the gauchos could only find temporary work on the *estancias*, and they moved from one place to another, branding cattle or shearing sheep. These itinerant laborers were paid by the day or task.

were put to work at the service of the *estancieros*. Their skills were employed to round up, brand and maintain the herds. Wages were pitifully low.

However, the gauchos maintained their pride. They refused to do any unmounted labor, which was seen as the ultimate degradation. Chores such as the digging of ditches, mending of fences and planting of trees were reserved for the immigrants who were arriving in increasing numbers from Europe. As the opportunities for exports to the Euro-

Left, early gaucho, with toe-held stirrups. **Above**, roundup in Corrientes.

Through the 19th century a whole new order came to rest on the pampa; the gaucho had ceased to be his own man. His new status as a hired ranch hand did not sit well with the gaucho's rebellious spirit. But the forces working against him were strong. The landowners had powerful friends in the capital, and the politicians saw the ordering of the countryside as a major priority. Argentina was finally beginning to take its place among the developing nations, and the traditional life of the gaucho could only be seen as a hindrance to that course.

Informal armies: However, while the gaucho ceased to present an independent threat, he still had a role to play in the new social structure of the rural areas. As the domestication of the gaucho increased, new bonds of loyalty were formed between the worker and his master.

Powerful *caudillos* were gaining control over large parts of the interior, backed up by their gauchos, who served as irregular troops in private armies. This formation of regional powers was in direct contradiction to the goals of centralized government.

Years of civil warfare followed Argentina's independence from Spain, and it was only when the Unitarians, led by José de San Martín, gained the upper hand, late in the 19th century, that the powerful Federalist

bands were finally brought under control.

Gauchos were also, at various times, put to work in the defense of the central government. These skilled horsemen were first used in the armies that routed the British invasion forces in 1806 and 1807, and by all accounts, their services were invaluable. Although they were forcibly inducted, they fought bravely and did not have the high desertion rates of other groups.

Gaucho squadrons were next used in the war of independence from Spain, and again they displayed great valor. The last time that the gauchos fought as an organized force in the nation's army was during the Desert

Campaign of the 1880s. Ironically, the gauchos, many of whom were of mixed Indian blood, were being used this time to exterminate the Indian tribes who were seen as an obstacle to territorial expansion. The campaigns opened up vast new areas for Europeans to settle on, but gaucho songs from the period lament their compromise of honor in the endeavor.

Las Chinas: The family life of the gaucho was never a very settled one. Supposedly, the women of their early camps were captives from raids on nearby settlements. This primitive theft was perhaps one of the practices that made the gauchos so unpopular with the forces of civilization. But even when women later moved voluntarily out onto the pampas, the domestic arrangements were rather informal. Church weddings were seen as inconvenient and expensive, and common law marriages were the norm.

The *chinas*, as these women were called, were rarely welcome on the *estancias* where the gauchos worked. The few that were allowed were employed as maids, wet nurses, laundresses, and cooks. They also participated in the sheep shearing. Home life for the *china* reflected the primitive conditions on the *estancias*. Shelter was usually a simple adobe hut, thatched with grass. Crude furniture was fashioned from the bones and skulls of cows. Some women managed to find independent employment as midwives and faith healers.

Snappy dressers: Although gaucho clothing was designed for comfort and practicality, the men were born dandies, and their outfits were always worn with a certain amount of flair.

The *chiripá*, a loose diaper-like cloth draped between the legs, was very suitable for riding. It was often worn with long, fringed leggings. These were later replaced by *bombachas*, pleated pants with buttoned ankles that fitted inside their boots.

Although store-bought boots with soles became popular with gauchos in later years, the first boots were homemade, fashioned from a single piece of hide, slipped from the leg of a horse. This skin was moulded to the gaucho's foot while still moist. Often the toe was left open. This had a practical function, as the early stirrups were nothing more than a knot in a hanging leather thong. The rider would grasp the knot between his first and

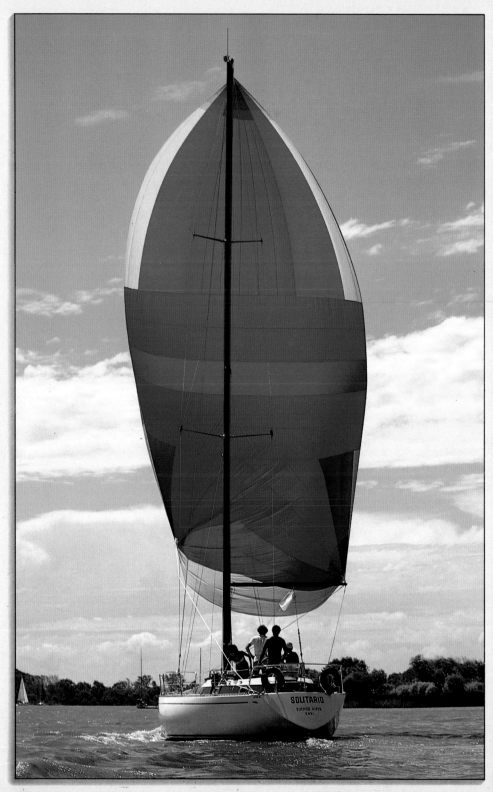

It should be an average enough day in Buenos Aires, yet the streets are strangely deserted. The banks are empty, the restaurants are quiet and an eerie silence has settled over the entire city. The only people in sight are huddled around portable radios or television sets, their attention tightly focused on the latest news.

The outbreak of war? Some national disaster? Election returns, perhaps? Quite the contrary. This scenario occurs every time Argentina's national soccer team takes to the field, ample evidence of that sport's hold on the country. Every match commands the nation's rapt attention, and victories are cause for unrivaled celebration.

When Argentina won the 1986 World Cup tournament in Mexico, the highest honor in football, several hundreds of thousands of fans flooded the streets of Buenos Aires, Córdoba, Rosario, La Plata and beyond. Make-shift parades materialized out of nowhere, thousands of cars jammed the avenues and sidestreets, and the nation found itself swathed in blue and white.

The world championship was actually the second for Argentina, which also captured the cup in 1978. But that tournament, hastily staged in Argentina by the ruling military government that had come to power not long before, fostered little of the pride and enthusiasm seen in 1986. The 1978 World Cup was perceived by many as a simple exercise in public relations designed to avert the world's eyes from Argentina's soaring inflation, mounting national debt and human rights violations.

That Argentines flocked to the match, still cheered their players, and still celebrated wildly when it was all over, shows their affinity with the sport.

Soccer was introduced to Argentina in the 1860s by British sailors who passed the time in port playing pick-up games before the curious onlookers.

The large British community in Buenos Aires finally organized the game in 1891, and the balls, goalposts and nets imported

from Europe were checked through customs as "some silly things for the mad English."

But by the turn of the century, Argentina had established its own soccer league. The Quilmes Athletic Club was formed in 1897, making it the oldest soccer team in Argentina. Rosario Central (1899), River Plate (1901), Independiente (1904) and Boca Juniors (1905) quickly followed suit.

Argentina's national team also progressed rapidly, as proven by its performance in the inaugural World Cup held in Uruguay in

1930. Although still amateur and lightly regarded, Argentina defeated such established soccer powers as France and Chile en route to a place in the finals, before narrowly losing to Uruguay, 4–2.

Soccer became a professional sport in Argentina in 1931, and the league games began to draw large, vociferous crowds. River Plate and Boca Juniors, two teams that emerged from the Italian Boca district in Buenos Aires, quickly became the two most popular teams in Argentina. Even today, 50 percent of the nation's fans support one of the two clubs.

Such unbridled support is not necessarily

Preceding pages: a polo match. **Left**, sailing. **Right**, windsurfing.

a good thing – Argentine soccer has been increasingly troubled in recent years by crowd violence at its league matches, especially when rival fans like River Plate and Boca Juniors meet.

As a result, many of the country's stadiums – including La Bombanera, Cordero, Cordiviola and Monumental – have been turned into something resembling armed camps, complete with moats, fences and barbed wire designed to keep fans off the field and rival factions apart.

Nineteen teams compete annually in the Argentina First Division, playing a total of 36 matches between September and June. In addition, many of the top clubs compete

try's star spectator sport, Maradona is the Carlos Gardel of the Argentine sports scene. He still commands the unconditional support of most Argentine soccer fans, despite his suspensions by FIFA for drug abuse while playing for the Naples team in Italy and for the Argentine First Division in the 1994 World Cup in the United States.

After two failed attempts at coaching second-line clubs in Argentina, Maradona returned to his first love, Boca Juniors, to play as center forward.

But soccer is not the only sport in Argentina. Blessed with a climate that allows for a wide variety of sports year round, Argentina is also known for its polo, rugby, horse and

concurrently in international tournaments such as the World Club Cup and the Libertadores Cup.

Argentines, like most South Americans, seem to have a special skill for soccer. The name of Diego Maradona readily comes to mind, but he was a national hero long before he gained international prominence at the 1986 World Cup.

When Maradona threatened to leave his club, Boca Juniors, for Europe in 1982, the government unsuccessfully attempted to intervene by declaring him to be part of the "national patrimony."

As the leading all-time star of the coun-

auto racing, and tennis.

Polo: The first thing many visitors ask upon arrival in this country is where they can see polo being played. Although it did not originate in Argentina, polo has evolved into an integral part of the national sporting heritage. Many of the world's best players and teams have come from this country. In addition, Argentina has top-flight breeding programs for ponies.

As with soccer, polo was introduced to Argentina by the English in the mid-19th century. The inherent riding skill of the Argentines and the abundance of space helped ensure that the sport flourished. At present, there are more than 6,000 polo players registered in the country.

Polo tournaments are held all over the country throughout the year, but the bulk are played in spring and autumn. The top teams compete each November in the Argentine Open championship in Buenos Aires, which was begun in 1893.

There is no distinction between amateur and professional polo in Argentina. But many of the top players are regularly hired by foreign teams for huge sums. In fact, the favorite team in an international tournament is often the one that can sign up the most Argentine players.

Polo ponies are also regularly exported.

Pato is Spanish for "duck," and the duck certainly got the worst of it in the game's formative stages. Placed inside a leather basket with handles, possession of the duck was contested by two teams of horsemen – often farm workers or Indians – who attempted to grab the basket and return to their *estancia*. Any number could play, and anything from lassoing an opponent to cutting free his saddle was permissible.

The sole rule of the sport was that the rider in possession of the *pato* had to keep it extended in his right hand, thus offering it to any opponent who caught up with him. Such skirmishes inevitably resulted in a fierce tug-of-war, and the riders unfortunate enough

Specially trained by *petiseros* (laborers) at an *estancia* where polo is played, the short, stocky ponies are prized for their speed, strength and ability to work with their riders.

Pato: The game of *pato* has been described by some observers as basketball on horseback, and it is one of the few sports that are indigenous to Argentina. The earliest references to the game can be dated back as far as 1610, and the game was probably played long before that.

Left, famous – and infamous – national soccer hero, Diego Maradona. <u>Above</u>, the Pumas face off against France in rugby.

to be pulled from their saddles were often trampled to death.

The government banned *pato* in 1822, but a group of ardent supporters revived the game in 1937. They drew up a set of rules, refined the sport, and established a federation in 1938.

Today, *pato* is played by teams of four horsemen with a basket (like the type used in basketball) at each end of a regulation field. The duck has been replaced by a leather ball with handles, and points are scored by passing the ball through the basket.

Pato has steadily grown in popularity and is now as socially acceptable as polo. The annual national open championship is held each November in Buenos Aires.

Other equestrian sports: In a country where horses are plentiful and breeding is a big business, horse racing and show jumping are also quite popular.

There are racetracks in most Argentine towns and plenty of opportunities for off-track betting, although the government oversees the official odds. The big races are held in Buenos Aires, often at the Jockey Club in the suburb of San Isidro.

Horse shows are staged at numerous clubs in Buenos Aires and other major cities almost weekly from March to December. There is a fine tradition in this sport – as there is for

dressage – and only the regular exportation of top horses has kept Argentina from gaining international stature.

In Buenos Aires, most horses are privately owned and kept at riding clubs. Club instructors give individual riding classes in the arena, but do not hire out horses. Many seaside resorts along the Atlantic coast offer instruction and organized outings.

For those who want to have a real adventure on horseback, there are splendid trail riding opportunities in Salta, Mendoza, the Patagonian provinces, the Iberá wetlands, and the province of Buenos Aires. Two of the Buenos Aires travel agents specializing

in such excursions are Lihué (tel: 311-9610) and Caminos Action Travel (tel: 311-4111).

Tennis for the masses: Tennis has been played in Argentina since the last century, but it has always been a game largely for the middle and upper classes – until now. Fueled by the meteoric rise of Guillermo Vilas, an energetic and talented player who gained international prominence in the 1970s, tennis has experienced an unprecedented boom ever since.

The driven, dashing Vilas won the Masters in 1974 and the US Open in 1977, and became an international playboy. Linked romantically with such women as Princess Caroline of Monaco and countless Hollywood starlets, Vilas emerged as a hero at a time when Argentina had none.

Virtually overnight, every young Argentine dreamed of being a professional tennis player. The number of players skyrocketed, as did the sales of racquets, balls and shoes. Courts sprang up all over the suburbs of Buenos Aires – both municipal and privately owned – and Argentine players flooded the pro circuit.

One of the products of that boom is Gabriela Sabatini, the teenage sensation who emerged as one of the top women's players of the mid-1980s. Dubbed "Gorgeous Gabby" by the international press, Sabatini played her way into the top 10 rankings in 1986, quickly rising to the third spot, but later falling to seventh or eighth, despite winning two Masters and one US Open.

Although few Argentine players have yet equaled the accomplishments of Vilas and Sabatini, the sport remains very popular in Argentina. Countless courts are available for hire, and the Buenos Aires Lawn Tennis Club regularly sells out its 6,500-seat stadium for its top matches.

Rugby: As with soccer and polo, rugby was introduced to Argentina by the British. But the sport inexplicably failed to catch on until the mid-1960s. That was when the Pumas, Argentina's national rugby team, rose to prominence with a string of international successes. Like tennis, the sport experienced a rapid growth of interest and a massive infusion of young talent.

Today, Argentine rugby ranks among the best in the world. Virtually every province has its own federation, and attendance continues to grow impressively. International

All around the campground one will see the plains vizcacha, a large gray and be-whiskered rodent of social burrowing habits. These creatures are extremely tame. Indeed, campers must be tidy, as anything that is left out at night is stolen and carted off to the dens. Vizcacha males weigh up to 9 kg (20 lbs), and their nocturnal vocalizations are loud, varied and unnerving.

Pampas gray and crab-eating foxes and the capybara (a pig-sized aquatic grazing rodent, the largest in the world) are to be seen on the walks. There are European hares and wild boar (unfortunate introductions of the last century), and the greater rhea, the archaic ostrich of the area.

only out of the summer season; Christmas to Carnival is booked solid.

Between Lavalle and San Clemente is a wildlife sanctuary, managed by Fundación Vida Silvestre Argentina (the local wildlife group), where the last specimens of the once numerous pampas deer can be seen in the wild. The bird sanctuary and observatory at Punta Rasa is also run by the foundation. Along with the local species, many migrant shore birds from North America spend their "winters" here.

A diverse combination of dunes, sandy beaches, planted trees for shelter, mud flats, rivers of grass and sedges, salt marshes and brackish sloughs give this area a highly

Pristine pampas: Perhaps the most representative pampas left, due to the absence of plowing, is the area surrounding General Lavalle and south to Madariaga. Route 2 as far as Dolores, some 320 km (200 miles) southeast from Buenos Aires, has abundant wildlife all along it.

Route 11, in places, offers views of the vast open plains as they were before the Europeans arrived with their fences, wind-pumps and shelter tree belts. **San Clemente del Tuyú** is the best town to lodge in, but

concentrated array of habitats and, consequently, of fauna.

All of this is within easy reach of San Clemente, but it is in a military zone, as the local lighthouse is operated by the navy. Be friendly towards any navy personnel you may encounter. A smile, a wave of the hand and the single word *aves* (birds) should be enough to open the gates.

Marsh drives: Two drives can be recommended as well worth your time. One is out and back along Canal 2, some 32 km (20 miles) east of San Clemente, where the road-crowned embankment gives an overview of the extensive marshes and all they contain.

Left, a puma picks up a scent. **Above**, a wildcat keeps a lookout.

The other drive is along the **Estancia El Palenque Camino Vecinal**, down the access road to the farms behind. The elevated road skips from one grassy island to another, and offers one a superb view of the marshes and water below. However, these roads are made of earth, and the drives are not to be attempted after rains.

Given good conditions, all the earth roads in the area are well worth exploring as far south as Madariaga. The circuit can be completed by returning to Buenos Aires by the coast road (Route 11), through Punta Indio and Magdalena, where the *estancias* El Destino and San Isidro are. Take an ACA (Automobile Club of Argentina) map, a smatter-

animals in an unspoiled and beautiful setting. Be careful and sensible about clothing and about orientation, as mists can descend unexpectedly. Part of the hills are a provincial reserve, Ernesto Tornquist, and it may be wise to consult the ranger, if you can find him at headquarters.

Endangered trees: The subtropical jungles or rain forest are best represented in Argentina at Iguazú, site of the internationally famous waterfalls. The falls have no equal and are a must on the itinerary of any visitor. The **Iguazú National Park** was established to preserve both the falls and the 54,000 hectares (135,000 acres) of varied jungle terrain that surround them.

ing of Spanish, an adventurous spirit and a reliable car, and drive around to see what you can see in two or three days. The best months for visiting the coastal pampas are September to December.

Hill hikes: Only one outcrop of hills breaks the regularity of the pampas' sea of grass. Between Tandil and Tornquist a range of ancient granite and limestone hills rises gently in a southwesterly direction, and attains its highest points in the **Sierra de la Ventana** and **Tres Picos**, both around 1,200 meters (4,000 feet) high. For those who like hill walking, these small mountains offer opportunities to view guanaco and other

It is a shame to see that Misiones' native hardwood forests are coming under the axe. The trees are being replaced by crops that give a more immediate yield, cash crops on a yearly cycle, or in some cases by grazing land. Some areas are being planted with pines for the budding paper pulp industry.

Thunder and mist: Iguazú National Park's waterfalls offer one of the most breathtaking natural sights to be seen anywhere. In a wide swing above the drop, the river splits up into many channels of varying sizes, and each plunges into the ravine below in one or two steps, a total of some 76 meters (250 feet). The waters then join in the furious racing rapids of the boxed-in lower river, which still has some dozen miles to go before becoming an anonymous part of the ten times greater Paraná river.

A choice of walks at the falls offers a variety of views and experiences. Especially attractive because of the sheer force of the spectacle is the **Garganta del Diablo** (Devil's Throat), which at present can be reached only by boat because the previous catwalk, washed away by a flood, has not been repaired. Standing at the railing on the edge of the drop, one is made to feel quite small.

The best time to see the falls is in the afternoon, for the angle of the light, and in the evening, for the spectacle of thousands of

their rapid flap-then-glide flights from treetop to treetop.

Tracks and trails in the park encourage visitors to get to know the marvels and rich diversity of the jungle: some 2,000 species of higher vascular plants, nearly the same number of butterflies and moths, 100 species of mammals from the jaguar on down, nearly 400 kinds of birds from the hummingbird up. All this, as well as thousands of varieties of insects, spiders, reptiles, frogs and fish can be seen.

Most wildlife activity in such hot places as Iguazú is limited to the early morning, from about an hour before sunrise to two or three hours after, and the evening, from just before

great dusky swifts returning to roost on the bare basalt walls between the falling waters.

Toucans: Perhaps the best known birds of the South American jungles are the toucans. The biggest, the least shy and the classic toucan of advertisements and brochures, is the toco toucan. Its dry croak, which passes for a call or song, is as distinguishing as its enormous orange bill.

From the top of the water tower, or from the lawn in front of the park's visitors' center, the colorful toucans can be seen doing

Left, flamingos along the Patagonian coast.
Above, a group of alert vicuñas.

to just after sunset. Avoid being out there between 11am and 4pm.

Hide and seek: Don't think, however, that all this abundance is to be found and observed on a brief visit. In this kind of habitat it is notoriously difficult to see anything other than that which is immediately at hand. The thick surrounding vegetation forms a curtain which effectively hides anything that may be behind it. Some creatures are only to be seen when they cross gaps in the forest canopy at great speed.

The **Macuco Trail** is for walkers only, and in its 4 km (2½ miles) it varies as much in types of vegetation as it does in species of animals and birds. There are tapirs, jaguars, capuchin monkeys, small deer called brockets, pacas and agoutis, coati-mundis and even peccaries (two species) to be found, if one is quiet and lucky. Anyhow, look for their tracks. **Yacaratia Trail**, though suitable for vehicles, is little used by them, and one can return from the end of Macuco along it with hopes of seeing even more of the wonderful creatures of this habitat.

An observation blind over a marshy area is for those who enjoy waiting for the wildlife to pass by. Cayman, stealthy tiger herons, muscovy ducks (the original wild species), coypu and many others are the reward for the patient.

The **Wet Chaco** has undergone some major clearing for agriculture in the past 25 years, but there are still some very beautiful tracts of Wet Chaco woods interspersed with marshes. West from Corrientes or Resistencia, Route 16 should be explored at least as far as the **Chaco National Park**.

The wet season (summer) is to be avoided, for the heat is great and the roads become impassable. Between April and November, with a tent in preference to the available lodging, search the Chaco Park for howler monkeys, guans, and chachalacas (of the pheasant family, but with dull colors and loud voices). Or you could take a look at the many and varied forms of marsh life: whis-

There are plenty of other trails and roads to explore on foot or by car. Get all the information at the desk in the visitors' center. Here, too, you can obtain copies of the bird, mammal and tree lists to help you. Don't hesitate to approach a ranger, even in sign language, to help you identify and enjoy the sights all around you.

The Chaco: The Chaco covers areas of Bolivia and Paraguay as well as the north of Argentina. It is divided into two recognizable parts, of which only one will concern the traveler. The **Dry Chaco** is crossed by very few and dreadful roads, and there are no amenities for visitors.

tling herons, jabiru storks, jacanas, and ducks galore.

From Corrientes, both east and south, there are some very rich woodlands interspersed with wide open grasslands and enormous marshes. Route 12 is paved in both directions, but the earth roads which run northeast–southwest between the paved stretches, through places like **Mburucuya** and **San Luis del Palmar**, generally get into the better habitats.

The **Iberá Marshes** are hard to get to and, except for the edges, are virtually devoid of life. On the edges, however, water birds of many kinds provide a great spectacle. In

Corrientes, in the region of the headwaters of the Iberá complex, where grass seas stretch from horizon to horizon, one may come across a maned wolf. This rare species is still fairly abundant here, though shy. Here, too, the marsh deer survives – albeit in small numbers. On the larger *estancias* where there is a consciousness of the conservation ethic, one can even see the endangered pampa deer in its last refuge.

This region is also the best place to look for the capybara. The best of the ranches near the marshes from which to see the wildlife are **Capí Varí** and **El Dorado** near Mercedes, and **San Juan de Poriajú** near Itá Ibaté. The bird nesting season starts in Au-

Puna sickness of nausea and general discomfort from lack of oxygen. After Humahuaca, the only other town in the region with hotels offering any real comfort is San Antonio de los Cobres.

Going over the ridge to the west of **Abra Pampa** into the huge valley of **Pozuelos**, there are usually vicuña to be seen as one descends. Laguna Pozuelos is a national park monument. Thousands of flamingos of three species, mixed in with waterfowl and waders, form a blanket over the water. Walk slowly along the shore, binoculars in hand, or if feeling the height too much, take the car, but be careful of muddy spots. Look for Puna teal, avocets, and giant, horned and aAndean

gust, but the best (less rainy) season for getting about on dirt roads is from October through December.

Northwest Argentina: The provinces of Jujuy, Salta and Tucumán have some extraordinarily scenic areas and good wildlife. Don't miss the Humahuaca Valley, which is on the way to the Puna zone. Take side roads to places like Purmamarca. As this area rises above the altitudes one may be used to, it should be covered in stages, over two or three days. This is the best way to avoid the

Left, the elusive Andean condor. **Above**, the noisy Toco Toucan.

coots. At **Lagunillas**, on the western side of Pozuelos, there is a small lake some miles from the road that one can walk to, or perhaps drive to in order to get a better look at all these birds. The Puna rhea is usually somewhere to be seen in the Pozuelos area, so keep an eye open.

Varied vegetation: A visit to **Calilegua National Park**, on the eastern slopes of the Andes, between 600 and 4,500 meters (2,000 and 15,000 feet), is only to be attempted in the dry season – June to October/November, as the roads are washed out the rest of the year. The road through the park rises steeply, so a series of vegetation zones is traversed in short order. This starts with the Chaco vegetation at the foot, with the palo borracho (drunken or bottle trees, *Chorizia*), jacarandas and tabebuias, both yellow and pink. Then one passes up through a transition jungle dominated by tipa (*Tipuaria*) and into the cloud forest of podocarpus and alder (*Alnus*).

As a consequence of the variation in vegetation, there is a change in the fauna. Jaguar, puma, ocelot and jaguaroundi are the larger cats to be seen. Their prey are brockets, tapir, peccaries, agoutis, even capuchin monkeys, squirrels and a large variety of birds. There is a campground at the foot of the park, in **Aguas Negras**, and there are many trails and river and stream beds to explore.

Córdoba: Córdoba is the starting point for exploring the hills to the north and west of the city itself. The Pampa de Achala, with its condors and mountain species, is not a long drive away. Nor is it far to the Sierras Chicas, where the spectacular red-tailed comet (a hummingbird) is common.

In the south of La Pampa province there is a very special national park, Lihue Calel. Here, guanacos, vizcachas, rheas and the introduced European boar are easily seen on walks, and special birds such as the yellow cardinal and the spot-winged falconet (both endemic Argentine species) are also encountered. There is an Automobile Club motel at the entrance to the park.

Andean playground: The Patagonian Andes, which stretch from Neuquén, through Río Negro, to Chubut and Santa Cruz, are a scenic delight, and vary quite a lot with the latitude. Here lies one of the playgrounds of Argentina, with winter sports, fishing, hunting, boating, canoeing, riding, camping, and all that makes up a good outdoor holiday. Towns are spread along the foothills where the steppe meets the woodlands and mountains, and they offer all the commodities one could need.

From Zapala, a short distance west, is the Laguna Blanca National Monument. It lies at a considerable elevation on the open steppe, where thousands of water birds congregate. Chief among these is the majestic and beautiful black-necked swan.

Lanín National Park has communities of the primitive Araucaria tree, and the southern beeches of the genus *Nothophagus*, both *obliqua* and *nervosa*. Together with Nahuel

Huapi National Park, just to the south, this park is the most developed in terms of roads, communications and lodging (San Martín de los Andes and San Carlos de Bariloche are the major towns in the region).

There is a sharp increase in the precipitation as one moves westwards, so the richness and variety of the flora increases markedly in the 30–65 km (20–40 miles) from the steppe to the Chilean border. There is no parallel increase in the types of birds and animals to be found, perhaps because their numbers are not regulated by the availability of resources in the good months but rather by the severity of winters. Few of the local woodland species migrate.

Condors and parakeets: There is a much greater variety of birds in the steppe and transition zones. Here, it is definitely more clement in spring and summer into autumn. One can see huge flocks of upland geese in the grassy valleys, ashy-headed geese in the clearings in the woods near lake shores and rivers, and noisy buff-necked ibises nearly everywhere.

In the woods one meets flocks of Austral parakeets and the greenbacked firecrowns (another hummingbird), vestiges of more temperate climates, which are now isolated and adapted to colder areas. The Andean condor is fairly common, though the enormity of the landscape tends to reduce it to an unrecognizable size. Sighting one is a thrill, nevertheless. The most spectacular bird of the woods is certainly the Magellanic woodpecker, the giant of his family. The male sports a scarlet head with a small crest, while his all-black mate has a very long and floppy crest that curls forward.

Here, too, one can find the torrent duck. As its names implies, the black and white striped drake with its fire-brigade red bill is only seen in white water rivers and streams. Torrent ducks sport, dive and swim around in these furious and frightening rapids as if they were in a pond.

Mountain parks: South along the Andes chain are spread a series of parks, large, small, well-visited, or off-the-track, all similar but each with its own special attractions and character. From El Bolsón one can visit **Puelo National Park**. There is good fishing for the introduced trout, along with camping and boating. As for wildlife, the only sight of special interest is the rare Chilean pigeon.

Los Alerces National Park is most easily reached from the town of Esquel. *Alerces*, strictly translated, means larch. This is the local misnomer of *Fitzroya Cupressoides*, the giant evergreen equivalent of the redwood of the western United States. Though it is present in several other parks, it is here that it reaches its greatest size. A boat trip takes one to the more beautiful stands of these giants. Above the treeline is the rare and unafraid Andean huemul, a type of deer, waiting for the intrepid hill-walker.

Francisco P. Moreno National Park is very far from any amenities. Camping equipment and extra gasoline are a must. The eastern steppe section of the park, some

Andes, in virtually permanent cloud. This icecap area is what Eric Shipton, the famous mountaineer, called "the Land of Tempest." It is some 240 km (150 miles) long and, at times, 70 km (45 miles) wide.

The Moreno Glacier, the one accessible by car, is about 80 km (50 miles) west of the town of **Calafate**, on the shores of Lago Argentino. From just in front of the glacier, one has a grandstand view of the ice tumbling into the milky waters of the lake and creating just such an ice dam as was formed in Alaska in 1986. This damming and flooding cycle has happened with increasing regularity since 1937, when it first occurred. The cycle now runs for three to four years,

260 km (160 miles) west of **Gregores**, lies at about 900 meters (3,000 feet). Here, two species of the peculiar seed-snipe are to be seen in abundance, along with many upland geese, huemuls and some mountain caracaras. One can often see guanacos on the peninsula of **Lago Belgrano**.

Glaciers at their best: The next park southward is **Los Glaciares**. Both by land and on lake excursions one can see glaciers at their best in this region. They all originate as overspillage from the South Patagonian Icecap, which is out of view on the crest of the

with the pressure building until it is sufficient to tear away the front. Few people have the opportunity to witness the rupture, as it is unpredictable, and even folks from town are often late for the show because it goes so fast. Add the 40 percent likelihood that it will break during the hours of darkness and you can see it's not worth waiting around for.

The lake trip to the **Upsala Glacier** starts from **Puerto Bandera**. The shores leading to Bandera are always good for sighting waterfowl, maybe even some black-necked swans. The trip on the boat starts early and takes most of a day. Look for black-chested buzzard-eagle nests on the *elefantes* rock

<u>Above</u>, sea lions at the Valdés Peninsula.

formations and condor nests on the low cliffs over the water. Upsala is a classic, with icebergs all around the front, in incredible tones of blue. The medial moraines stand out just like they do in the textbooks.

Tierra del Fuego: The wildlife of Tierra del Fuego and the national park there (19 km/12 miles west of Ushuaia) comprise just about everything one has encountered all the way south from Lanín, with species dropping out as conditions get more severe. However, there is a marine coastal environment here along the north shore of the Beagle Channel. One can see the kelp goose, the stunning white male against the black coastal rock, and the flightless steamer duck, a local

special, whose name derives from the paddlewheel-like spray it generates as it chases or escapes from a rival.

One may also get a chance to see Austral parakeets, buff-necked ibises and condors. A sighting, this far south, of the torrent duck is a rare treat indeed.

Beavers and muskrat were introduced in the 1940s and are creating havoc with the woodlands by felling, damming, and flooding. Early sailors introduced rabbits, which now thrive here. There is a very good boat trip available on the Beagle Channel, where one can see cormorants, sea lions, fur seals and some penguins.

In Tierra del Fuego, the scars left by road construction, gas line digging, petroleum exploration, uncontrolled forest fires, convict clear-cutting of the native woods and the filth and litter of both Río Grande and Ushuaia, especially, are shocking, and it is a relief to get away from such disrespect for nature into the less disturbed national park. Here, the autumn foliage (from March on) is a real sight.

The Valdés Peninsula: Once back on the mainland, the dominant scene all the way up to Buenos Aires and its surrounding pampas is the Patagonian steppe and coastline. These are best represented in **Chubut**, a pioneer province in the conservation of nature in Argentina. Throughout the year there is some spectacle of sea life frolicking on land or in the sheltered gulfs north and south of the Valdés Peninsula.

The wildlife calendar looks like this:
January–March: Southern sea lions breed in rookeries (Punta Norte, Pirámides).
March–May: Killer whales visit these rookeries to prey on sea lion youngsters.
June: Arrival of southern right whales starts in both gulfs.
September: Elephant seals start breeding and are finished by mid-October; Magellanic penguins arrive to nest at Tombo and stay until March, when they start migrating.
December: Last whales leave for feeding grounds south.

One can see that it is a busy year, and that spring and summer offer the promise of greater activity.

In the Valdés region there are also many steppe animals: guanacos at their best, Darwin's rhea, maras (Patagonian cavy) and the elegant crested tinamou, a game bird that looks like a squat guinea fowl, and the hairy armadillo or its smaller relative, the Patagonian pichi armadillo.

Heading north, you will arrive back in Buenos Aires, and the circuit has been completed. Some things may have been missed en route but others encountered unexpectedly, as if in consolation. By this time, certainly, the dedicated nature lover should have a full appreciation of Argentina, with its unique geography and its stunning array of both flora and fauna.

Left, a fox sits for a portrait. **Right**, Magellanic penguins at Punta Tombo.

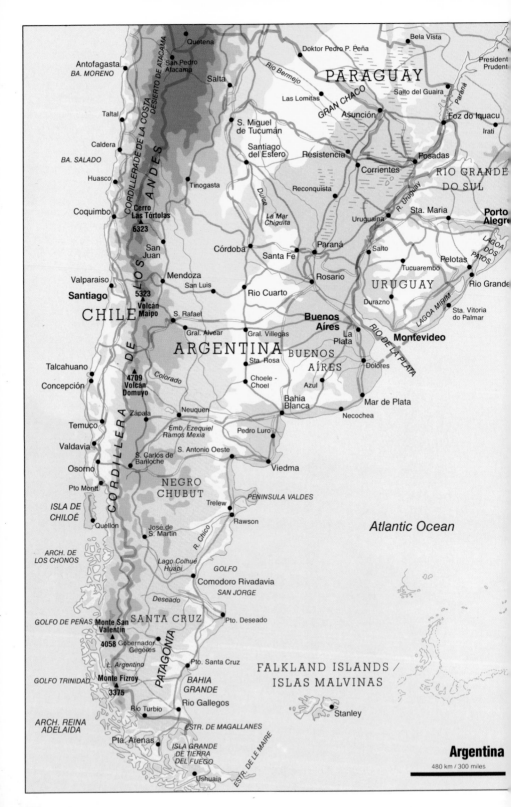

Quetena

Antofagasta
BA. MORENO
San Pedro
Atacama
Salta

Doktor Pedro P. Peña
Bela Vista

President
Prudent

Río Bermejo
PARAGUAY
GRAN CHACO

Las Lomitas
Salto del Guaira

Taltal
S. Miguel
de Tucumán
Asunción
Foz do Iquacu
Irati

Caldera
BA. SALADO

Huasco

Santiago
del Estero
Resistencia
Posadas
RIO GRANDE
DO SUL

Tinogasta
Reconquista
Corrientes

Sta. Maria
Porto
Alegre

Coquimbo
Cerro
Las Tórtolas
6323
La Mar
Chiquita
Uruguaiana
LAGOA
DOS
PATOS

San
Juan
Córdoba
Santa Fe
Paraná
Salto
Pelotas
Tucuarembó

Valparaiso
Mendoza
Rosario
Río Grande

Santiago
5323
Volcán
Maipo
San Luis
Río Cuarto
URUGUAY
Durazno
LAGOA MIRIM
Sta. Vitoria
do Palmar

CHILE
S. Rafael
ARGENTINA
Buenos
Aíres
La
Plata
Montevideo
RIO DE LA PLATA

Gral. Alvear
Gral. Villegas
BUENOS
AÍRES

Talcahuano
4709
Volcán
Domuyo
Colorado
Sta. Rosa
Choele-
Choel
Dolores

Concepción
Azul

Temuco
Zapala
Neuquen
Bahia
Blanca
Mar de Plata

Valdavia
Emb. Ezequiel
Ramos Mexia
Pedro Luro
Necochea

Osorno
S. Carlos de
Bariloche
S. Antonio Oeste

Pto Montt
Viedma

ISLA DE
CHILOÉ
NEGRO
CHUBUT
Trelew
PENINSULA VALDES

Quellon
José de
S. Martin
Rawson

ARCH. DE
LOS CHONOS
Lago Colhué
Huapi
GOLFO

Atlantic Ocean

Comodoro Rivadavia
SAN JORGE

Deseado

GOLFO DE PEÑAS
Monte San
Valentín
4058
SANTA CRUZ
Pto. Deseado

Gobernador
Gegóres

GOLFO TRINIDAD
L. Argentino
Monte Fizroy
3375
PATAGONIA
Pto. Santa Cruz
BAHIA
GRANDE
FALKLAND ISLANDS /
ISLAS MALVINAS

Río Turbio
Río Gallegos

ARCH. REINA
ADELAIDA
Stanley

Pta. Arenas
ESTR. DE MAGALLANES
ISLA GRANDE
DE TIERRA
DEL FUEGO
ESTR. DE LE MAIRE

Ushuaia

Argentina
480 km / 300 miles

CORDILLERA DE LA COSTA
DESIERTO DE ATACAMA
ANDES
CORDILLERA DE LOS ANDES
CORDILLERA DE LOS
Dulce
R. Uruguay
Río Chico
R. Chico

134

PLACES

While it is possible to get package tours to Argentina, this is by far the least preferable way to see the country. Independent visitors can familiarize themselves with the points of interest, through the Places chapters that follow, and then set about planning an itinerary. And it does take planning, for Argentina is a huge country and destinations often lie far apart. Getting from the deserts of the northwest to the coastal wildlife of Patagonia requires organization, and the likelihood of fitting everything in on one visit of course depends on how much time one has.

Fortunately, Argentina has a solid infrastructure geared for tourism. Comfortable hotels are available in all popular spots, and in even the most remote reaches there are usually at least camp grounds. Planes, trains and buses run on convenient schedules and cars can be rented. In some areas, one might even prefer to get around on foot or horseback. Air passes on the national carriers enable one to cover the larger distances at reduced rates.

In the following chapters the country has been divided up into territories that one is likely to see as a whole: Buenos Aires, the vacation coast, the central sierras, the northeast, the northwest, the western wine country, Patagonia, and Tierra del Fuego. How much of an adventure you make of it is up to you.

Be mindful of the conditions dictated by the time of year when you visit. During the regional high season, reservations may be hard to come by; winter rains may make a park inaccessible; wildlife one will see in a particular spot depends on migration patterns. These chapters will help you decide whether you'd like to be sunning on the beaches of Mar del Plata in January, gliding down the ski slopes of the Andes in August, or eating a *bife de chorizo* in Buenos Aires any time of the year.

Preceding pages: a condor tours his domain; a chilly vantage point; a gaucho surveys his territory.

settlement. A fortress was built facing the river, and the town square, Plaza de Mayo, was marked off to the west. At the far end of the plaza they built the Cabildo (the Town Council) and on the northern corner, a small chapel. Although new buildings have been constructed on the ruins, the plaza maintains this basic structure and is still the center of the city's activities.

Buenos Aires was the last major city in Latin America to be founded. It was not only geographically cut off from more developed trade routes, but, under Spanish law, the use of its ports for European imports and export of precious metals from Potosí and Lima was prohibited. Logically, the English, Portuguese and French took advantage of the lack of Spanish presence on the Río de la Plata, and illegal trade flourished. The settlement was able to survive in large part due to this contraband.

Manufactured goods were exchanged for silver brought from northern mining centers, and for cow hides and tallow. Construction materials also began to be imported, since the pampa had neither trees nor stones. Homes were originally built of adobe and straw.

Faced with competition in the region from other European nations, in 1776 Spain declared what is now Argentina, Uruguay, Bolivia, Paraguay and the northen section of Chile a viceroyalty. Buenos Aires was made the site of the central goverment. With its new judicial, financial and military role, the city burgeoned as a regional power. Functionaries, lawyers, priests, military personnel, artisans and slaves arrived, and the small village began its transformation into a major cosmopolitan city. In Latin America, only Lima and Mexico City exceeded the economic development at the time.

The *porteños* were accustomed to a certain economic and political independence from Spain. When, alone, they were able to repel two British invasions in 1806 and 1807, pride in the city's military prowess, and what later was to be called nationalism, ran high.

Independence and development: In 1810 the city's residents took advantage of Spain's preoccupation with Napoleon, and won an increased amount of autonomy for themselves. However, it was not until 1816 that independence was declared for the whole country.

In the subsequent decades, the government of Buenos Aires was consumed with the struggle for control over the rest of the country. The Federalists, represented by Juan Manuel Rosas, the governor of Buenos Aires from 1829 to 1852, believed each province should maintain considerable power and independence. The Unitarians, who came to power when General Urquiza overthrew Rosas, sought the dominance of Buenos Aires over the rest of the country. The tension between residents of the interior and the *porteños* still exists, but at a social, rather than political, level.

Finally, in 1880 the dispute was resolved in a small street battle, and the city became a federal district, rather than simply the capital of the province of Buenos Aires. This was also to be a decade of intense change for the city. Under President Julio Roca, the mayor of the city looked to Europe and especially Paris as a model for change in Buenos Aires. Hundreds of buildings were constructed in imitation of the latest Parisian styles. New neighborhoods were created for the wealthy by filling in huge sections of the river, particularly in the northern parts of the city, where Retiro, Recoleta, and Palermo lie.

It was also in the 1880s that the massive immigration from Europe began, principally from Italy and Spain although also from Germany, Poland and Britain, as well as Lebanon and Syria and later Russia. By 1910 the city had reached a population of 1,300,000. Public services such as the tramway, running water, schools and police protection were well under way. The city's literature, opera, theater and other arts were becoming known around the world. Suddenly, Buenos Aires was the Paris of Latin America for upper-class European and North American tourists.

In the last 20 years the city has lost out to other major cosmopolitan cities. The results of political and economic insta-bility can be seen in the old cars, buildings in disrepair, and lack of construction. Where buildings have sprung up, there is little regard for maintaining the beauty of the old city, and virtually no urban planning for a new city.

The incongruous architecture of some areas of Buenos Aires may disappoint those who had imagined a picturesque European city. But it's the real city; a city in crisis, a city whose future is undefined and a city that reflects the special character of its residents.

Mix of old and new: To understand Buenos Aires, one must venture beyond the downtown area. One must walk the streets of residential areas, ride buses, hang out in cafés, dine on *parrilladas* and pizza and, above all, talk to the people. Their conflicting and emotional feelings about the city and the whole country are contagious.

Buenos Aires is not only enormous in relation to the population of the rest of Argentina, but is also one of the largest cities in Latin America. The Federal District occupies 200 square km (77

A view from the port.

square miles) and the entire metropolitan area spans over 2,915 square km (1,121 square miles). Approximately 12 million people, or one third of the country's population, live in the city and surrounding areas. Three million reside within the Federal District.

Buenos Aires is marked to the north and east by the Río de la Plata and, on a clear day, one can see all the way across the mud-colored river to the Uruguayan coast. To the south, the city limit is marked by the Riochuelo, a shallow channel constructed to permit entrance to the major ports.

The city's landscape is varied. There are wide boulevards and narrow cobblestone streets. The downtown area boasts charming boutique windows, outdoor cafés, simple but elegant restaurants, and grand old cinemas and theaters. In residential districts, ornamental old apartment buildings, with French doors that open onto plant-filled balconies, stand side by side with modern buildings up to 12 stories high, most with sliding glass doors that open onto balconies. Sycamore and tipuana trees line the streets, providing shade for little boys playing soccer. There are innumerable parks and plazas, where one may feel comfortable jogging, or simply sitting quietly near old men playing *truco* (a card game) or chess in the summer.

A city of barrios: There are 46 *barrios* (districts) in Buenos Aires, each with its own special history and character. With few exceptions, the neighborhoods have a Roman grid structure around a central plaza with a church. Most *barrios* also have a main street for commerce, with a two-story shopping mall, as well as a butcher, baker and vegetable and fruit stand. A sports club, a movie theater, a pizzeria, and an ice-cream parlor also form part of the typical *barrio*.

Needless to say, the social atmosphere in these neighbourhoods is much warmer than in the busy downtown area, where pedestrians, as in most other big cities, are on the run and will barely stop to give the time of day. In a *barrio*, a lost traveler will be accosted by helpful and curious residents.

ther and enjoy an rnoon ee.

To grow up in a *barrio* is to have a special allegiance to it. Soccer teams from each club compete in national competitions that create natural rivalries among many of the districts.

In order to get a sense of Buenos Aires' layout, it is useful to simplify and talk about major blocks of the city. From Plaza de Mayo, two diagonal avenues extend to the northwest and southwest. The central track between the two is the most populated area of the city. To the south is the oldest part of the city, including San Telmo and La Boca, where working and some middle-class people live. To the north, are the *barrios* of Retiro, Recoleta and Palermo, where the wealthy moved when yellow fever hit the southern district in the 1870s.

A fourth zone may be delimited to the west. With the establishment of two railway lines – the Once line that runs along Rivadavia Avenue, and the Retiro line that runs northwest along the river – new *barrios* began to spring up.

(Do not be deceived by the many maps of Buenos Aires that are tilted, and show west at the top of the map as though it were north. The Rio de la Plata runs southeast, not west.)

The center of Buenos Aires: The center of Buenos Aires is truly the city's "downtown", and while most *porteños* live in outer *barrios*, everyone comes downtown, either to work, to eat, or to find entertainment. Residential *barrios* have their own mini-commercial areas, so that except to visit friends, many *porteños* never cross the city; they simply make a bee-line downtown.

As in every big city, there are lots of hurried, well-dressed business people in the center of Buenos Aires, but there are also Argentines here enjoying the bookstores, the movies, the theater, the round-table discussions and conferences on every imaginable topic, the plazas, the shopping and the political and cultural street life. Some streets, like Florida, Corrientes and Lavalle are for strolling, and are filled with leisurely visitors come to walk, watch and be watched.

A two-hour jaunt starting at the Plaza de Mayo, along Avenida de Mayo and

Left: the Casa Rosada. **Below**: the mix of architectur fronting th Plaza de Mayo.

back down Corrientes and Lavalle to Florida Street, provides a quick introduction to the government buildings as well as the commercial, financial and entertainment districts.

Plaza politics: Buenos Aires began with the **Plaza de Mayo**, today a strikingly beautiful plaza with its tall palm trees, elaborate flower gardens and central monument, set off by the surrounding colonial buildings. The plaza has been and still is the pulsating center of the country. Since its founding in 1580, as the Plaza del Fuerte (fortress), many important historical events have been celebrated or protested against.

The most eye-catching structure in the plaza is unquestionably the **Casa Rosada** (Pink House), the seat of the executive branch of the government. Flanking it are the Bank of the Argentine Nation, the Metropolitan Cathedral, the City Council and the *Cabildo* (Town Council).

The Casa Rosada was originally a fortress overlooking what is now the **Plaza Colón**, but was at that time the river's edge. When the Indians' attacks subsided, the plaza became Plaza del Mercado, a market place and social center. The name and role of the plaza changed again with the British invasions of 1806 and 1807, when it became the Plaza de la Victoria. Finally, following the declaration of independence, the plaza assumed its present name, in honor of the month of May in 1810 when the city broke away from Spain.

The date also marks the first mass rally in the plaza, on this occasion to celebrate independence. Subsequently, Argentines have poured into the plaza to protest and celebrate most of the nation's important events. Political parties, governments (de facto and constitutional), and even trade unions and the church, call people into the plaza to demonstrate a symbolic power.

Salient events in the history of the Plaza de Mayo include the 1945 workers' demonstration, organized by Eva Perón to protest her husband's brief detention. Ten years later, the airforce bombed the plaza while hundreds of

ne of the ndiose lpture ng ertador nue.

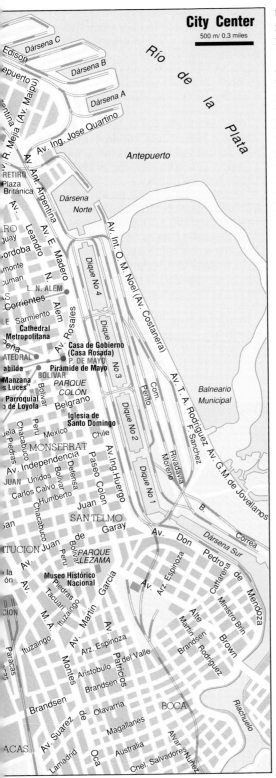

thousands of Perón's supporters were rallying to defend his administration from the impending military coup. In 1982, Argentines flooded the plaza to applaud General Galtieri's invasion of the Malvinas/Falkland Islands. A few months later, they were back again, threatening to kill the military ruler for having lied about the possibilities of winning the war with the British. More recently, in 1987, the plaza was jammed with 800,000 *porteños* demonstrating against a military rebellion, and again at the end of 1989, protesting President Menem's pardon of convicted generals.

But the most famous rallies have been those of the Mothers of the Plaza de Mayo, who still protest every Thursday afternoon, demanding information on the whereabouts of their children who disappeared during the dirty war, and calling for the punishment of those responsible. Their presence in the plaza is perhaps the best illustration of the symbolism of occupying space here. During the last years of the military regime, young people accompanying the Mothers would chant at the menacing army and police units, "Cowards, this plaza belongs to the Mothers…"

The Pink House: Leaders traditionally address the masses from the balconies of the Casa Rosada, a building constructed on the foundations of earlier structures in 1894. Sixteen years earlier, President Sarmiento had chosen the site for the new government house. There are several explanations for why he had it painted pink, the most credible of which is that it was the only alternative to white in those days.

The special tone was actually achieved by mixing beef fat, blood and lime. Some insist that Sarmiento chose pink to distinguish the building from the White House. Still others say that pink was selected as a compromise between two feuding parties whose colors were white and red.

The **Museo de la Casa Rosada** is a small gallery, located in the basement, that contains antiques and objects identified with the lives of different national heroes. The entrance is on Avenida Yrigoyen, and it is open 11am–6pm every day except Wednesday and Saturday, with guided tours at 4pm.

The Grenadiers Regiment guards the Casa Rosada and the president. This elite army unit was created during the independence wars by General San Martín, and they wear the same blue and red uniforms that distinguished them during those times. Between 6 and 7pm each day, soldiers lower the national flag in front of the Government House. On national holidays the Grenadiers often parade on horseback, and they accompany the president during all his public appearances.

Another historic building in the Plaza de Mayo is the **Cabildo** (Town Council), located at the western end of the plaza. This is perhaps the greatest patriotic attraction in Argentina. School children are brought here and told how their forefathers planned the nation's independence in the Cabildo.

The town council has been on this site since the city's founding in 1580, although the present building was constructed in 1751. Originally, it spanned the length of the plaza with five great arches on each side. In 1880, when Avenida de Mayo was built, part of the building was demolished. And once again, in 1932, the Cabildo was further reduced, this time to its current size, with two arches on either side of the central balconies.

The Cabildo also has an historic museum, the **Museo del Cabildo**, exhibiting furniture and relics from the colonial period. It is open Tuesday to Friday 12.30–7pm and Sunday 3–7pm. Behind the museum is a pleasant patio, which features a simple outdoor snack bar and on Thursday and Friday afternoons a small arts and crafts fair.

Across Avenida de Mayo, to the north, is the **Consejo Municipal** (City Council), an ornamental old building known for its enormous pentagon-shaped clock in the tower.

Church and state: The **Catedral Metropolitan** is the next historic building on the plaza. It is the seat of Buenos Aires' archbishopric, and lies at the northwestern corner of the plaza. The

The graceful Cabildo.

cathedral's presence in this highly political plaza is appropriate. The Catholic church has always been a pillar of Argentine society, and since the city's founding, the church has shared the Plaza de Mayo. In a mural at the northern end of Avenida 9 de Julio, two symbols are used to illustrate the founding of the city: a priest and a spade, representing the military.

The cathedral was built over the course of several decades and was completed in 1827. It was built, like the Cabildo and the Casa Rosada, upon the foundations of earlier versions. There are 12 severe neo-classical pillars at the front of the cathedral that are said to represent the 12 apostles. The carved triangle above reputedly portrays the meeting of Joseph and his father Jacob. This section is generally considered to be the work of architects. Yet a theory persists among some that it was created by a prisoner, who was then set free as a reward for its beauty.

Inside are five naves with important art relics. The oil paintings on the walls are attributed to Rubens. There are also beautiful wood engravings by the Portuguese Manuel de Coyte.

For Argentines, the most important aspect of the cathedral is the tomb of General José de San Martín, liberator of Argentina, Chile, Peru, Bolivia and Uruguay. San Martín, who actually died during his self-imposed exile in England, is one of the few national heroes to be revered by Argentines of all political persuasions.

At the northeastern corner of Plaza de Mayo is the **Banco de la Nación**. The old Colón Theater was on this site before it reopened on Lavalle Plaza in 1908. The imposing marble and stone bank was inaugurated in 1888.

The Plaza de Mayo has a central pyramid that was constructed on the first centennial of the anniversary of the city's independence. Among other purposes, it serves as the centerpiece for the Mothers of Plaza de Mayo's weekly rounds.

Ornamental lunch: The view from Plaza de Mayo down Avenida de Mayo to the National Congress is spectacular, and the 15-block walk is a wonderful

introduction to the city. The avenue was inaugurated in 1894 as the link between the executive branch and the Congress, most of which had been completed by 1906. It was originally designed like a Spanish avenue, with wide sidewalks, gilded lamp posts, chocolate shops and outfitters emporiums, and old Zarzuela theaters. Today, however, there is a mixture of influences with local adaptations that defy classification. As in much of the city, "neo-classical", "French" "Italian" and "art nouveau" are terms that do not adequately describe the special combination of influences seen here. Nor is there a traditional coherence from one building to the next; ornamental buildings stand side by side with others that are simple and austere.

There are several well-known restaurants along the way. One of the oldest is **Pedemonte** (676 Avenida de Mayo), dating back to the turn of the century. This is a favorite lunch spot for government functionaries and politicians who have links with activities in the neighboring executive branch.

Further down, is the **Tortoni Café** (825 Avenida de Mayo), a historic meeting place for writers and intellectuals. Apart from the famous customers said to have frequented the café, the ornamental interior makes the place worthy of at least a quick glimpse. Marble tables, red leather seats, bronze statues and elaborate mirrors create the most regal of atmospheres.

In the evenings the café hosts various theater and music productions, the most common being tango or jazz.

Traditional Spanish restaurants are also a prominent feature of Avenida de Mayo. At the 1200 block and turning left on Salta street, is **El Globo** (98 Salta), known for its *paella valenciana* and *puchero* (stew). Similar restaurants are also located on Avenida de Mayo and down some of the smaller side streets. Another well-frequented and classic *parrilla* (restaurant featuring *asado*, grilled beef) is **Don Pipón** (1249 Avenida de Mayo).

World's widest avenue: You could not have missed **Avenida 9 de Julio** at the 1000 block, the world's widest avenue, according to the Argentines. It is 140 meters (460 feet) from sidewalk to sidewalk, and everything about it is big – big billboards, big buildings, big *palo borrachos* (drunken trees) with pink blossoms in the summertime, and, of course, the big obelisk.

The military government of 1936 demolished rows of beautiful old French-style mansions to build this street. Much of the central block is now occupied by parking lots. The only mansion to survive was the **French Embassy**; its occupants refused to move, claiming it was foreign territory. There is a sad view of its barren white wall facing the center of town, testimony to the tragic disappearance of its neighbors.

The **Obelisco**, which marks the intersection of Diagonal Norte, Corrientes, and 9 de Julio, was built in 1936 in commemoration of the 400th anniversary of the first founding of the city. One assumes that because of its phallic appearance, it was the subject of much public joking. Three years after it was

Left, the obelisk is : the center the city's nightlife. Below, life imitates a

has gained momentum in recent years, despite the economic crisis, and has undoubtedly been bolstered by the new freedoms under democracy. For visitors, both these centers are a wonderful introduction to the contemporary cultural scene in Buenos Aires.

There are many restaurants for both lunch and dinner right in the heart of this theater district. **Pepito** and **Pippo**, the latter known for its economical menu, are next door to each other on the 300 block of Montevideo, half a block from Corrientes. At the end of this block, on the corner of Montevideo and Sarmiento is **Chiquilín**, a classic *parrilla*. Continuing down Corrientes towards 9 de Julio is **Los Inmortales**, a famous pizzeria decorated wall to wall with photos, posters and paintings of tango stars.

Plaza Lavalle is another center of activity in the area. It is two blocks north of Corrientes at the 1300 block. The **Federal Justice Tribunals** are at one end of this historic plaza, and the internationally renowned Colón Theater (Teatro Colón) is at the other. The plaza first served as a dumping ground for the unusable parts of cattle butchered for their hides. In the late 19th century, it became the site of the city's first train station, which later moved to Once.

The Colón Opera House: The **Teatro Colón**, Buenos Aires' opera house, occupies the entire block between Viamonte, Lavalle, Libertad and Cerrito (part of 9 de Julio). It is the symbol of the city's high culture, and part of the reason Buenos Aires became known in the early 20th century as the "Paris of Latin America."

The theater's elaborate European architecture, its acoustics, which are said to be near perfect, and the quality of performers who appear here, have made the opera house internationally famous.

Three architects took part in the construction of the building before it was finally finished in 1907. The original blueprint, however, was respected. It is a combination of styles – Italian Renaissance, French and Greek. The interior includes some great colored glass domes and elaborate chandeliers. The principal

nting for
gains
ng
rrientes.

auditorium is seven stories high and holds up to 3,500 spectators. There is a 18 meters by 34 meters (60 feet by 110 feet) stage on a revolving disk that permits rapid scenery changes.

Over 1,300 people are employed by the theater. In addition to opera, the National Symphony Orchestra and the National Ballet are housed here. In a recent rehaul that cost millions of dollars, a huge basement floor was added – creating storage space for the sets, costumes and props and working space for the various departments.

The Colón's season is approximately from April to November, and it offers an interesting guided tour of the opera house Monday to Friday, on the hour, from 9am–4pm, and on Saturday 9am until noon.

Pedestrian thoroughfares: Crossing 9 de Julio one enters the **Mini-centro**, an area for pedestrians only during working hours. The other restricted zones are Rivadavia, Leandro Alem and Córdoba.

Here, it is worth going across to **Lavalle street**, since Corrientes is at its best between Callao and 9 de Julio. Lavalle, like Florida several blocks down, is a pedestrian street. At night, it is filled with young couples strolling on their way to or from the movies. In a four block stretch, there are no less than 20 movie theaters on this street. There are also pizza parlors, cafés, restaurants, including **La Estancia** (941 Lavalle), famous for its barbecue pit in the front window and, of course, their *asado*, and several shopping malls, most of them specializing in clothing.

Avenida Florida, also closed to motor vehicles, is the principal shopping district downtown. The promenade is packed with people, as well as *kioscos,* folk musicians, pantomime artistes and others passing the hat. There is a leisurely pace here, and because of the crowds, it is not a good thoroughfare for anyone in a hurry.

There are two tourist information booths located at opposite ends of Florida, one being at Diagonal Roque Sáenz Peña and the other between Córdoba and Paraguay.

Café La Pa

The shopping on Florida is slightly more expensive than in other districts outside of downtown. As elsewhere, most shops are one-room boutiques, many in interior shopping malls that exit onto adjacent streets. They sell clothes, leather goods, jewelry, toys, and gifts. Leather continues to be the best buy for foreigners.

One of the most famous malls is the **Galería Pacífica**, between Viamonte and Córdoba. It is part of a turn-of-the-century Italian building that was saved from demolition because of the frescoes on the interior of its great dome. These are the work of five Argentine painters: Urruchua, Bern, Castagnino, Colmeiro and Spilimbergo.

Books, burgers and art: Probably the largest bookstore in the country, **El Ateneo**, at 340 Florida, carries a wide selection of guidebooks, maps, and books in English.

There are also cafés along Florida, which offer a chance to relax from the busy street. **Richmond** (468 Florida) is an elegant café/tea room with a reserved

atmosphere. At the far noisier **Florida Garden** (corner of Florida and Paraguay) one can stand at the bar in front for a quick coffee, or have a seat and sample some of their tempting sweets or *medialunas* (croissants) or *tostados* (toasted sandwiches).

Just past Paraguay on the last block of Florida is the **Centro Lincoln** (935 Florida), a library and reading room run by the US Embassy. Here one may read *The New York Times* and *The Washington Post*, as well as major magazines, all in English. Library hours are confined to weekdays from 1.30–5.30pm. The street dead ends right at the entrance to **Ruth Benzacar's Gallery** (1000 Florida). It's literally an underground art gallery, dedicated to promoting Argentine contemporary artists.

Below Florida, on the 300 block of Paraguay Street, is **Kelly's**. It is an unlikely name for the best stocked and cheapest Argentine handicrafts store. They sell traditional artisans' goods from different provinces, including doublelayered sheepskin slippers (the inside

opulent
ón Opera
use.

layer is for wearing in bed), brightly colored wool scarves that are astonishingly inexpensive, leather bags, wooden plates for barbecues, gaucho belts and smaller souvenirs.

A couple of restaurants are worth mentioning just a few blocks from Florida, and right near Kelly's. One of the newest and hippest places to dine in Buenos Aires is **Filo** (975 San Martin). There's nothing traditional about it, especially the arty decor, and definitely no *asado*; they serve unusual salads, pizzas, and pastas, lunch and dinner. Definitely on the more traditional side is **El Establo** (431 Paraguay), a cozier, kitschier version of a typical *parrilla*.

South towards Plaza de Mayo is the financial district. Tall banks and exchange houses line the narrow streets. Weekdays, the district is filled with well-dressed business people, and the only vehicles pressing their way through the crowds are the armored bank trucks. Weekends, with booming Lavalle and Florida just blocks away, the financial district is eerily silent.

The southern quarter: The expansion of Buenos Aires in the 17th century first occurred towards the south, making the southern quarter one of the oldest residential areas of the city.

There are three areas of interest to most tourists: Manzana de las Luces (Block of Enlightenment); San Telmo, historically a fascinating *barrio* and today inhabited by artists and antique dealers; and La Boca, at the southeastern tip of the city, which is famous for the pastel colored tin houses where dock workers used to live, and for the raucous restaurants where working-class Argentines and lively tourists come to enjoy themselves.

La Manzana de las Luces refers to a block of buildings that were constructed by the Jesuits in the early 18th century. The San Ignacio Church, the old Jesuit school and underground tunnels are bordered by Bolívar, Alsina, Peru and Moreno streets.

The area was originally granted to the Jesuits at the end of the 17th century. In 1767, the Spanish Crown withdrew the

Along Avenida Florida.

gift, in light of what was perceived as the group's increasing power. In fact, of principal concern in this case, as with Jesuit missions throughout the world during this period, were the egalitarian principles practiced by the priests within their social organizations. Today, La Manzana de las Luces serves as a cultural center, but tours of its historical past are available.

Despite the repression against the Jesuit order, many of the churches still stand, the oldest of which is **San Ignacio**. This church, which is also the oldest of the six colonial churches in Buenos Aires, was constructed between 1710 and 1735. It is an impressive baroque structure, at the corner of Alsina and Bolívar.

Walking south on Defensa Street from the Plaza de Mayo, one finds the **Estrella Farmacia** (402 Alsina), a 19th-century drugstore with marvelous metaphorical murals on the ceiling and walls portraying disease and medicine.

On the second floor of the same building is the **Museo de la Ciudad** (412

Alsina) open Tuesday to Friday 12.30–7pm and Sunday 3–7pm. The museum features rotating exhibitions of aspects of the city's past and present, including architectural photo studies, as well as more curious shows, such as old postcards of the city. And continuing just a few doors down Alsina is **La Puerto Rico**, a pleasant café.

Also on the corner of Defensa and Alsina is the **San Francisco Basilica** and the **San Roque Chapel**. The main church, finished in 1754, is the headquarters of the Franciscan Order. Parts of the neo-classical building were rebuilt at the end of the 19th century, in imitation of the German baroque styles in vogue at the time. The chapel was built in 1762.

San Francisco was severely damaged in 1955, as were a dozen other churches, when angry Peronist mobs attacked and set fire to the historic structure. The violence was a response to the Catholic church's opposition to the Peronist government, and its support for the impending military coup.

shop in
n Telmo.

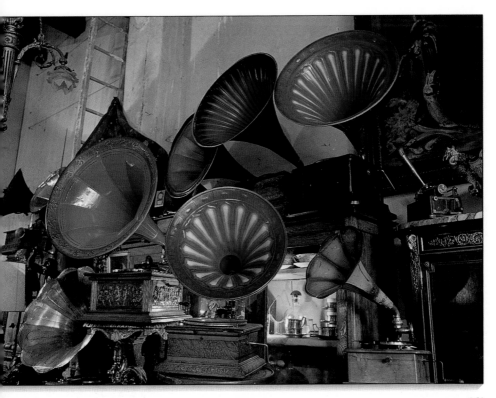

Art, architecture, antiques: San Telmo, like Greenwich Village in New York, used to be one of the more run-down sections of the city, until history, architecture, and low rents in the 1960s caught the attention of artists and intellectuals who began to revive the area. Attractive studios, restaurants and antique shops began to replace the decaying tenements. An open-air flea market held each Sunday in the central plaza has brought in enough tourists to nourish the new business ventures.

While San Telmo is now one of the principal tourist stops, the neighborhood maintains its historic authenticity and its vitality. Plaza Dorrego, the site of the Sunday flea market, is proof of this. Weekdays, it remains a fascinating spot, where old people who have lived all their lives in the *barrio*, many of whom still speak with an Italian accent, meet to talk and to play chess and *truco*.

San Telmo emerged during the 18th century as a rest stop for merchants en route from the Plaza de Mayo to the warehouses along the Riochuelo. Next to the Plaza Dorrego was a trading post for goods coming in from the ports. On adjacent streets, *pulperías* (bar/grocery stores) quickly sprang up to accommodate passersby.

Except for the Bethlemite priests that had established themselves in the San Pedro Church, the area's first residents were Irish, blacks and Genoese sailors, whose rowdy drinking habits made the *pulperías* famous.

In the early 19th century, many important families built their homes along **Defensa Street**, which connects Plaza de Mayo and Plaza Dorrego. During this period, a typical home had three successive interior patios, and only the facade would change, as new architectural styles arrived. They were called *chorizo* (sausage) houses, because of their linear shape. The first patio was used as living quarters, the second for cooking and washing, and the third for the animals.

In the 1870s, a yellow fever epidemic hit the area. At the time, it was widely believed the fog off the Riochuelo carried the disease. Those who could fled Rounding out the national die of beef.

162

San Telmo and built homes just west of the downtown area, approaching what is now called Congreso, and in the northern section, now called Barrio Norte.

In the 1880s and the subsequent three decades, San Telmo received poor European immigrants, particularly Italians, who were arriving in Argentina. Many of the old mansions and *chorizo* houses were converted into *conventillos* (one room tenements that open onto a common patio), in order to accommodate the flood of new families.

Tango bars: A walk through San Telmo begins at Balcarce and Chile Streets, the northern edge of the *barrio*. There are several old tango bars nearby, such as **La Casablanca, Media Luz, La Cumparsita**, and two blocks back towards Belgrano Avenue, one of the oldest, **Michelangelo**.

Crossing Chile on Balcarce, one comes to a two-block long cobblestone street called **San Lorenzo**. To the right are a number of beautiful old houses. Many are now nightclubs. Others, some with interior patios, have been converted into apartments, studios and boutiques. At 319 San Lorenzo are **Los Patios de San Telmo**, a renovated house open to the public, which contains numerous artists' studios and a bar located just inside the entrance. The brick and wood ceilings date back at least 200 years. Just up the block is yet another old tango bar, **Ultimo Tango**.

Balcarce Street continues across Independencia and is one of the prettiest streets in San Telmo for strolling. The next block is **Pasaje Giuffra**, another narrow, cobblestone street, where many of the old *pulperías* used to be. Up the block on the right is **La Scala de San Telmo** (371 Giuffra), a popular nightspot which hosts live music, usually classical, jazz, or tango. Continuing down Balcarce at the corner of Estados Unidos is another tango bar, **Bar Sur**, a cozy and intimate venue with small wooden tables and candles.

Further down is **Carlos Calvo**, especially charming because of its numerous restored colonial houses.

Good restaurants: To the right on Calvo are several picturesque restaurants.

One, **La Tasca de los Cuchilleros**, has a lovely plant-filled patio in front with outdoor tables, and offers both Spanish and Argentine cuisine. Further up is **La Convención** (375 Carlos Calvo), with a wooden interior and an interesting array of historic relics. French dishes are served and most evenings feature a live pianist. And on the corner of Calvo and Defensa is **La Casa de Esteban de Luca**, the restored colonial-era home of "the poet of the revolution," with a more typical and economical menu.

Half a block past Carlos Calvo on Balcarce is the old home of the Argentine painter **Castagnino** (1016 Balcarce), whose murals from the 1950s may be seen on the ceiling of Galeria Pacífica on Florida Street. Since the artist's death, his son has converted the building into an art museum.

On this same block on the right is the **Galería del Viejo Hotel** (1053 Balcarce), another old *conventillo* that has been renovated and now serves as an art center. Two stories of studios open onto a central plant-filled patio. Visitors may

wander through the complex and watch the artists at work. Weekends are the best time to visit.

Humberto 1 Street is the next block. Turning right, one comes upon the old **Iglesia de Nuestra Señora de Belén**. The church was built by the Bethlemite priests in 1770.

Across the street is the **National Council of Education**. Next door, there is a small plaque that calls attention to the site of an old *pulpería*, run by a woman named Martina Cespedes. During the British invasion, the woman and her many daughters enticed British soldiers into their bar one by one, tied them up and turned them over to the Argentine army. Although one of her daughters reputedly married a British victim, the mother was rewarded for her brave deeds with the honorific title of Captain of the Argentine Army.

Sunday flea market: Finally, we are upon **Plaza Dorrego**, the center of San Telmo's commercial and cultural life. It is the site of the Sunday flea market, with junk jewelry, secondhand books,

antiques and some handicrafts. Surrounding the plaza are several restaurants, bars and antique shops that are fun to wander through. One of the prettiest is the old *chorizo* house, **Pasaje de Defensa**, a block south of the plaza. Another charming shopping mall on Defensa is **Galería El Solar de French**. It was redone in a colonial style, with flagstone floors, narrow wooden doors, bird cages and plants hanging from wrought iron hooks along the long patio.

For those who like to sample open-air food markets, just a block past the plaza, on Carlos Calvo, there is a large municipal market.

Lezama Park is just four blocks south of Plaza Dorrego on Defensa. Many believe that this little hill was the site of the first founding of the city. Later it was the home of Gregorio Lezama, who converted it into a public park. By the end of the 19th century, it was an important social center, with many amenities such as a restaurant, a circus, a boxing ring and a theater.

Today, the park is somewhat rundown, and the view is no longer attractive due to the surrounding construction and heavy traffic. However, the old mansion still holds nostalgic memories and has been converted into the **Museo Histórico Nacional** (1600 Defensa), the national history museum, open Tuesday to Friday 2.30–6pm.

La Boca: The working-class neighborhood of La Boca is at the southern tip of the city, along the Riochuelo Canal. The *barrio* is famous for its houses made from sheet-iron and painted in bright colors, and for its history as a residential area for Genoese sailors and dock workers in the 19th century.

La Boca came to life with the mid-19th century surge in international trade and the accompanying increase in port activity. In the 1870s, meat salting plants and warehouses were built, and a tramway was constructed that facilitated access to the area. With the expansion of the city's ports, the Riochuelo was dug out to permit the entrance of deep-water ships. Sailors and longshoremen, most of whom were Italian immigrants, began to settle in the area.

A conventill *house.*

The sheet-iron homes that can still be seen throughout La Boca and across the canal in Avellaneda were built from materials taken from the interiors of abandoned ships.

The idea was taken from the Genoese. The style, as well as the bright colors, so unusual in Buenos Aires, became a tradition in La Boca.

One painter's influence: The famous painter Benito Quinquela Martín also influenced the use of color in the neighborhood. Quinquela was an orphan, adopted by a longshoreman family of La Boca at the turn of the century. As an artist, he dedicated his life to capturing the essence of La Boca. He painted dark stooped figures, set in raging scenes of port action.

In one of his works (that Mussolini reputedly tried unsuccessfully to buy from him with a blank check), an immense canvas splashed with bright orange, blues and black, men hurriedly unload a burning ship.

Neighborhood residents took pride in their local artist, and were influenced by his vision of their lives. They chose even wilder colors for their own homes, and a unique dialogue grew between residents and artist.

Quinquela took over an alleyway, known as the **Caminito**, decorated it with murals and sculpture, and established an open-air market to promote local artists. The brightly painted homes and colorful laundry hanging out to dry provide the background to this charming one-block alley. There are small stands, manned by the artists themselves, where watercolor paintings and other art are sold to tourists.

A stroll through La Boca begins at the Caminito. Heading north from the river on the alley, it is worth walking around the block and back to the riverside in order to get a sense of the normal residential street.

The tin houses were not created for tourists; they are, in fact, comfortable homes. Most have long corridors leading to interior apartments, and are graced by wood paneling. The cobblestone streets are shaded by tall sycamore trees,

and elevated sidewalks are some defense against frequent flooding.

The **Vuelta de Rocha**, where the Caminito begins, consists of a small triangular plaza with a ship's mast. It overlooks the port area, which may be more accurately described as a decaying shipyard. More boats lie half sunken on their sides than upright and functioning. Depending on which way the wind is blowing, the visitor may be accosted by the foul odors of the canal, which is so polluted that reputedly there is no life in its waters. Residents blame the old slaughterhouses upriver, which used to dump waste into the canal.

East along Pedro de Mendoza, the avenue parallel to the canal, is the **Museo de Bellas Artes de La Boca** (1835 Pedro de Mendoza), La Boca's very own fine arts museum, open Tuesday to Friday, 9am–5.30pm and Saturday, 9am–12pm and 2–6pm. The top floor was used by Quinquela as an apartment studio. Many of his most important paintings are here, and one may also see the modest apartment he used in his last years. The museum is a fun stop, if only to get the view of the shipyard from the window of the studio, the same shipyard depicted in his paintings.

Rowdy cantinas, rowdy soccer: Just past the Avellaneda Bridge is **Necochea Street**, where rowdy cantinas form a sharp contrast to the sedate restaurants in other areas of Buenos Aires. These were originally sailors' mess halls, and their high spirits recall the jazz clubs of New Orleans.

Brightly colored murals of couples dancing the tango, speakers set out on the sidewalk blaring loud music, and somewhat aggressive doormen who compete for the tourists, may combine to frighten off those who are not prepared. But the scene is not as seedy as it might appear. Families from the interior of the country are there for a festive night out. Old people are singing their favorite tunes and dancing amidst balloons and ribbons. And the idea that a night out on Necochea Street is a celebration of sailors returning home is definitely preserved. Much of the action is

concentrated between Brandsen and Suarez streets. Two blocks west is **Avenida Almirante Brown**, the main commercial street in La Boca.

The avenue holds no particular charm, except for its excellent pizzerias. Here the specialties include *pizza a la piedra*, a thin crust pizza baked in a brick oven, *faina*, a baked *garbanzo* bean dough eaten on top of the pizza, and *fugazza*, an onion and herb pizza. One of the most well known pizzerias is **Banchero Rancho**, at the corner of Suarez and Almirante Brown.

La Boca also boasts the country's most famous soccer team, Boca Juniors, and their stadium **La Bombonera** (the candybox), located in the heart of the neighborhood, draws fans from all over the city. Diego Maradona, the internationally famous soccer star who carried Argentina to victory with his spectacular goals in the 1986 World Cup, played here for Boca Juniors.

The northern quarter: The northern district, which includes Retiro, Recoleta and Palermo *barrios*, is the most expensive residential and commercial area of the city. Elegant mansions built at the turn of the century immediately remind the visitor of Paris, although the architectural styles are actually a mixture of different influences.

Until the end of the 19th century, this area was unpopulated, except for a slaughter house on the site of the Recoleta Plaza. Much of the area was under water. In the 1870s, following the yellow fever epidemic, many of the wealthier families from the south moved north.

Great changes came in the 1880s when President Roca began a campaign to turn Buenos Aires into the Paris of Latin America. Prominent Argentines had traveled to Paris and were deeply influenced. They brought back materials and ideas for the transformation of Buenos Aires into a cosmopolitan city.

Roca's policies were and still are controversial. Critics supported a more nationalistic policy, oriented toward the development of the interior of the country. And yet, unquestionably, what was called the "Generation of the 80s" was

Left and right, the colorful architecture of the La Boca district.

responsible for making Buenos Aires the great city that it became.

A tour of the area begins at the eastern edge of the city, where Florida Avenue ends in Plaza San Martín.

Standing at the top of the hill in **Plaza San Martín**, amidst the spectacular old palms, jacaranda, tipus and palo borracho trees, there is a wonderful view of the *barrio* of Retiro. Across the Avenue at the bottom of the hill, Leandro Alem, is the old **Retiro train station**. Next to the station is the **British Tower**, renamed following the Malvinas/Falklands War as the Air Force Plaza. The Sheraton Hotel is also in view, and still further to the south, a series of highrise glass and chrome office buildings known as the **Catalinas**. The Catalinas were completed in the late 1970s, and except for a few buildings like the Rolero, a tall, round structure on Libertador Avenue, the Catalinas are the only large-scale additions to the downtown area since the 1940s.

From Plaza San Martín, one may also see the **Kavanagh Building**, just to the right, built in 1936 and reputedly Latin America's first highrise. Next door, is the **Plaza Hotel**, where such notables as Isabel Perón, the Shah of Iran, and Fidel Castro have stayed.

On the other side of the plaza are two fantastic old mansions. One is the Anchorena family's residence, built in 1909. Now it is used by the foreign ministry to welcome and entertain foreign diplomats. Another beautiful private residence, constructed in 1902, is at Maipu and Santa Fe. It is now used as a social club for military officers, and doubles as an arms museum.

Chic shoppers: Before setting off to visit the Recoleta, those interested in shopping may want to detour to **Santa Fe Avenue,** one of the principal commercial districts. The busiest area is between Callao and 9 de Julio avenues. Here, there are innumerable shopping malls, replete with little boutiques selling clothing, shoes, chocolates, leather goods, linens, china and jewels. But perhaps the greatest attraction is watching the young *porteñas* from Barrio

A moment of calm in the Plaza San Martín.

Norte, decked out in the latest Parisian styles, and simply out for a sunny stroll.

The **Recoleta**, often referred to as Barrio Norte, is adjacent to Retiro on the northern side. A 20 minute walk from San Martín Plaza to **Recoleta Cemetery** provides a pleasant introduction to what some *porteños* call their golden years (1880 to 1920). Many of the city's most sumptuous palaces lie along Tres Arrollos and Alvear Avenues.

The **French Embassy** at 9 de Julio and Alvear is hard to miss, not only because of its luxurious appearance, but because it is the only building left standing in the middle of the wide avenue. Two blocks further, at 1300 Alvear, is the **Carlos Pellegrini Plaza** where there are two other great mansions, the **Brazilian Embassy** and the exclusive **Jockey Club** are located.

Some of the best quality and most expensive shops are situated along **Alvear**. At 1777 and 1885 there are elegant malls, ideal for window shoppers. And at the 1900 block is the stately **Alvear Palace Hotel**.

Running parallel to Alvear one block down the hill towards Avenida Libertador is **Posadas** street, where at the 1200 block is **Patio Bullrich**, probably the most exclusive shopping mall in Buenos Aires. It stretches through to the next street, and houses not only stores and boutiques, but a cinema and various cafés. Directly across from it lies the modern **Ceasar Park Hotel**.

Also parallel to Alvear but on the other side runs **Avenida Quintana**, home to more boutiques. This street ends at the **Ramon Cárcano Plaza** and the Recoleta Cemetery. Here, it is worth stopping for croissants and coffee at **La Biela** or **Café de la Paix**, or one of the other numerous sidewalk cafés overlooking the plaza. This is one of the places to see and be seen among the Argentine wealthy and beautiful.

And just to the left, along the pedestrian street **Ortiz** (which merges with **Junín** street after a couple of short blocks), are some of the most renowned restaurants of the city, most with indoor and outdoor seating. Under the shade of a giant rubber tree, one has a view of the

entrance to the famous Recoleta Cemetery, the handsome Pilar Basilica, an American baroque convent which is now used as a cultural center, as well as a series of attractive and well-kept parks and gardens.

This civilized plaza, ironically, has a very gory past. It used to be the sight of a *hueco de cabecitos*, a dumping ground for heads of cattle slaughtered for their hides. As in the case of other *huecos*, a little stream flowed past the area, where other wastes were also thrown. The meat was not consumed, and black women were reputedly employed to drag away the carcasses.

The stream was piped underground in the 1770s and the Recoleta priests began to fix up the area, converting it into an orchard and vegetable garden. Until the 1850s, the Río de la Plata ran up to the edge of the plaza, covering what is now Libertador Avenue. Under Rosas' administration this area began to be filled in. It was not until the 1870s that the population, mostly the wealthy, started to migrate to this northern *barrio*.

adorned bute to the eat erator San artín.

The **Basilica of our Lady of Pilar** was built between 1716 and 1732. Subsequent restorations have been faithful to the original Jesuit simplicity of its architects, Andres Blanqui and Juan Primoli. Much of the building materials were brought from Spain, such as wrought iron gates and stone. It may be recalled that there is no rock in Buenos Aires, since the city lies on part of the pampa, and it was not until much later that stone was transported from an island in the delta.

Among the historic relics contained in the church is a silver-plated altar, believed to have been brought from Peru. Like many other colonial churches, during the British invasions, it was used as a hospital by the foreign soldiers.

The **Centro Cultural Recoleta**, just next door to the church, is housed in what used to be the convent. There is always a flurry of activity inside this large arts center, which features changing photography, painting, and sculpture exhibits, plus theater, dance and music. And on Sunday, the grassy plaza which slopes down towards the river fills with people enjoying one of the largest arts and crafts fairs in the city.

Evita's final resting place: The **Cementerio de la Recoleta** is the burial ground for the rich and famous, and the most expensive property in the country. Entering the gates, one has the sense of walking into a city in miniature, and, in fact, it is an architectural and artistic history of Buenos Aires from its inauguration in 1882. The great leaders and their enemies are buried here.

The history of the place should be indisputable, since the tombs and cadavers are material proof. Yet the schisms of the rest of Argentine society are reflected here, not only in terms of the conflicting architectural styles, but, astonishingly, in disagreement about who is buried here and why.

For example, one of the most visited tombs is that of Evita Perón. Nevertheless, tourism officials have been known to deny that she is buried here, explaining that she is not of the "category" of people buried in the Recoleta. In fact,

The colonial grace of the Pilar basilica.

she is 9 meters (30 feet) under ground to keep her enemies from stealing her body, as occurred in 1955.

Parks and patriachs: Down the hill from the Recoleta is Avenida Libertador, and on the far side, before one reaches Avenida Figueroa Alcorta, there are a series of parks and gardens that are great for joggers interested in seeing more than the pretty woods and fields of Palermo. On the way down the hill, is one of the most spectacular of Buenos Aires' monuments, a mounted statue of **General Alvear**. Across the street at 1473 Libertador is the **Museo Nacional de Bellas Artes**, the national fine arts museum. It has an excellent collection of Argentine and foreign paintings and sculpture, and is open Tuesday to Sunday 12.30–7.30pm and Saturday 9.30am–7.30pm.

Almost at the end of this row of plazas is the **Chilean Embassy**. Behind it is one of the prettiest public gardens in the area. Nearby is the reconstructed home of the hero of the Independence Wars, General José de San Martín, and a series of statues sits in front of the building, representing different friends of the liberation fighter.

Palermo Chico, a neighborhood of the rich and famous, is just around the bend. In fact, one must weave around several bends in order to get a sense of this exclusive neighborhood. It is a cozy nest of palaces, set off from the rest of the city by its winding streets that seem to exclude those from outside its boundaries. An assortment of movie stars, sports heroes, and diplomats make up this unusual community.

The area was built up together with the Recoleta area in the 1880s. Many of the old French-style mansions are now used as embassies, since the original owners have been unable to maintain such an exorbitant standard of living. There are also many new wood and brick-built homes with classic red tile roofs, but apart from their well-kept gardens, they can hardly compete with the great stone palaces.

The rest of Palermo is known for its parks and gardens, although there are other quite beautiful residential sections.

e cropolis of Recoleta.

There are hundreds of acres of exotic vegetation that include strange juxtapositions of pines and palms. There is an equally eclectic array of entertainment.

There are few cities in the world with such an infrastructure for recreation, and this is undoubtedly a key to understanding *porteños*. Here, the frenzy of the city subsides and *porteños* refuel with the oxygen from the sumptuous vegetation. There are families picnicking, men working out with their buddies, young couples in the grass who have escaped the stern supervision of their parents, and, of course, lots of babies. The park is a constantly changing scene of people, bicycles and dogs.

Sports and snacks: A pleasant, but lengthy jaunt through Palermo may begin in Palermo Chico. The heart of the park area, **Parque 3 de Febrero**, is six blocks further down Figueroa Alcorta Avenue from the tip of Palermo Chico.

The park includes 400 hectares (1,000 acres) of fields, woods and lakes. There are several points of interest near and within it. Approaching Sarmiento Avenue on Figueroa Alcorta, one passes the National Cavalry on the right, and immediately after, the **KDT Sports Complex**. A small entrance fee permits access to excellent sports facilities. There are tennis courts, a running track, an indoor pool, and a café with a terrace overlooking the track. Many simply come, however, to sprawl out on the well-trimmed grass to begin work on their tans before hitting the beaches of Mar del Plata or Punta del Este.

The **Japanese Botanical Garden** is across the avenue. Extraordinarily lush gardens, with fish ponds spanned by white, wooden footbridges, provide a nice spot for strolling.

The intersection of Figueroa Alcorta and Avenida Sarmiento (not to be confused with Sarmiento Street downtown), the wide avenue that crosses the park, is marked by an enormous statue of **General Urquiza**, who became president when he overthrew Rosas in 1852.

To the right on Avenida Sarmiento there is the **Planetario de la Ciudad** which sits next to a small artificial lake.

Enjoying the sun.

172

The planetarium features a changing astronomy show on Saturday and Sunday at 3 and 4.30pm. To the left on Sarmiento is **Avenida Iraola**, which leads to the heart of Palermo's parks and lakes. There are paddle boats for hire, and a storybook pedestrian bridge that leads to rose-lined gravel paths with stone benches every few yards. Ice-cream vendors also sell warm peanuts, sweet popcorn and candied apples, and still others specialize in *choripan* (sausage sandwich) and soda. An indoor/outdoor café, **Green Grove**, overlooks the most crowded area of the lake.

Iraola weaves around the lake and back to Libertador and Sarmiento, where another large monument marks the intersection. This one was a gift from the Spanish community, and is surrounded by a pretty fountain pool.

Kiddies and creatures: Avenida Sarmiento continues up away from the parks and dead ends at **Plaza Italia**. Here at the intersection is the entrance to the **Jardín Zoológico**. The zoo is pleasant, and has a variety of monkeys and birds native to South America. The real attractions, however, are the hundreds of local children racing from one cage to the next. The zoo is open Tuesday to Sunday 9.30am–6pm.

Across Sarmiento from the zoo's main entrance is the **Sociedad Rural**, an exhibition complex run by the powerful association of Argentina's large-scale farmers. Their biggest event of the year is the Exposición Rural, a cattle, horse and agro-industries show, but many other events are held here as well, from auto shows to tributes to foreign countries. The exhibitions are open to the public for a fee.

Plaza Italia is at the intersection of Las Heras, Santa Fe, and Sarmiento avenues. The plaza holds no special charm except that it is the site of so much activity. Weekends in the area are especially fun. To the right down Avenida Santa Fe, there is a street fair, known as the "hippie market," since the individual stands are often run by young bearded-and-sandalled types, who make the ceramic mugs and ashtrays, leather

shoes, belts and handbags, the jewelry, and embroidered and tie-dyed clothes sold at the fair. On the last block, the stands are dedicated to secondhand books and magazines.

Heading back down Avenida Sarmiento and taking a left on Avenida Libertador are two of Palermo's other attractions. The **Hipódromo**, or horserace track, is located at the corner of Libertador and Dorrego, and races are usually held on Monday, Friday and Sunday, starting around 3 or 4pm. Right across the street is the **Campo de Polo**, the attractive polo fields where in springtime the Argentine elite come to take in afternoon matches. Walking down Dorrego street one can get a peek through the bushes surrounding the fields.

Side trips: From Buenos Aires there are innumerable possibilities for day trips to small towns in the pampa and north along the river to the delta and its many islands. Here are three suggested all-day outings:

Tigre: Tigre is an old town situated at the mouth of the delta. Fruit brought by boat from the northern provinces is deposited here en route to Buenos Aires. But the principal economic activity revolves around the summer tourists and weekenders who come to fish, row, water ski and cruise the winding channels that flow past hundreds of little islands.

While it is only 28 km (17 miles) from downtown Buenos Aires, the air is clear, the vegetation subtropical, and the rhythm of activity less hurried. Those who live all year round on the islands rarely venture into the big city. They go into Tigre or simply buy their food off a grocery boat that swings by once a day. There is almost no crime, and it is said that the dogs never get sick because of special immunities gained from drinking the brown river water.

After touring the charming plant-filled residential area of the town, one heads for the main drag along the riverside, **Paseo Victorica**. Old English rowing clubs and *parrilla* restaurants line the street. There are several small docks, where *lanchas* (taxi boats) depart. Several larger ferries run two-hour cruises.

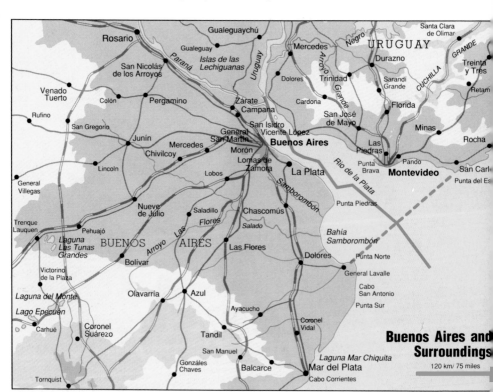

Buenos Aires and Surroundings
120 km/ 75 miles

174

They leave from the dock next to the train station. One even has a restaurant on board. Boats may also be rented for floating parties, and there is a ferry that crosses over to the Uruguayan beaches.

A train runs from the Retiro station to downtown Tigre, taking about 45 minutes. Or the bus number 60 starts in Constitución and winds through downtown to reach Tigre. Be sure to ask before getting on the bus because there are many different lines, and be prepared for a long journey.

Lujan: Lujan is one of the oldest cities in the country and today is visited by Argentine tourists because of its religious importance. It is situated 63 km (40 miles) west of Buenos Aires, along the Lujan River. Trains leave from Once and take two hours, stopping at every little town in the pampa along the way.

The **Basílica Nuestra Señora de Luján** is a magnificent gothic structure, built over a period of 50 years and completed in 1935. The great attraction is a statue of the **Virgen de Luján**, which is housed in its own chapel behind the main altar. Legend has it that the statue was sent by wagon from Brazil, and the wagon wouldn't continue until the virgin was taken off. Here she has remained, and now she is the patron saint of Argentina. Each October, hundreds of thousands of young Catholics make a pilgrimage from Buenos Aires, making the journey on foot in honor of the saint.

The Lujan River runs through the city, and in colonial times, boats heading to the northwest were checked here for contraband. When there have been no recent rains, the river is a place of recreation for residents and tourists.

There are several museums in Lujan. The **Complejo Museográfico Enrique Udaondo**, in a beautiful old colonial building, shows relics of Argentina's customs and history. In an annex is the **Museo de Transporte**. There is also the **Museo de Bellas Artes**, in Florentino Ameghino Park, dedicated principally to contemporary Argentine art.

On national and religious holidays there are gaucho competitions on horseback that are quite spectacular. Most of

the competitors are in fact descendants of gauchos and now work as farm hands, although costumes and saddles are saved for these special occasions.

A highly recommended restaurant is **L'Eau Vive** (Constitución 2106), run by a group of women missionaries. The specialty of the house is trout. It's closed on Monday and Tuesday, and reservations are suggested.

For those driving, there is a fun stop available on the way to Lujan. It is an open-air zoo called **Mundo Animal** (Animal World). Llamas, sheep, horses, cows and deer will follow your car begging for food. Lions, monkeys and other wild animals are enclosed in special areas where one is not permitted to get out of the car.

La Plata: La Plata is the capital of the Province of Buenos Aires, and despite being only 56 km (35 miles) south of Buenos Aires, it is representative of many provincial cities in Argentina. Life is less frantic here, the city is clean and orderly, and boasts independent political and cultural activities.

From **Constitution train station**, there is a 1½-hour train ride to La Plata. South of the city, one passes through an industrial belt populated by poor, working-class people. A number of shanty towns line the tracks.

Some 38 km (24 miles) from Buenos Aires, where Routes 1 and 14 split, is an *estancia* that used to be owned by the Pereyra family. It was expropriated by Perón and transformed into a recreational park, where working-class people who live in the area can come to relax. Adjacent is a zoo, where the animals run wild, and visitors can drive safari-style through the countryside.

Fourteen km (9 miles) further south is **La República de los Niños** a marvelous recreational center for children, built by Evita Perón in the early 1950s.

A few more miles down Route 1 is the city of **La Plata**, founded in 1882 by Dr Dardo Rocha. The city was conceived by Pedro Benoit, and takes the logical form of a rectangle with horizontal/vertical streets which are numbered, and diagonal avenues.

Order and cleanliness permeate the atmosphere of the tree-lined streets, public squares and parks.

The **Legislatura**, is located off **Plaza San Martín**, as is the **Palacio del Gobernio**, and the **Pasaje Dardo Rocha**, a large cultural center. The gothic **Catedral de La Plata** is on the **Plaza Moreno**, and just across the plaza is the **Palacio Municipal**. One block away, between 9th and 10th streets, is the **Teatro Argentino**.

There are a series of pretty parks in the center of the city called **Paseo del Bosque**, with lakes, a zoo that is actually much more complete than the Buenos Aires zoo, an observatory and a theater, **Anfiteatro Martín Fierro**. La Plata is most famous for its **Museo de Ciencias Naturales**, which was founded in 1884. This museum has many fascinating geological, zoological, and archaeological exhibits, and is located in the Paseo del Bosque. The **Museo Provincial de Bellas Artes**, at 525 51st Street, has an excellent collection of Argentine paintings and sculpture. The large **Universidad de La Plata** is only blocks away.

Left: a bit of preserved heritage.
Right: inner peace at La Plata cathedral.

If your interests on a vacation tend at all toward the sociological and anthropological, then when on a vacation to Argentina, this is the place to come. Here along the extensive Atlantic coast where the hills roll down to the sea (giving rise to the popular name Mar y Sierras) is an array of resorts for all tastes and bank accounts. Here one can see the Argentines at play. Although their country is enormous, and has an astonishing variety of appealing destinations, few Argentines seem interested in exploring it. Instead they head for the beach. Year after year, they return to the same spot, often to the point of renting the same changing cabana every time.

This fostering of a second home leads to a real sense of community in each resort. Families who may live far apart during much of the year, see each other each summer, watch each other's kids grow up, and keep up with the community gossip.

Along these beaches, the older folks pass the day playing the card games of *truco* and canasta, while the young swim and play paddle ball and volleyball. Young women prance about in their *cola-less* bikinis (this translates roughly into tail-less; the backsides of these suits are strikingly short on fabric) and everyone seems relaxed and happy to escape the mania of city life.

There is a fierce sense of pride among Argentines about their riviera. Keen competition exists among all the resorts of the South Atlantic, and some of Argentina's hot spots consider themselves rivals of such places as Punta del Este, in Uruguay. Fashions are kept up to the minute, and many fads actually start here. Those of the smart set insist on being seen here at least once during the summer season.

So if your exposure to Argentine society has been mostly to those living under the pressures of *porteño* life, it's not a bad idea to visit the coast, where everybody is smiling. It's not a bad spot to take a vacation either.

Preceding pages: an off day near Mar del Plata. **Left**, net maintenance is part of a fisherman's job.

THE ATLANTIC COAST

Popularly known as the Costa Atlántica, or sometimes Mar y Sierras (Sea and Hills), fertile rolling hills and occasional sand dunes come right to the edge of the sea to make up this scenic coastline.

The main strip of this popular vacation coast extends from San Clemente del Tuyú to Mar del Plata, the hub of the Atlántica area. Though founded late in the 19th century, Mar del Plata was at first a resort for well-to-do *porteños*, i.e. for those residents of Buenos Aires who could afford the 400-km (250-mile) journey to the then solitary cliffs near Punta Mogotes. Early on, this journey was made by train, and later by car. Only in the mid-1930s did Mar del Plata really start to boom and swing. This was due mainly to two developments: the opening of the Casino, with its 36 roulette tables (in those days the largest gambling place in the world), and the paving of the Ruta Nacional 2, which brought Mar del Plata to within four hours by car from Buenos Aires.

With the construction of still another road along the coast (Ruta Provincial 11), other smaller seaside resorts started to sprout up north and south from Mar del Plata. Before long, each of these places acquired a character of its own; some preferred by the elderly, others by youth, some by those who like rock music and some by the lovers of smooth tango dancing.

How to get there: If an excursion to the vacation coast was a small adventure not so many years ago, mainly because of the muddy condition of access roads to most of the smaller villages, today the entire coastline is easily reached by car, bus, and in some places, train or plane. Mar del Plata and Miramar can be reached by the Roca train which departs from the Constitution station in Buenos Aires twice a week, taking about four hours to make the journey south. A growing number of vacationers also use airline services, which are inexpensive and frequent in summer. Most flights

The Mar del Plata Golf Club.

connect between the Buenos Aires city airport, Aeroparque Jorge Newbery, with Mar del Plataís Camet airport, but some of the smaller resorts can be reached by air, including Santa Teresita, Pinamar, Villa Gesell, Miramar, and Necochea. The principal airlines are Aerolineas Argentinas, Austral, LAPA, and SAPSE.

Fishermen's retreats: Heading south on Route 11 from Buenos Aires, the first resort town is **San Clemente del Tuyú**, located at the northern point of **Cabo San Antonio**, the most easterly point of continental Argentina. It is adjacent to Bahia Samborombon, the muddy mouth of the Rio Salado and other, smaller rivers of the pampa. The bay is rich with fish that here come to feed.

A small stretch of land juts out between the bay and the ocean, an area called **Punta Rasa**. Here one can visit the **El Faro San Antonio** (lighthouse), which is over 100 years old, and at 58 meters (190 feet) high, offers remarkable views. Also in Punta Rasa is an ecological reserve and biological station for migratory birds, which visit in spring and autumn on their journey between Alaska or Canada and Tierra del Fuego.

The town of San Clemente boasts one of the few "marine worlds" in South America, as well as many sports facilities and numerous well-equipped campsites. But the place is most popular among fishermen, who, starting in October, like to catch the *corvina negra* or *corvina rubia,* a delicacy used in soups and stews.

Another 22 km (14 miles) south on Route 11 is another well developed resort town, **Santa Teresita**. In addition to the popular beach, long fishing pier, and many seafood restaurants, there is a golf course, horseback riding, and various campgrounds.

Continuing south on Route 11, there are numerous resort towns, including **Mar del Tuyú**, **Costa del Este**, **Aguas Verdes**, **La Lucilla del Mar**, **Costa Azul**, **San Bernardo** and **Mar del Ajó**. They fall together in a rather developed 26-km (16-mile) stretch of coastline,

:olorful
ʰing fleet.

one after the other, just off the main road. These towns attract many tourists, but the beaches are wide and services abundant. San Bernardo is the largest of these, with highrise condominiums and hotels. Most visitors to this area come to swim, sunbathe and walk along the narrow beach beside the high sand dunes, but many others come to fish. One of the most popular pursuits is shark fishing, with catches reportedly ranging up to 1 meter (3 feet). This, however, is simply for sport; when it comes to mealtime, most of these visiting fishermen retire to one of the area's countless tiny seafood restaurants, many of which specialize in Italian fare. South from Mar de Ajó, the beach becomes increasingly solitary. The spaces between settlements become wider, and one can find more stretches of isolated pristine shore.

Old wrecks and lighthouses: Along this part of the coast, one can see many old lighthouses made of iron and brick. Previously mentioned is El Faro San Antonio, in San Clemente. Another is near Punta Medanos, at the southern tip of Cabo San Antonio, and still others can be found halfway to Mar del Plata (**Faro Querandi**), on the southern outskirts of Mar del Plata (**Faro Punta Mogotes**) and at Monte Hermoso.

Some of these towers are over a century old, and are worth a visit from both an architectural and a historical point of view. Many of them have shared in the area's long and fascinating history of maritime adventures and misfortunes. In a walk along the beach one will frequently encounter the stranded and disintegrating hull of some old windjammer or steamer.

Pines and shade: Probably one of the loveliest of all the urban areas along the Costa Atlántica is the one that comprises Pinamar, Ostende, Valeria del Mar and Cariló.

Pinamar is a very fashionable spot. It is bordered by a pine forest, and the scent of the pines mixed with the salty sea air gives the town a bracing atmosphere. There are no sand dunes at Pinamar, which makes access to the beach easy, even by car. The town has a

Beachfront at Mar del Plata.

variety of sports facilities, including an attractive golf course amid the pines. Accommodations range from four-star establishments down to modest, inexpensive pensions. Although hotels of all categories are available all year round, most people come for two weeks or a full month and therefore choose to rent a flat at prices which are much cheaper than that of the most humble pension. These apartments of one, two or three bedrooms may be rented on the spot, or in advance in Buenos Aires.

The greater Pinamar area includes **Ostende** and **Valeria del Mar**, where some very high dunes are to be found. A gambling casino, formerly located in Pinamar, is now south of Valeria. South of that, **Cariló** is a country club-style community dotted with elegant villas and shaded by pines. About 20 km (12 miles) south of Cariló lies **Villa Gesell**. It is especially popular with young people, due to its plethora of bars, discotheques and skating rinks. Villa Gesell also has several excellent campsites.

The main attractions between Gesell and Mar del Plata are the shady campsites at **Mar Chiquita** and **Santa Clara del Mar**, both some way from the beach.

Pearl of the Atlantic: Shortly before **Mar del Plata**, the landscape changes dramatically. Approaching the city on the coastal Ruta Provincial 11, the high cliffs of Cabo Corrientes and the downtown skyscrapers built upon this rocky peninsula seem to grow from the sea like a fata Morgana (mirage). It is a truly striking first impression. As one gets closer, secondary impressions should not disappoint the visitor, either.

This city is proudly called *La Perla del Atlantico* (the Pearl of the Atlantic) by its half-million residents. Accommodations range from first class hotels to apartments available for short-term lease all year round. The city has well-groomed plazas, parks, boulevards and several golf courses. Beyond the beaches and the sun lies perhaps the biggest attraction for the two million summer visitors, the colossal **casino** where, if you feel lucky, you can try your hand at roulette, poker, *punta banca*, and other games.

Another major pastime in Mar del Plata is to see and be seen. All of fashionable Buenos Aires feels obliged to be seen here at least once a year. During the peak of the season, the boutiques and galleries of **Calle San Martín** and the adjacent streets bustle late into the night with the tanned and the beautiful.

A visit to Mar del Plata would not be complete without a sampling of a few of the area's specialties. First, a visit to the fishing port, with its red and yellow boats along the quays is a must. A nest of restaurants in the area serve good, fresh fare. Next, be sure to try one of the famed *alfajores marplatenses.* These are biscuits filled with either chocolate or caramel, and are a favorite for afternoon tea. And lastly, visitors should avail themselves of the opportunity to buy well-made inexpensive woolens here. The sweaters, gloves and other items are made by the locals during the winter months.

Solitary beaches: From Mar del Plata, the coastal road runs past the Punta Mogotes lighthouse toward Miramar.

The scenery along this 40- km (25-mile) stretch is very different from that at the northern end of the Costa Atlántica. Instead of dunes and sandy beaches, the sea is met by cliffs. The road runs along the very edge, offering the traveler a splendid view of the sea, and the spectacle of Mar del Plata disappearing into the distance.

Miramar is infinitely less developed and much quieter than Mar del Plata, yet the main beachfront is overshadowed by towering apartment buildings. But the beach is very wide here and it's not difficult to escape the crowds. There is plenty of open space for many outdoor sports, including bicycling, horseback riding, tennis, jogging or just walking. For a break from the sand and surf, Miramar boasts a large, lovely, wooded park, Vivero Florentino Ameghino, complete with picnic spots and walking trails.

Between Miramar and **Necochea** the seaside resorts become sparser. Along this 80-km (50-mile) of shore there are only three places with facilities for vacationers: **Mar del Sur**, **Centinela del Mar** and **Costa Bonita**.

At Necochea, a pleasant city 125 km (78 miles) from Mar del Plata, the Río Quequén empties into the sea. There is a large port, where fishing excursions depart daily, a developed beachfront, and a proper city center. Beyond the beach, another interesting trip is 15 km (9 miles) up the river, to the Parque Cura Meucó, to relax and enjoy the various small waterfalls.

Even scarcer still are the developed beaches south of Necochea. **Claromeco**, about 150 km (93 miles) to the south, is one of the most attractive.

One place that comes heavily recommended is **Monte Hermoso**, some 700 km (435 miles) south of Buenos Aires near Bahia Blanca. Visited by Darwin during his voyage on the *Beagle*, and since then well known for its wealth of fossils along the shore, it has a broad beach of fine, white sand, shady campsites and a venerable lighthouse. The peace and quiet of this site promise a relaxing getaway for the traveler.

It is here, at Monte Hermoso, that the Argentine vacation coast ends.

there were three or four main languages and many dialects in the area.

There is no consensus as to the original population numbers but it is estimated that there were between 12,000 and 30,000 Indians in the area at the time of the Spanish conquest.

The discovery by the Spaniards of metal sources and stone for quarrying in the mountains more than justified in their eyes and in the eyes of Spain the foundation of a new city.

One hundred years after its foundation, Córdoba manifested the characteristics which are still seen as its trademark. The little village had flourished religiously and culturally. By that time it boasted an astonishing number of churches, chapels and convents erected by the Jesuits, the Franciscans, the Carmelites and others; it had a Jesuit-run university, the oldest in the country, erected in 1621 (now called the Universidad Nacional de Córdoba); the local economy was supported by a variety of agricultural products (corn, wheat, beans, potatoes, peaches, apricots, grapes and pears) and by extensive and ever-growing herds of wild cattle.

The tree: In Córdoba one finds the stark juxtaposition of the impossibly flat pampas with the rolling sierras, the first mountain chain one encounters when moving west towards the Andes. As one approaches across the plain, the hills appear as great waves breaking on a beach.

There are three chains of mountains in the western part of the province of Córdoba, all of which run parallel to each other, from north to south. They are the Sierras Chicas in the east, the Sierras Grandes in the center and the Sierras del Pocho (which turn into the Sierras de Guasapampa) in the west. The highest peak in the province is Champaqui, which reaches a height of 2,884 meters (9,517 feet).

The Sierras de Córdoba are neither as high nor as extensive as many of the other mountain formations east of the Andes. Their easy accessibility, their beauty, their dry weather, magnificent views, and good roads, as well as the

myriad of small rivers and water courses have established for Córdoba a strong reputation as an ideal spot for rest and recuperation.

Most of the rain falls in the summer and is heavier in the eastern section where the hills look very green and lush. In truth the vegetation on these hills is mostly of the *monte* type, bushes and low thorny thickets. Towards the piedmont of the eastern hills, larger trees grow in greater abundance. Among these trees, the friendly algarrobo deserves special mention. From prehistoric times right up to the present it has been used by the local populations as a shade-giving tree, and as a source both of fruit and wood for fence posts and for fires. It is also one of the trees most resistant to drought, and because of all these virtues, it is sometimes simply called "the tree" by the locals.

Bird songs: The fauna of the region is not as rich as when the Spaniards first arrived, but is still plentiful enough in some hidden areas to support seasonal hunting. Pumas or American lions still roam the hills but are few and isolated. Guanacos are not a common sight around most of the vacation resorts but can be seen toward the higher western areas. Hares abound and are hunted and eaten, as are partridges and vizcachas. Several types of snakes can be found, including rattlesnakes and coral snakes, but the steady invasion of most places in the mountains by residents and visitors has decreased their numbers. Foxes are also occasionally seen. The countless species of birds, including condors, in the area are a source of attraction and delight for many people.

Córdoba has a continental climate. Though the summer, with its hot days and cool nights, is the favorite season for most visitors, the winter is not without its charm. Because the rains are seasonal, occurring in spring and summer, the views change dramatically.

Across the flats: The easiest access to the city and province of Córdoba is from the south and east. Leaving from Buenos Aires, the visitor has the choice of traveling by plane, bus or car.

One of Córdoba's central walkways.

194

Buses are fast, offer a wider variety of schedules and are all new, spacious and comfortable units. There are several companies that make the Buenos Aires–Córdoba run with options to stop in Rosario and a few other large towns (the "express" takes about 9 to 9½ hours). The two principal airlines, Aerolineas Argentinas and Austral, have several daily flights to Córdoba which take about an hour.

If the trip from Buenos Aires is made by land, there are two main ways to go to Córdoba. The shortest is via Rosario, a city of 1,000,000 inhabitants located 300 km (185 miles) from Buenos Aires, using Route 9. The other choice is using Route 8, a slightly longer but quieter and quainter road. In both cases, the visitor will pass through miles and miles of pampas (plain, flat and very rich terrain) dotted with small towns and huge plots planted with corn, wheat, soya and sunflower. Everywhere there are enormous herds of cattle (Aberdeen Angus, Hereford, Holando-Argentina) and horses. The roads are quite good

and offer the basic commodities (hotels, small restaurants, cafés, gas stations) in almost every town along the way. Córdoba can also be reached easily from the west (either Santiago de Chile or Mendoza) by plane and bus and from the north (Santiago del Estero, Salta, Tucumán, Jujuy) by plane, bus and train.

Spanish grid: The city of **Córdoba** is one of the largest in the country, with a population of approximately 1,200,000. The basis of its economy is agriculture, cattle and the automotive industry. Its key location in the country, at the crossroads of many of the main routes, established its early importance and fostered its rapid growth. Although Buenos Aires, with its excessive absorption of power and people, has always tended to overshadow the rest of the country, Córdoba and its zone of influence is the strongest nucleus of resistance found in the vast interior of Argentina.

Córdoba, like most Spanish-settled cities, was designed with a rectangular grid of streets, with the main plaza (in this case Plaza San Martín), the cathe-

e
ndonga
urch, in
Córdoba
s.

dral and the main city buildings in the center of town. It is therefore easy for travelers to find on a map the different sites of historical, architectural or artistic interest within the city.

Because many of the early buildings of Córdoba were either religious or educational, time and progress have spared a great number of them, leaving visitors and residents with a rich treasure-trove of colonial chapels, churches, convents and public buildings amid the modern surroundings.

There are several different tourist offices, including downtown, at the airport and inside the bus terminal. The main office for city tourism is located in the Recova del Cabildo, Independencia 30, with information about walking tours, special events, museum exhibits, maps and historical background. If planning a trip to the countryside, make sure to visit the provincial tourist office at Tucumán 360, which offers a wide range of information about the nearby sierras.

Church circuit: The religious *circuito* (circuits being the various tours that are recommended) covers most of the oldest colonial religious buildings. Alone or with a guide the traveler can visit the following:

The cathedral: Though its site was decided on in 1577, the final consecration took place in 1784, after collapses, interruptions and changes. These delays account for the many artistic styles visible in the architecture. It has been described by the architect J. Roca as having a classic Renaissance portico and a baroque dome and steeple, with influences of indigenous origin. A large wrought iron gate completes the picture.

The interior of the church is divided into three large naves, separated from each other by wide, thick columns (which replaced the smaller original columns which were not strong enough to support the building).

The main altar, made of silver, is from the 19th century; it replaced the original baroque altar which is now in the church of Tulumba.

The cathedral is located across from **Plaza San Martín**.

A river through the sierras.

The Jesuit complex: This complex is located on the spot where there was originally a small shrine, dating from 1589. It is located on Caseros Street, two blocks from the cathedral.

The group of buildings is made up of the church, the Domestic Chapel and the living quarters. Originally it also encompassed the Colegio Maximo and the university, both of which are now national institutions.

The church dates to the 17th century. One of its outstanding details is an arch made of Paraguayan cedar, in the shape of an inverted boat's hull, fitted with wooden pegs. The church interior is lined with cedar beams and the roof is made up of beams and tiles. The tiles were joined with a special glue, which after 300 years is still tightly weatherproof. Many of the baroque altars, including the one made of cedar, date to the 18th century and the Carrara marble work on the walls is 19th century.

The Domestic Chapel (with its entrance on Caseros Street) is also from the 17th century. Here, the ceiling was constructed of wooden beams, and canes tied with rawhide, which were placed between the beams and then plastered and covered with painted cloth.

The Jesuits and their work occupy a special place in the history of Argentina and the rest of South America, up to the time of their expulsion in 1768 by the Spanish Crown. Córdoba has its share of their legacy, and for those interested in Jesuit lore and work, visits to the **Santa Ana Chapel** in the city, and the towns of **Alta Gracia**, **Colonia Caroya**, **Estancia La Candelaria** and **Jesus Maria** are recommended.

The Church and Monastery of the Carmelite Nuns (also called Las Teresas) was founded in the early 17th century. It was heavily renovated during the 18th century and many of the buildings date to this later period. The main altar has a large baroque sculpture of Saint Teresa of Jesus and the wooden choir is an example of fine woodwork. In the monastery there is a religious art museum, in which many of the objects once belonging to the cathedral are now ex-

e golf club
La
mbre.

hibited. The entrance is on Independencia Street and the complex is located opposite the cathedral.

The Church and Convent of Saint Francis: The land for the church was given to the Franciscan Order by the founder of the city, Jeronimo Luis de Cabrera. The first chapel was built in 1575; this original chapel and a second one which replaced it no longer exist. The current structure was initiated in 1796 and finished in 1813. Within the complex, a room named Salon de Profundis is original.

The church is located at the corner of Buenos Aires and Entre Rios streets and is only two and a half blocks from the cathedral.

The La Merced Basilica: Located in the corner of 25 de Mayo and Rivadavia, only three blocks from the cathedral, the present building was finished in 1826 over foundations from the 1600s.

The main altar, executed in 1890, and the polychrome wooden pulpit from the 18th century are two of the outstanding attractions of the interior.

Also worth mentioning is the **Sobremonte Historical Museum**, an outstanding example of colonial residential architecture. It hosts a very comprehensive collection of Indian and Gaucho artifacts, old musical instruments, ceramics and furniture.

It is located on Rosario de Santa Fe and Ituizango Streets, three blocks from the cathedral.

The contemporary city: Córdoba might be better known for its historical and colonial charm, but the modern city also has much to offer visitors. A few blocks from the city center is **La Cañada**, the tree-lined canal that runs through town, a lovely place to walk in the evening or when there is not too much traffic. On Saturday and Sunday there is an art and crafts fair on the corner of La Cañada and A. Rodriguez.

The Rincon de los Pintores (the Painter's Corner) is a gallery devoted to the work of local painters, located downtown inside the Centro Muncipal de Exposiciones Obispo Mercadillo at Rosario de Santa Fe 39.

Alta Gracia' old Jesuit complex.

The *peatonales* (pedestrian streets) in the city center are lined with cafés, bookstores and boutiques, and many students coming and going from the university. This is a good place to sit and relax, do some window shopping and watch the people strolling by. Also close by are numerous movie theaters featuring current releases.

A traditional evening out in Córdoba would include attending a *peña*, where locals and visitors drink wine, eat *empanadas* and listen to folk music.

Village fiestas: Once the city of Córdoba has been explored, a trip to the surrounding countryside is highly recommended for those with the time. The local tourism authorities have laid out a number of routes which will lead the dedicated traveler up into the mountains, along paved and unpaved roads to lakes, streams, campsites and spectacular views. While these routes can be done by bus, a car is necessary to really explore the area.

One of the most popular areas is **El Valle de la Punilla**, which extends north from the city of Córdoba on Route 38 towards **Cruz del Eje**. This route passes through or near most of the small resort towns of the region.

The first stop is **Carlos Paz**, famous for its night life, its casinos, restaurants and clubs, and the sports activities centered around Lake San Roque. This town surprises the visitor with its handsome chalets, comfortable hotels and streets packed day and night with tourists (if one visits during the high season).

Eighteen km (11 miles) directly north of Carlos Paz is **Cosquin**, a quaint village famous for its Argentine and Latin American folk music and dance festival in the second half of January. Another 15 km (9 miles) north along the narrow but well-paved road brings one to the village of **La Falda**, which holds a festival celebrating the folk music of Argentina's immigrants, along with the tango, in the first week of February. During other times of the year, golfing, swimming, hiking, horseback riding, and sailing can be enjoyed in these and neighboring towns. Numerous small hotels

and pensions are available throughout the region.

About 11 km (7 miles) further north lies **La Cumbre**. This town boasts excellent trout fishing from November to April (as do many other towns in the area) as well as facilities for golf, tennis and swimming. Its altitude of 1,142 meters (3,768 feet) makes the climate extremely pleasant and for that reason, as well as for its serenity, it has become known as a writers' haven.

Another 15 km (9 miles) along the same road (now one has traveled 106 km/66 miles from Córdoba) will take the visitor to **Capilla del Monte**, a town which celebrates its Spanish Festival in February. One can enjoy hiking, rock climbing, swimming and serenity in this town in the heart of the sierras.

By taking Route 5 south of Córdoba the traveler will find another tourist haven, **El Valle de Calamuchita**, which lies between Las Sierras Chicas and Las Sierras Grandes.

Chalets and cakes: Arriving in **Alta Gracia**, one finds a charming, prosperous town which welcomes tourists but does not live off them, so one is not overwhelmed by the kinds of crowds or tourist establishments found in Carlos Paz. Life seems to move at a very slow pace here, with shops closing at 12.30pm for lunch and opening again at 4pm. There are a number of modest but clean hotels and several decent restaurants. One of the main attractions is the **Jesuit Church and Monastery**, veritable jewels of colonial architecture.

A short excursion into the hills behind Alta Gracia toward **La Isla**, on the **Anizacate River**, leads over a passable dirt road, past small farms and spectacular views of the beautiful river. With luck, somewhere along this route, or another in the Sierra region, the visitor just might come upon a group of locals branding their cattle and be invited to eat a barbecue (*asado*), drink strong red wine and throw the *taba* (a gaucho game of chance played with the left knee bone of a horse) with some rough looking but friendly country people. Traditionally, when the meal is over, a simple gourd is packed with *mate* (Argentine green tea)

and drunk through a silver straw with the same seriousness and enjoyment with which New York bankers would sip cognac after a meal.

Leaving Alta Gracia behind and returning to the main route, one continues on south and enters the Sierras on a well-paved, but winding road. Twenty picturesque kilometers (12 miles) later the **Los Molinos Dam** and **Lake** appear. This is a favorite spot for the people of the region to practice various aquatic sports. One can eat a decent meal overlooking the dam, high above the lake.

Another 20 km (12 miles) brings one to **Villa General Belgrano**, a town purportedly founded by seamen from the ill-fated Graf Spee, who chose not to return to Germany. The town has a decidedly German character, with its charming chalets and well-kept gardens. As might be expected, the town celebrates an Oktoberfest during the first week of that month. And don't leave town without sampling some of their famous homemade cakes.

The tiny town of **La Cumbrecita** is nestled at the foot of Las Sierras Grandes, 40 km (25 miles) down an unpaved road west of Villa Belgrano. Visitors will find many nature paths just outside town, crossing small rivers and waterfalls, and meandering among varied plant life, including a small forest of cedar, pine and cypress trees. The town is relaxing and quiet, with attractive houses and gardens along the side streets. Hotels and restaurants are plentiful. On the road between Villa Belgrano and La Cumbrecita there's a view of Champaqui, at 2,800 meters (9,186 feet), the highest peak in the sierras of Córdoba.

A less developed and more tranquil part of the sierras is Traslasierra (which means behind the mountains), reached by taking **El Camino de las Altas Cumbres** to the west, on the other side of the mountains from the valleys La Punilla and Calamuchita. Some of the towns worth visiting are **Mina Clavero**, **San Javier**, and **Cura Brochero**.

The Sierras of Córdoba offer infinite possibilities to explore off the main tourist routes, following dirt roads to quiet villages in the mountains.

A gaucho i▸
the making

hours and goes along a network of waterways, wending between islands with wooded shores.

Carnival color: The cities of **Resistencia** and **Corrientes** are linked by a huge bridge. Following the rule of most of the river, Corrientes, on the east bank, sits high, and Resistencia is amongst the swamps. Neither is high on the tourist's agenda, but Corrientes does have a carnival celebration of note, with floats, music, drums, dancing, fancy-dress and all. This takes place during the last days before Lent, so consult a calendar, as the date for the feast varies.

Inland from Corrientes, the small town of **San Luis del Palmar** has retained the flavor of colonial times and is well worth a visit.

Just past Corrientes one reaches the confluence with the Paraguay river. It is about here, at **Paso de la Patria**, that fishermen from all over the world congregate to try for dorado, the "fightingest fish in the world." Lodging, boats, guides and equipment are available from July to November.

Incongruous and totally out of the blue, the huge church dome at **Itatí** can be seen for up to 24 km (15 miles) across the plains. This dome is said to be the "most impressive" after St Peter's. It tops the basilica where many pilgrims converge to venerate the miraculous Virgin of Itatí, housed in the adjoining shrine. She has quite a following. For sheer bad taste it is hard to beat the local *santerias*, which sell plaster statues of the virgin, saints and other religious articles, all gaudy, all grotesque, and all in the cheapest souvenir tradition.

The gigantic **Yacyretá Dam** has become the chief tourist attraction of the once-sleepy Corrientes town of **Ituzaingó**, which is also recommended for its beaches, zoo and dorado and surubí fishing. The **San Gará Ranch** offers expeditions into the Iberá wetlands.

Just southwest of Posadas, the character of the river changes; the wide, shallow sweeps change to a boxed-in area between steep. high banks in rolling countryside. From here on up, the river cuts through a basalt flow originating some 1,290 km (800 miles) distant in Brazil. Here even the soil changes; the red lateritic soil of Misiones province deceives one into thinking it is quite fertile, as the vegetation here is very lush. This is, however, a complete hoax: the vegetation provides its own growth as the constant fall of leaves makes a rich compost.

Jesuit missions: Posadas is the provincial capital of Misiones, very provincial, with some 150,000 inhabitants and nothing much to attract the visitor. A bridge crosses the river to Encarnación in Paraguay. Posadas' Paraguayan market is open every day at San Martín and Roque Pérez Streets.

The Jesuits were the real pioneers in Misiones; indeed, it is from their work that the province gets its name. They arrived early in the 17th century, and proceeded to settle and convert the local Guaraní natives. They soon began to be pushed around, first by slave traders in the area and then by the Iberian governments, first Portugal, then Spain. They were finally expelled in 1777, and left behind them the mission buildings and

r a rain he town olón.

lots of unprotected and slightly Christian souls.

There are 12 known mission ruins in Misiones, but first among them is **San Ignacio Miní**. Started early in the 17th century, it was by no means safe from slave raids from the Portuguese colony. At the peak of its existence, it housed some 4,000 to 5,000 Indians. San Iganacio is the most cleaned-up and restored of all the sites.

It is best to amble around the ruins at dawn or dusk, when one can be alone and when the light plays wonders on the red stone. It is then that one can commune with the spirit of what was begun in the name of humanity. The surviving Indians are worse off today than they were 200 years ago.

Muddy waters: It is a sad reflection on the short-sightedness of man that all the streams which run into the upper Paraná, save one, are muddy. Clear-cutting, lack of soil protection and the use of slash-and-burn techniques are all chronic problems, and have led to severe ecological deterioration in the area. The Paraná, too, suffers from these ravages in its own headwaters.

Some of the villages of Misiones have a flavor peculiar to themselves. Wooden houses and churches are made from local materials, but the ideas which inspired them came from northern Europe, the origin of most of the settlers. Immigrants from Germany, Poland, Switzerland, Sweden and France settled in this area, which accounts for the fair-haired people seen everywhere.

One finally disembarks in **Puerto Iguazú**, the head point of navigation, now that the Itaipú Dam has closed off the Paraná and since the Iguazú River has its own natural barrier. This small town is fully geared for tourism, with a number of hotels, restaurants, taxis, exchange houses and so on. As a town, it has not much to save it from mediocrity, but it just happens to be the nearest settlement to the **Iguazú National Park** and the world-famous **waterfalls**.

The Devil's Throat: Amidst a spectacular jungle setting, the **Iguazú Falls** lie on the Iguazú river, which runs along

The vortex called the Devil's Throat.

ANCIENT SETTLEMENTS

The northwest of Argentina is in large part a colorful, wind-sculpted montane desert traversed by green river valleys. Blessed with as many minerals as rock colors, it is the epicenter of Argentina's colonial and pre-Columbian cultures; its elevation and dry, sunny climate have long made it an ideal agricultural region. The Calchaquí Valleys, named after one of the pre-Incan tribes that inhabited the region, occupy a 250 by 70-km (155 by 44-mile) area in the provinces of Salta, Catamarca and Tucumán, inhabited by small farmers and artisans.

Slow-paced village life enhanced by comfortable inns, many recycled from colonial structures, tasty local cuisine and numerous wineries, make a leisurely drive through the valleys an unforgettable experience. Cafayate, Salta's second-largest city, the heart of the Calchaquí Valleys, sums up the history of the area in its archaeological and colonial, vine and wine museums, as well as the workshops of local artists and artisans.

The city of Salta, one of Argentina's oldest provincial capitals, is graced by numerous colonial and neo-colonial homes, and is the jumping-off point for the 14-hour Tren a las Nubes (Train to the Clouds) trip to the highland town of San Antonio de los Cobres. In the surrounding Valley of Lerma are numerous century-old *fincas* (ranches) that accept tourists. Day trips from Salta to the Indian villages of Humahuaca and Purmamarca and the pre-Columbian Tilcara fort in Jujuy Province are an opportunity to see a Bolivian-influenced culture.

The tiny province of Tucumán, the country's biggest sugar producer, is renowned for the mysterious Tafí culture menhirs near the mountain hamlet of El Mollar, and the largely reconstructed ruins of the pre-Columbian stronghold of Quilmes near Cafayate. The parks of the provincial capital of San Miguel de Tucumán have flowers all year round thanks to a mild climate, and its lakes and rivers are a fisherman's paradise. In La Rioja, the 225-million-year-old Talampaya Valley, an important paleontological and archaeological site and wildlife reserve, is just across the border from Ischigualasto in San Juan. Ischigualasto is one of the world's biggest fossil reserves.

THE MAGNIFICENT NORTHWEST

Northwest Argentina is a large territory sometimes known as the NOA (Nor Oeste Argentino). It comprises the provinces of Jujuy, Salta, Tucumán, Santiago del Estero, Catamarca, and La Rioja, though the latter two are occasionally considered part of the Cuyo region.

The vast and varied Northwest can be divided into three very distinct regions. It is most famous for the part best described as *quebradas*, the arid, high mountains of the *precordillera* (foothills of the Andes), characterized by painted desert hillsides, cacti and dry shrubs, deep canyons, and wide valleys. In stark contrast, the *yungas*, or subtropical mountainous jungle, is identified by dense green vegetation, mist-covered hillsides, and trees draped in vines and moss. And finally there is the *puna*, the cold, high altitude and practically barren plateaus found close to the Chilean and Bolivian borders.

Beyond the beauty of its natural landscapes, Northwest Argentina offers the opportunity to explore pre-hispanic culture and history. This part of the country has been inhabited for more than 10,000 years, and many traces of previous settlements remain. There are interesting yet modest ruins scattered throughout the region, historical museums and monuments, traditional foods and music, and arts and crafts which still use ancient techniques.

Moon Valley: There are two remarkable natural monuments near the border between the provinces of San Juan and La Rioja: the Valle de la Luna (Moon Valley) and the Talampaya Canyon. Excursions to both can be made by bus from the capitals of either of the two provinces, or by car.

The **Valle de la Luna** is a large natural depression where constant erosion by wind and water through millennia has sculpted a series of sandstone formations of strange shapes and an abundance of colors.

Beyond its beauty, the Valle de la

Luna has great geological and palaeontological significance. In prehistoric times (even before the birth of the Andes) this area was covered by an immense lake. Around this, during the triassic period, a rich fauna and flora thrived. A 2-meter (6-foot) long reptile, the Dicinodonte, was one of the most typical specimens in the area. In all, 63 different species of fossilized animals have been found and described by palaeontologists.

The small towns of San Agustín del Valle Fértil, to the south, Patquía, to the east, and Villa Unión, to the west, are ideally suited as base camps for those who intend to explore the remote past of the planet.

Canyons and condors: Talampaya lies about 80 km (50 miles) west of the provincial road that runs between Patquía and Villa Unión. Although palaeontologically not as significant as the Valle de la Luna, this impressive gorge, with cliffs towering to more than 145 meters (480 feet), was occupied by pre-hispanic people. Uncounted rock paintings and

engravings (pictographs and petroglyphs) offer an interesting archaeological contrast to the impressive geological nature of the canyon. Watch for condors soaring high above the canyon walls, because the cliffs harbor dozens of condor nests.

Nearby **Villa Unión** offers a chance to sample the exquisite white wines of the region. The *patero*, a homemade variety made in the traditional way (the grapes being crushed underfoot), is especially good. From this town one can make an excursion to **Vinchina**, which has an old water mill and a strange, multicolored, ten-pointed star built by the natives as a ritual site. One can also visit **Jagüe**, a tiny hamlet cradled at the foot of the giant **Bonete Volcano**, on the old muletrack which connects the green meadows on the Argentina side with the Chilean mining towns in the southern Atamarca Desert.

Another place well worth a stopover is **Chilecito**. Connected to Villa Unión by the tortuous and colorful **Cuesta de Miranda** pass, this small town lies on the eastern slopes of the majestic Famatina range. Chilecito's attractions include its excellent wines, the very old chapel of Los Sarmientos, a good hotel (Hosteria ACA), two museums and a pleasant climate. La Rioja, the capital of the province, has ancient churches, among them the oldest in ·Argentina (Santo Domingo, built in 1623), and interesting folkloric and archaeological museums.

Salt flats and volcanoes: A little farther to the north, **Catamarca** offers surprising geographical and historical highlights. Catamarca is a province with the greatest altitude differences imaginable; toward Córdoba and Santiago del Estero in the east, the vast **Salinas Grandes salt flats** are barely 400 meters (1,300 feet) above sea level, while in the west, near the Argentine–Chilean border, the **Ojos del Salado Volcano** reaches the vertiginous height of 6,930 meters (22,869 feet), making it the highest volcano in the world.

If passing through the capital, **San Fernando del Valle de Catamarca**, points of interest include the famous church and convent San Francisco, archaeological and historical museums, and a year-round arts and crafts fair, best known for rugs and tapestries.

The countryside around the capital is lovely, and two side trips are worth mentioning. Provincial Route 4 winds up north through hills and canyons, passing the two small towns of **El Rodeo** 37 km (23 miles) and **Las Juntas** (another 15km/9 miles), both with services for visitors and recreational activities. Heading east out of town on Route 38 is the well known **Cuesta El Portezuelo**, a winding road climbing out of the valley and up the lush mountainside, offering stunning views of the valley below.

Time permitting, a trip to the old indigenous settlements scattered on National Route 40 is highly recommended. The road crosses the province through a series of valleys and riverbeds, surrounded by dusty mountains. These towns are now slightly more developed than they were hundreds of years ago, but their small museums, traditional chapels, and the spectacular landscape of the road

In the Valle de la Luna.

make for a worthwhile trip. The most visited of these towns are **Tinogasta**, **Belén**, and **Santa Maria**. Look for the thermal spas along the route, one of the most developed being at **Fiambalá**, 48 km (30 miles) north of Tinogasta. For the adventurous, there is **Antofagasta de la Sierra**, about 250 km (155 miles) north of Route 40, located in the *puna* region of northern Catamarca. The remote Antofagasta is 3,500 meters (11,482 feet) above sea level and nearby are lagoons, volcanoes and salt flats. Be sure to ask locally about road conditions before embarking very far off Route 40.

Dusty flats: To the east of Catamarca lie the dusty flats of the province of **Santiago del Estero**. The capital of the province, bearing the same name, was founded by Spanish conquistadors in 1553, making it the oldest continuously inhabited city of the region.

There is not much to see in this region beyond algarrobo forests and the cotton fields. However, there is one major attraction: the thermal spas at **Río Hondo**.

Near an artificial lake, which offers a variety of sporting activities, the city of Río Hondo has developed into one of the most fashionable spas in Argentina, with fine restaurants, first-class hotels and even auditoriums suited for conventions. Life here is as bustling in the winter months as it is on the beaches of Mar del Plata in the summer.

A tropical garden: Not far from Río Hondo the dusty desert gives way to a subtropical spectacle which surprises everybody who visits Tucumán for the first time. Here the almost endless aridity and scenic boredom of Santiago del Estero, Formosa and the Chaco provinces is replaced abruptly by a cornucopia of tropical vegetation. It is for this reason that the province of Tucumán – the smallest of the 24 Argentine federal states – is popularly known as the Garden of the Nation.

This climatic and visual contrast is most vividly marked along the Aconquija range, which has several peaks of more than 5,500 meters (18,000 feet). Here the intense greenery is juxtaposed with gleaming snow-capped peaks.

rail ough lilegua tional rk.

Favored with copious rainfall, the province of Tucumán is one of the loveliest and economically richest of Argentina. On the plains, farming is the major economic activity. Around San Miguel de Tucumán, the provincial capital, one finds the smoky *ingenios* (sugar mills), and industrial factories built since the mid-1960s.

The city of **Tucumán** has a unique character. The spacious **Nueve de Julio Park**, the baroque **Government Building** and several patrician edifices, together with a number of venerable churches, are reminders of the town's colonial past. This may best be appreciated by visiting the **Casa de la Independencia**. In a large room of this stately house, part of which has been rebuilt, the Argentine national independence ceremony took place on July 9, 1816.

Side trips: However, it is not so much the town but its surroundings which make San Miguel de Tucumán worth a break during a tour through the Northwest area. Short excursions definitely should be taken to **Villa Nougués** and to San Javier, high up in the Aconquija range. From here the onlooker gets a splendid view of Tucumán, its outskirts and the extensive sugar cane and tobacco fields surrounding it.

A half-day excursion to nearby **El Cadillal**, with its dam, artificial lake, archaeological museum and restaurants (where fresh *pejerrey* fish is served) is quite pleasant. It may also be worthwhile taking a guided tour to some of the sugar mills.

Once finished with the sightseeing tours in and around San Miguel de Tucumán, the traveler may choose between two different roads to carry on toward the north. One choice is the main Ruta Nacional 9, which passes by Metán and the Rosario de la Frontera spa and then winds through dense scrub forest and bushland to Salta and from there to Jujuy. But perhaps the better choice is to leave Tucumán, heading south towards **Acheral**. From Acheral, a narrow paved road starts climbing up through dense tropical vegetation, until it reaches a pleasant green valley, which is frequently

Harvesting in the great salt flats of the *puna*.

covered by clouds. The valley is dotted with tiny hamlets, the principal one being the old aboriginal and Jesuit settlement of Tafí del Valle.

Stone circles: Tafí del Valle, situated in the heart of the Aconquija range at an altitude of 2,000 meters (6,600 feet), is considered the sacred valley of the Diaguita natives, who, with different tribal names, inhabited the area. The valley is littered with clusters of aboriginal dwellings and dozens of sacred stone circles. By far the most outstanding attractions at Tafí are the menhirs or standing stones. These dolmens, which sometimes stand more than 2 meters (6 feet) high, have recently been assembled at the **Parque de los Menhires**, close to the entrance of the valley.

From Tafí, a dusty gravel road winds up to **El Infiernillo** (Little Hell), at 3,000 meters (10,000 feet) above sea level. Just past this point the landscape changes drastically once again, from rolling grass-covered mountains to the desert highlands.

Local tradition has it that at **Amaicha del Valle** the sun shines 360 days of the year. Some hotel owners are said to be so fond of this bit of lore that they reimburse their guests if an entire visit should pass without any sun at all. Whatever the weather, the local handwoven tapestries and the workshops certainly merit the visit.

Sun-blessed valleys: Leaving Amaicha you enter the colorful, sun-blessed **Santa María** and **Calchaquí valleys**. Together they constituted one of the most densely populated regions of pre-hispanic Argentina. Shortly after Amaicha, the road splits into two branches. To the left (the south) one soon reaches **Santa María**, with its variety of fine artisan products and wines. It also has an important red pepper industry.

However, still better is to go straight ahead toward the north. Soon after one reaches Ruta Nacional 40 (the same Route 40 recommended for exploring Catamarca, and Argentina's longest road), a short approach road leads to the archaeological ruins of **Quilmes**. This vast aboriginal stronghold, which once

ying red
ppers near
nta Maria.

had as many as 2,500 inhabitants, is a paradigm of fine pre-hispanic urban architecture. Its walls of neatly set flat stones are still perfectly preserved, though the roofs of giant cacti girders vanished long ago. Local guides take the visitor to some of the most interesting sites of this vast complex, its fortifications, its huge dam and reservoir and its small museum.

On goes the journey through forlorn villages like **Colalao del Valle** and **Tolombón** to **Cafayate**, leaving the Tucumán province and crossing into Salta. In Cafayate, the exquisite white wines made from the Torrontes grape are produced.

Shady patios: Though situated only 260 km (160 miles), (about three-and-a-half driving hours) from San Miguel de Tucumán, Cafayate should be earmarked in advance as a place to spend at least one night.

There is more to Cafayate than its cathedral, with its rare five naves, its excellent colonial museum, seven *bodegas* (wine cellars), tapestry artisans and silversmiths. It is the freshness of the altitude of 1,600 meters (5,300 feet) and the shade of its patios, overgrown with vines, that really enchant the visitor. The surroundings of this tiny colonial town are dotted with vineyards and countless archaeological remains.

Some of the bodegas worth visiting around Cafayate are Etchart and Michel Torino, where guided tours and wine tasting are available.

There are two routes which lead from Cafayate to Salta. To the right, along Route 68, the road winds through the colorful **Guachipas Valley**, also called **La Quebrada de Cafayate**. Along this valley, water and wind have carved from the red sandstone a vast number of curious formations which delight the traveler at every bend. It is a pleasant drive of less than four hours (about 180 km/112 miles), and is especially ideal for those who are in a hurry.

The long way: Others, who have more time to spare and who are equally interested in natural beauty and history, should by all means follow Ruta Na-

Baking bread.

cional 40. It snakes along the scenic **Calchaquí Valley**, which is irrigated by the Calchaquí, one of Argentina's longest rivers.

Every one of the many romantic villages along the Calchaquí Valley deserves at least a short sightseeing walk, in order to gain an appreciation of the fine colonial architecture and hispanic art still largely preserved in this region. A stop at **San Carlos**, not far away from Cafayate, is especially worthwhile. This sleepy spot, with a comfortable ACA Hosteria, is said to have been founded no fewer than five times, first by the Spanish conquistadors as early as 1551, and later by waves of missionaries.

Soon after San Carlos the road becomes even more winding. From the chimneys of humble houses lining the way, the tempting smell of traditional dishes is frequently perceivable. The observant traveler may sniff *locro* (a corn and bean soup), *puchero* (a meat and vegetable stew) or *mazzamorra* (a hot drink made from corn meal and sugar), as well as fragrant bread being baked in the adobe ovens that are hidden behind the dwellings.

The route briefly leaves the river bed and crosses the impressive **Quebrada de la Flecha**. Here, a forest of eroded sandstone spikes provides a spectacle, as the play of sun and shadow makes the figures appear to change their shapes.

Angastaco, the next hamlet, was once an aboriginal settlement, with its primitive adobe huts standing on the slopes of immobile sand dunes. In the center there is a comfortable *hosteria*. Angastaco lies amid extensive vineyards, though between this point and the north, more red peppers than grapes are grown.

Molinos, with its massive adobe church and colonial streets, is another quiet place worth a stop. *Molino* means mill, and one can still see the town's old water-driven mill grinding maize and other grains by the bank of the Calchaquí River.

Across the river is a recently formed artists' cooperative, housed in a beautifully renovated colonial home, complete with a large patio, arches and an

st food in
rmejo,
ar Salta.

inner courtyard. The local craftspeople sell only handmade goods, including sweaters, rugs and tapestries.

Also, at **Seclantás** and the nearby hamlet of **Solco**, artisans continue to produce the famous, traditional handwoven *ponchos de Güemes*, red and black blankets made of fine wool that are carried over the shoulders of the proud gauchos of Salta.

Cactus church: By far the loveliest place along the picturesque, twisting Calchaquí road is **Cachi**, 175 km (108 miles) north of Cafayate.

Cachi has a very old church with many of its parts (altar, confessionals, pews, even the roof and the floor) made of cactus wood, one of the few building materials available in the area. Across the square lies the archaeological museum, probably the best of its kind in Argentina. With the advice and permission of the museum's director, the traveler may visit the vast aboriginal complex at **Las Pailas**, some 18 km (11 miles) away and partially excavated. This is one of countless archaeological sites in the Calchaquí region, which was densely populated before the arrival of the hispanic peoples.

Here, as in Cafayate, the visitor may decide to stay for more than just one night. An ACA Hosteria is situated magnificently atop a hill above old Cachi.

So clear is the atmosphere here that the mighty **Mount Cachi** (6,300 meters/20,800 feet) seems to be within arms' reach. Inhabitants of this region are said to benefit from the crisp mountain air, and many live to a very old age.

For closer views of Mount Cachi and a glimpse of the beautiful farms and country houses, be sure to visit **Cachi Adentro**, a tiny village 6 km (3½ miles) from Cachi proper.

Ruta Nacional 40 at this point becomes almost impassable, although you can visit the sleepy village of **La Poma**, 50 km (30 miles) to the north and partly destroyed by an earthquake in 1930. But the main tourist route runs to the east over a high plateau called **Tin-Tin**, the native terrain of the sleek, giant *cardon*, or candelabra cactus. **Los Cardones** **Spot the see-saw.**

230

National Park has recently been opened in this area.

Down the spectacular **Cuesta del Obispo Pass**, through the multicolored **Quebrada de Escoipe** and over the lush plains of the **Lerma Valley** the road stretches to Salta. From Cafayate to Salta, via Cachi, without stopovers, it is a demanding eight-hour drive.

In the whole Northwest region many roads are impassable during the rainy summer season (approximately Christmas to Easter). Autumn and spring (April–May and September–November) are the most advisable times for a visit.

Colonial gems: Salta is probably the most seductive town of the Northwest, due both to its setting in the lovely Lerma Valley and to the eye-catching contrast of its old colonial buildings with its modern urban architecture.

The city itself is a fascinating place for the tourist. It cradles such valuable colonial gems as the **San Bernardo Convent**, the **San Francisco Church**, and the **Cabildo** (city hall), with its graceful row of arches. The Cabildo

houses a very fine historical museum. The **Archaeological Museum** and the **Mercado Artesanal** (artisans' market), with handicrafts by some of the tribes living in the vast province of Salta, are two more musts for the tourist. A superb view of the city can be enjoyed from atop **San Bernardo Hill**.

Also an excellent way to pass an evening in Salta is at a local *peña*, where a dinner of traditional dishes is served and folkloric music is performed live by local musicians.

Train to the clouds: Both the Tren a las Nubes and El Rey National Park deserve brief descriptions. The train, fully equipped with dining car, leaves Salta's main station around seven o'clock in the morning and enters the deep **Quebrada del Toro** gorge about an hour later. Slowly, the train starts to make its way up. The line is a true work of engineering art, and doesn't make use of cogs, even for the steepest parts of the climb. Instead, the rails have been laid so as to allow circulation by means of switchbacks and spirals. This, together with

The church of San Francisco in Salta.

some truly spectacular scenery, is what makes the trip so unique and interesting.

After passing through **San Antonio de los Cobres**, the old capital of the former national territory, Los Andes, the train finally comes to a halt at **La Polvorilla Viaduct** (63 meters/207 feet high and 224 meters/739 feet long), an impressive steel span amidst the breathtaking Andean landscape. At this point one has reached an attitude of 4,197 meters (13,850 feet) above sea level.

From here the train returns to Salta, where it arrives, after a journey of about 14 hours, in the late evening. Unfortunately, El Tren a las Nubes only runs from April through October, making the journey about four to six times a month. Tickets cost about $95 and can be purchased in both Salta and Buenos Aires (contact the local tourism offices for current ticket information).

Jungle retreat: El **Parque Nacional El Rey** is located in the heart of the *yungas* or subtropical jungle region, 80 km (50 miles) from Salta. It's a natural hothouse with tropical vegetation as dense and green as one can find almost anywhere in South America. Visitors who come to fish, study the flora and fauna, or just to relax, will find ample accommodations; there is a clean *hosteria,* some bungalows, and a campground. The park is only reachable by car or prearranged transportation from Salta, and the best months to visit are between May and October.

Salta as a base: For those who don't have much time, Salta is the ideal starting point for short but satisfying road trips. Less than two hours from Buenos Aires by plane, it is a base for visits by bus, organized tours, or car to some of the loveliest destinations in the Northwest, as described elsewhere in this chapter: **Cachi** and the **Valle Cachalquies,** 130 km (81 miles) west, for one day or an overnight trip; **Cafayate**, 180 km (112 miles) south via Route 68, for one day or an overnight trip; **El Rey National Park**, 125 km78 miles () for at least an overnight stay; **San Antonio de los Cobres** and the ruins at **Tastil**, either by car or the Tren a las Nubes; **Humahuaca**,

A cemetery in the Quebrada d Humahuaca

definitely worth a visit. The city has preserved as an historical monument the ruins of the **San Francisco Church**. Founded by the Jesuits in the 18th century, the church was destroyed by the earthquake in 1861.

Behind the rather unattractive **Government Palace**, is the **Giol Wine Museum**, an extension of the nearby state-owned winery. It is small, but has wine tasting events and some interesting old photographs. Some pleasing items can be picked up at the **Artisans' Market**, at Lavalle 97. The main **Tourism Office**, at San Martín 1143, is quite helpful.

The city's two major hotels are the **Aconcagua** and the **Plaza**. The first, built for the 1978 World Cup soccer championship, has air conditioning and a pool, while the second relies more on old style charm to lure its customers.

Those seeking a break from touring can sample the shopping along **Las Heras**, or pull up a chair at one of the shady sidewalk cafés clustered in the city center. Most of these have good fast food, and some offer pitchers of *clerico*, the Argentine version of sangria, made with white wine.

In this desert climate, hot summer days are followed by pleasantly cool nights, and there are restaurants which offer dining al fresco. **La Bodega del 900**, on the outskirts of town, has a dinner show on its patio, and a small wine museum in its cellar. In any of the finer eating establishments one is advised to try trout and wild asparagus.

There are several cafés and nightclubs perched along the foothills to the west. One of the most pleasant of these is **Le Per**, open until quite late, with its patio overlooking Mendoza.

Glory Hill: On the western edge of the city lies San Martín Park, crowned by the **Cerro de la Gloria** (Glory Hill). The park has facilities for a wide variety of sports, including a soccer stadium built for the World Cup. Further up the hill is the **City Zoo**, with shaded walkways wandering among open-air cages.

At the top of the hill sits an ornate **Monument to San Martín**, complete

e melted
ows
scend.

THE WINES OF ARGENTINA

Argentina is the world's fifth largest producer of wine, with an average of 21 million hectoliters per annum. Almost 90 percent is produced in the Andean provinces of Mendoza and San Juan, with Rio Negro, Salta and La Rioja producing the rest. Fine wines represent between 6 and 8 percent of production, with jug wine, regional wine and a few special wines (sherries, ports, vermouths, etc.) making up the balance.

Although per capita consumption has declined notably in recent years, it is still high, at approximately 61 liters per year. Wine has been made in Argentina since the time of the conquest but it has only been in the last 90 years that winemaking has become an important and organized activity; there are not more than four or five wineries with more than a century of uninterrupted production and only one with more than 140 years of continuous production (Gonzalez Videla, founded in 1840). Some 2,000 wineries now exist, though only a handful make fine wine, and even fewer estates bottle or sell under their own brand names.

Argentina possesses a vineyard based almost entirely on European grape varieties. Such noble names as Cabernet Sauvignon, Merlot, Chardonnay, Chenin, Riesling and Pinot Noir figure prominently. However, due to sloppy or ignorant registration in the early years of the industry, and poor ampelographic control in later times, much confusion still exists as to exactly what grapes are harvested. An organized and scientific examination of many of the better vineyards has shown that many varieties regarded as one thing are actually another. Such is the case with the Argentine Pinot Blanc, which ampelographers have now determined to be Chenin. Much Rhine Riesling is actually Italian Riesling (also known as Tokay Friulano). While this has not affected the quality or the character of the wines, it does lead to some confusion when local wines are compared with those of other countries.

Argentina has traditionally been a red wine country, and in the opinion of visiting foreign experts and local connoisseurs , the reds are still superior to the whites (with an exception or two). The most popular and expensive reds are those made entirely or overwhelmingly from the Cabernet Sauvignon grape, but recently the extraordinary qualities of the Malbec have been discovered. The Malbec is considered only second rank in its native Bordeaux, but it has developed exceptional characteristics in Mendoza. Such internationally famous experts as Hugh Johnson of Britain and Terry Robards and Joseph Schagrin of the United States have pronounced it the premier Argentine red grape. Its wine can be considered unique to Argentina as no other country in the world has managed to obtain the quality which it offers here.

Argentine white wines are largely Chardonnay and Chenin, with some good Rieslings coming along and a few minor wines (Geweurtztraminer, for example) filling out the list. However, just as there is a unique and superior quality wine in the Malbec, so is there a distinguished wine among the Argentine whites. It is not a Mendoza wine, although the grape is harvested there and in San Juan, but comes from the northern-most province of Salta. The grape is the Torrontes, of Spanish origin, but which only develops its full potential in the high Andean valley of Cafayate, approximately 160 km (100 miles) west of Salta city. Torrontes wines are overpoweringly aromatic – much more so than a good Geweurtztraminer, for example – with a rich, gold color, a sturdy body and a first impression of slight sweetness which is later proved false. It is probably the fruitiest wine the Argentines produce. They also bottle a line of sparkling wines of different qualities, some of which are surprisingly good, particularly those made by the Moët and Chandon and the Piper Heisdieck outfits.

Rosé wines, on the other hand, are barely drunk, although some interest has been caused by the introduction of a couple of "blush" wines based on the Cabernet Sauvignon grape. Brandy and fortified wines such as sherry and port are seldom seen on Argentine tables.

By and large, Argentines drink wine with their meals, but the fastest growing section of the wine industry is the sparkling wine sector, and this is due to the ever increasing fashion of drinking sparkling wine as an aperitif. Far behind, as a second choice, white wine is also drunk before a meal; it is rare indeed to see red wine drunk as an aperitif, although the practice of continuing to drink wine after a meal is fairly common. ∎

with bolting horses and Liberty breaking her chains. Bas-relief around the statue's base depicts various scenes of the liberation campaigns. The site also provides an excellent overview of Mendoza.

Around the backside of the park is the **Frank Romero Day Amphitheater**, site of many of the city's celebrations, including the grand spectacle of the *Festival de la Vendimia* (Grape Harvest Festival). This takes place every year in March, and lasts over three or four days. The first few days there are street performances and parades, and a queen of the harvest is chosen. The finale is a somewhat overproduced extravaganza, complete with dancing, fireworks and moving light shows. This is Mendoza's annual opportunity to show off its hard-earned wealth.

Bodega hopping: One of the most pleasant diversions in the Mendoza area is *bodega* hopping. Scattered up and down this stretch along the Andes are nearly 2,000 different wineries, some small family operations, others huge and state-owned. All of this cultivation is made possible through an extensive network of irrigation. The area is blessed with a heady combination of plentiful water, sandy soil, a dry climate and year-round sunshine, which makes for enormous grape yields.

The first vines were planted in the Cuyo by Jesuit missionaries in the 16th century, but production really took off in the mid-1800s with the arrival of Italian and French immigrants. Many of them simply worked as laborers in the fields, but a knowledgeable few contributed European expertise that greatly refined the industry.

A number of wineries are right on the outskirts of Mendoza. Tours can be arranged through a travel agent, but a more pleasant way to make the rounds is by getting a map, renting a car and finding them yourself. This provides the opportunity to meander down the lovely country lanes lined with poplars and wildflowers, and to get a sense of the Cuyo's lifestyle.

Local cycling fanatics are out in packs

and, with luck, one might even catch sight of old men playing a lazy afternoon game of *bocci*.

The most popular destinations for *bodega* hoppers are the major, streamlined operations at Trapiche producers **Peñaflor**, in the suburb of Maipú, and **Chandón** in Godoy Cruz. Visitors are taken on a standard tour (special arrangements must be made for tours in English) through the areas where the various stages of production take place. Huge oak casks are set on rollers as an antiseismic precaution. Tours end with an invitation to taste the company's wine. Of course bottles are also offered for sale, at reduced rates.

The most interesting time to be here is during the March harvest, when trucks spilling over with grapes congest the narrow roads.

Two of the less-visited but more interesting *bodegas* are **Gonzalez Videla** and **La Rural**. The first is located in the suburb of Las Heras, down a dirt road. It's a bit difficult to find, but one can stop to ask directions. Begun in 1840, this is the oldest surviving winery in the area. Visitors are not really expected, so you have to do your own looking around. Pieces of ancient equipment lie about, and the family house, filled with antiques, is next door. Part of the complex is the old community church, where Sunday evening masses are held.

The Bodega La Rural, whose house brand is San Felipe, is located in Maipú. Started in 1889, this winery retains a lot of charm, with its original pink adobe architecture. It has the nicest wine museum of the area, small but filled with old presses and casks and basins made from single cow hides. Mornings are the best time for visits.

Other bodegas to visit include **Toso** and **Santa Ana**, in the suburb of Guaymallén, and **Norton**, in Luján.

Mountain pass: One of the most spectacular trips to be made from Mendoza is up the **Uspallata Pass** to the border with **Chile**. It is an all-day excursion which should be started early in the morning to allow enough time to see all the sights. One can sign on for a com-

Bringing in the harvest

mercial tour, but hiring a car allows one to avoid being herded around.

However, unless you're carrying on through Chile, going on your own is only recommended outside the winter months (July–September). Road conditions in the upper reaches are often icily treacherous then, and snow and rock slides are common.

At any time of year a set of warmer garments are needed for these cooler altitudes. Also be aware that altitude sickness can be a problem, as one goes from 750 meters to 2,500 meters (2,500 feet to 8,200 feet).

Those requiring visas for Chile should get them in Mendoza, as they will not be issued at the border.

One begins the trip by heading south from Mendoza on Route 7 to **Luján**. Turning right at the town square, you get onto Highway 7, which carries you up into the pass. This stretch of road, the Camino de los Andes, is part of the vast complex known as the Pan-American Highway. Throughout the centuries, even before the time of the Incas, the pass was used to cross the mountains.

Immediately the landscape becomes more barren as one leaves behind the irrigated greenery of the lowlands to follow the Mendoza river up the valley. Trees give way to scrub and the occasional bright flower.

The first spot one will pass is the **Cachueta Hot Springs**, at a lovely bend in the river. Only those with a doctor's prescription can check in, however.

Next comes **Portrerillos**, a scenic oasis where many Mendocinos have summer homes to escape the heat. The **Portrerillos Hotel** has terraced gardens overlooking the valley, along with a swimming pool and facilities for tennis and horseback riding. There are campgrounds nearby.

Up from Portrerillos, at the end of a side road, is the modest ski resort of **Vallecitos**. The resort is open from July to September.

Continuing up the valley, one reaches the town of **Uspallata**, set in a wide meadow. Further up, the valley widens again at **Punta de Vacas,** Cattle Point,

pass at avicencio.

where long ago the herds were rounded up to be driven across to Chile. It is at Punta de Vacas that one submits documentation if wishing to continue across the border.

The ski resort of **Los Penitentes** is just beyond. Buses bring skiers up for day trips from July through September. Across the valley is the strange formation for which the resort is named; tall rock outcroppings look like hooded monks (the penitents) ascending toward the cathedral-like peak of the mountain. In winter, wind-swept ice on the rocks heightens the illusion.

The Redeemer: Off to the left of the road, a little further on, is a desolate, melancholy sight, a small graveyard for those who have died in the attempt to scale nearby Mount Aconcagua.

Just beyond this is the **Puente del Inca**, a natural stone bridge made colorful by the mineral deposits of the bubbling hot springs beneath it.

Just a few miles up the road lies the most impressive sight of the whole excursion. There is a break in the wall of rock, and looking up the valley to the right one can see the towering mass of **Aconcagua**, at 6,960 meters (22,834 feet) the highest peak in the Western Hemisphere, and the highest anywhere outside of Asia.

The name means stone watchtower in an old Indian dialect. It is perpetually blanketed in snow, and its visible southern face presents a tremendous 3,000-meter (10,000-foot) wall of sheer ice and stone. Most expeditions tackle the northern face. The best time to attempt the climb is mid-January to mid-February. Information can be obtained in Mendoza at the Club Andinista (Pardo and Ruben Lemos Streets).

The clear mountain air creates the illusion that Aconcagua lies quite close to the road, but the peak is actually 45 km (28 miles) away. One can walk as far as **Laguna de los Horcones**, a green lake at the mountain's base.

The last sight to see before heading back is the **Statue of Christ the Redeemer** that is situated on the border with Chile. On the way there, the road passes the beat town of **Las Cuevas**.

From there the road branches: to the right is the new tunnel for road and rail traffic to Chile (passenger rail service from Mendoza to Santiago has been suspended in recent years because of lack of customers).

To the left is the old road to Chile, which climbs precipitously over rock and gravel to **La Cumbre Pass**, at an altitude of 4,200 meters (13,800 feet). At the top is the Christ statue, which was erected in 1904 to signify the friendship between Argentina and Chile. It is most interesting for the little bits of colored rag tied onto it by visitors, in hopes of having prayers answered.

The best reward for having made it up this far is the view over the mountains. In every direction, the raw steep peaks of the Andes reach up, the tips still catching the late afternoon sun. If they don't take your breath away, the sharp icy winds of the pass surely will. The perfect cap for the journey is to catch sight of a condor soaring at this lonely altitude, so keep your eyes open.

Jet-set skiers: Another day trip from Mendoza is to the hot spring spa at **Villavicencio**, 45 km (28 miles) to the northwest along Alternate Route 7. The road continues on until it reaches the mountain pass at Uspallata, but this portion is not paved.

South of Mendoza, 240 km (150 miles) away, is the agricultural oasis of **San Raphael**. Nearby hydroelectric projects have created reservoirs which have become centers for vacationers. The river fishing is said to be excellent.

To the southwest of San Raphael, in the **Valle Hermoso** (Beautiful Valley), is the ski resort of **Las Leñas**. This is becoming quite the place for the chic set of both hemispheres to meet between June and October. It boasts 45 km (28 miles) of dry powder slopes and has beds for 2,000 people. Charter flights bring skiers from Mendoza to the nearby town of **Malargüe**, where buses take them the rest of the way.

Although **San Luis** does not really merit an extra trip, it lies on the road between Buenos Aires and Mendoza, so those going overland may want to rest here for a day or so. The town sits at the northwest corner of the pampas, and was for many years a lonely frontier outpost; it retains a slightly colonial atmosphere. Several resorts in the area, clustered around reservoirs, are popular with fishermen and windsurfers. There is a spa at **Merlo**.

The area has several quarries for onyx, marble and rose quartz, and these stones can be purchased inexpensively. The town of **La Toma**, to the northeast of San Luis, specializes in green onyx.

River rafting: The town of **San Juan** is 177 km (106 miles) north of Mendoza along Route 40. An earthquake in 1944 leveled the town, and it has been completely rebuilt since then. It was his theatrical and highly successful efforts to raise funds for the devastated town that first brought Juan Perón to national prominence.

San Juan is another major center of wine production. However, it is most famous for being the birthplace of Domingo Faustino Sarmiento, the noted historian and educator who was president of the republic from 1868 to 1874.

His former home is the site of the **Sarmiento Museum**. There is also a **Natural Sciences Museum** and an **Archaeological Museum**.

To the west there are mountains which involve less strenuous climbs than those of the Mendoza peaks. One can inquire at the local tourism bureau about the possibility of white water rafting on the area's rivers.

In the north of San Juan Province lies the sculptured **Valle de la Luna** (Moon Valley), which is a paleontological treasure. (For a complete description, see the *Northwest* chapter.)

Wherever one travels in the Cuyo, at whatever time of year, look out for local festivals. Small and grand scale celebrations are held for the harvest of everything from wine and beer to nuts and apricots. Local gauchos put together rodeo competitions that are a treat to watch, and in January there is a *cueca* festival east of Mendoza. The *cueca* is a courtship dance inherited from Chile, and the perky strains of its music can be heard throughout the region.

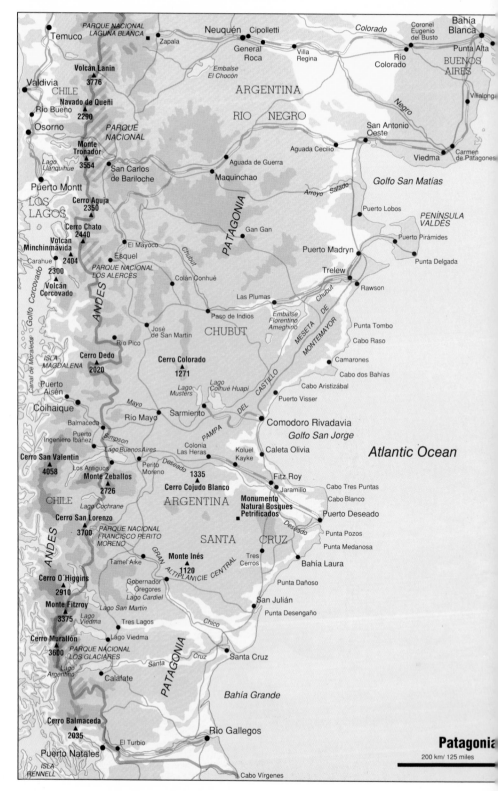

Patagonia

200 km/ 125 miles

purposes. They had been there long before the white man arrived and they stood their ground. The bravest were the Mapuche Indians, a nomadic tribe who lived on both sides of the border in the northern part of Patagonia. For 300 years they led a violent lifestyle on the northern plains by stealing and plundering the larger ranches of the rich pampas, herding the cattle over the Andes and selling them to the Spaniards on the Chilean side.

In 1879, the Argentine army, under General Roca, set out to conquer the land from the native Americans. The campaign, which lasted until 1883, is known as the Conquest of the Desert. It put an end to years of Indian dominion in Patagonia and opened up a whole new territory to colonization.

The land and its beauty remained, but the native inhabitants vanished: some died in epic battles, others succumbed to agonizing diseases that had been unknown to them, and others simply became cowhands on the large Patagonian *estancias*. Fragments of their world can still be found in this spacious land, in the features of some of the people, in local habits and in religious ceremonies still performed on Indian reservations.

European settlement: When the Indian wars ended, colonization began. The large inland plateau, a dry expanse of shrubs and alkaline lagoons, was slowly occupied by people of very diverse origins: Spaniards, Italians, Scots and Englishmen in the far south, Welsh in the Chubut Valley, Italians in the Río Negro Valley, Swiss and Germans in the Northern Lake District and a few North Americans scattered throughout the country.

These people inherited the land and reproduced in the far south a situation similar to the American West. Ports and towns developed on the coast to ship the wool and import the goods needed by the settlers. Large wool-producing *estancias* were established on these plains. To the west, where the plains meet the Andes, several national parks were designated to protect the rich natural inheritance, to develop tourism, and to secure the national borders.

The Patagonian towns grew fast. Coal mining, oilfields, agriculture, industry, large hydroelectrical projects and tourism attracted people from all over the country and from Chile, transforming Patagonia into a modern industrial frontier land. Some people came to start a quiet new life in the midst of mountains, forests and lakes. In the Patagonian interior, descendants of the first sheep-breeding settlers and their ranch-hands still ride over the enormous *estancias*.

A few geographical facts: With defined geographical and political boundaries, Patagonia extends from the Colorado River in the north, more than 2,000 km (1,200 miles) to Cape Horn at the southernmost tip of the continent. It covers more than 1 million square km (400,000 square miles) and belongs to two neighboring countries, Chile and Argentina. The final agreement on this long, irregular, international border took a long time to come by and was not an easy matter to settle. Although the land was still unexplored, there were times when both countries were almost on the brink

of war. Fortunately, it never reached that point, due to the common sense of both governments. An historical example of this attitude was the meeting of the Chilean and Argentine presidents in 1899 at the tip of the continent, in what is known as the Straits of Magellan Embrace. In 1978, a similar diplomatic encounter was carried out in Puerto Montt, Chile, where both countries agreed on the last stretch of undefined boundary, which concerned some small islands in the Beagle Channel.

The Argentine part of Patagonia includes approximately 800,000 square km (308,000 square miles), and can easily be divided into three definite areas: the coast, the plateau and the Andes. Only 4.5 percent of the Argentine population lives in Patagonia, at a rate of under one inhabitant per square mile (fewer than three per square km), and in Santa Cruz Province, this density drops to 0.19 inhabitants per square mile (0.5 inhabitants per square km).

Seasons are well defined in Patagonia. Considering the latitude, the aver-

Autumn comes to th plains.

age temperature is mild; winters are never as cold and summers never as warm as in similar latitudes in the northern hemisphere. The average temperature in Ushuaia is 6°C (43°F) and in Bariloche, 8°C (46°F). Even so, the climate can turn quite rough on the desert plateau. There, the weather is more continental than in the rest of the region. The ever-present companion is the wind, which blows all year round, from the mountains to the sea, making life here unbearable for many people.

The change of seasons: In spring, the snow on the mountains begins to melt, flowers (ladyslippers, buttercups, mountain orchids, etc.) bloom almost everywhere, and ranchers prepare for the hard work of tending sheep and shearing. Although tourism starts in the late springtime, most of the people come during the summer (December to March). All roads are fit for traffic, the airports are open, and normally, the hotels are booked solid.

The fall brings changes on the plateau. The poplars around the lonesome *estancias* turn to beautiful shades of yellow. The mountains, covered by deciduous beech trees, offer a panorama of reds and yellows, and the air slowly gets colder. At this time of the year, tourism thins out, and the foot of the Andes, from San Martín to Bariloche turns into a hunter's paradise. Los Glaciares National Park, in the far south, closes down for the winter. While the wide plains sleep, the winter resorts on the mountains thrive. San Martín de los Andes, Bariloche, Esquel and even Ushuaia attract thousands of skiers, including many from the northern hemisphere who take advantage of the reversal of seasons.

The two roads: Running from north to south, there are two main roads: Route 40 which runs along the Andes and Route 3 which follows the coast. The greater part of the former has yet to be paved. It starts at the northwestern tip of the country and runs parallel to the Andes through places of unusual beauty. In the Northern Lake District, Route 40 is very busy, but south of Esquel it becomes one of the loneliest roads in the

inter
mes to the
ountains.

world, until it joins Route 3 and ends in Río Gallegos on the Atlantic coast.

Route 3, completely paved, starts in Buenos Aires and runs along the coast for more than 3,000 km (1,800 miles) until it reaches its end on the Beagle Channel in Tierra del Fuego. This road connects all the main cities and towns on the Patagonian coast such as Bahia Blanca, Trelew, Comodoro Rivadavia, Río Gallegos and Ushuaia. In between these cities, the only inhabited places through miles and miles of desolation are the large Patagonian sheep-breeding *estancias*.

Many roads link the mountains to the coast. There is also a main railroad line connecting Buenos Aires to Bariloche, which follows the trail Musters rode a hundred years ago. On the voyage, the traveler will see the scenery change from the rich pampa of Buenos Aires province to the desert of Patagonia.

To some it might seem that time in Patagonia moves at a slower pace than elsewhere. The endless lonely roads, the long winters and the vastness of the sky have shaped a way of living that is simple and unpretentious. For the traveler, the kindness and hospitality of the local people will often make up for the occasional absence of some standard comforts, and those accustomed to European efficiency and fast pace will find things here a bit more relaxed.

Northern Patagonia: The northern boundary of Patagonia is the **Colorado River**. The steppe, or desert, as Argentines call it, starts farther north and extends uninterrupted through inland Patagonia and the coast, down to the Straits of Magellan. The **Río Negro**, south of the Colorado, flows into an oasis of intensive agriculture, which stretches for more than 400 km (250 miles). The valley itself is a narrow strip of fertile land, in sharp contrast to the desert surroundings that threaten to swallow it. Those interested in visiting agricultural areas specializing in growing fruit (apples, pears, grapes), cannot miss this place. Fruit farms, juice factories and packing establishments give an intense economic life to this oasis. **Neuquén, Cipoletti**, **Roca** and **Villa Regina** are the most important cities of this region.

Traveling along the Río Negro towards the Atlantic coast, past cultivated strips of land that alternate with sections of desert, one arrives at the twin towns of **Carmen de Patagones** and **Viedma**, having covered a distance of 540 km (330 miles) from Neuquén to very near the coast. Carmen de Patagones is one of the oldest settlements in Patagonia, founded in 1779 by the Spaniards. These settlers lived in constant fear of being invaded by foreign powers seeking to conquer Patagonia. Viedma, which lies on the opposite bank of the river, was slated in the mid-1980s by President Raúl Alfonsín to become the new capital of the Argentine Republic – the Argentine Brasilia – on the southern end of the continent, a symbol of the gradual shifting of economic and political interest. But as the cost of moving the capital from Buenos Aires became obvious, the plan was quietly forgotten.

Nearby, one can see the caves used for shelter by the first settlers. Where the river meets the sea, there is a sea lion colony similar to the many others along the coast. One hundred and eighty kilometers (110 miles) to the west lies the port of **San Antonio Este**, from where all the fruit production of the valley is shipped to foreign countries.

Dudes and swans: About 200 km (120 miles) southwest from Neuquén, on the road to Bariloche, is one of the many dude ranches in Patagonia. Near the small town of **Piedra del Aguila** is the enormous **Piedra del Aguila Hotel and Ranch**. It is open during the summer season and offers a variety of outdoor activities such as camping, horseback riding, sheep shearing and fishing.

Going west from Neuquén to the Andes, one reaches the top of the Northern Lake District. On the way there, close to the town of **Zapala** is a place no birdlife enthusiast should miss in spring: the **Laguna Blanca National Park** which includes a large enclosed lake. There are hundreds of interesting varieties of birds, the prime attractions in this park are the black-necked swans, which gather in flocks of up to 2,000 birds. Flamingos are also part of the scenery, and the surrounding hills give shelter to large groups of eagles, peregrine falcons, and other birds of prey.

Just one word of warning: this area has not been prepared as a tourist attraction. It is therefore not simple to reach. Try the approach from Zapala.

The Northern Lake District: The Patagonia lake district covers a stretch of land extending from Lake Aluminé in the north to Los Glaciares National Park in the south, over 900 miles (1,500 km) along the Andes. One can divide this region into two sections, the Northern and Southern Lake Districts. The zone that lies in between, where traveling is not easy and normal communications are scarce, is a challenge to be taken on by only the most adventurous.

The Northern Lake District covers the area between Lake Aluminé in the north and Lake Amutui Quimei in the south. It encompasses 500 km (300 miles) of lakes, forests and mountains divided into four national parks. From north to south we have the Lanín National Park and the town of San Martín de los An-

des, Nahuel Huapi National Park and the city of Bariloche, Lago Puelo National Park and the village of El Bolsón and, farthest south, Los Alerces National Park with the town of Esquel. This region connects to the Chilean lake area.

The three main cities of this district have their own airports, with regular scheduled flights all year round, and offer a complete range of traveler services (hotels, restaurants, car rentals, travel agencies). The railroad journey from Buenos Aires to Bariloche takes 32 hours. There are also daily buses from here to all parts of Argentina and to Chile, across the Tromen, Hua Hum and Puyehue passes.

If you want to reach Puerto Montt on the Pacific Ocean from Bariloche, try the old route the Jesuits and first German settlers used: across the lakes. The journey combines traveling by bus and boat across the beautiful Nahuel Huapi, Todos los Santos and Llanquihue lakes, through marvelous settings of forests, volcanoes and crystal waters. The route is open all year round; in summer the

trek is made every day and the rest of the year, three times weekly. You can book this trip at any travel agency.

There are two well-defined tourist seasons in this district: summer and winter. During the summer there is plenty to do. One can go on the regular tours, or rent a car and do some individual sightseeing. There are also many sports to keep one busy, from mountain climbing and fishing, to sailing and horseback riding. In winter, the main activity is skiing. July is the busiest month because of the Argentine schools' winter holidays. For a quieter time, try August.

Monkey puzzles and trout: The northern part of the Lake District, around Lake Aluminé, is well known for its Indian reservations where one can find handicrafts such as ponchos and carpets. This area is also home to one of the most peculiar looking trees in the world, the *Araucaria Araucana* or monkey puzzle. This tree, which grows at considerable altitudes, has a primeval look to it. Its fruit, the *piñon*, was a treat for Indians on their way across the Andean trails.

Lanín National Park, near San Martín de los Andes, is 3,920 square km (1,508 square miles) and gets its name from the imposing Lanín volcano, situated on the border with Chile. The volcano soars to 3780 meters (12,474 feet), far above the height of the surrounding peaks.

The national park is noted for its fine fishing. The fishing season is from mid-November through mid-April. The rivers and streams (Aluminé, Malleo, Chimehuin and Caleufu) around the small town of **Junín de los Andes** are famed for their abundance and variety of trout. Fly-casters come from continents away to fish for the brook, brown, fontinalis and steelhead. The best catch on record was a 12-kg (27-lb) brown trout – the average weight for this fish is 4–5 kg (9–11 lbs).

Although Junín has several good restaurants and pleasant hotels like the **Chimehuin Inn**, most anglers prefer the several fishermen's lodges located in the park. Two of these are the **San Huberto Lodge**, on the Malleo River

An ethereal vision of the Lanín volcano.

near the border with Chile, and the **Paimun Inn** on Lake Paimun at the foot of the Lanín volcano.

The Lanín National Park is also well known for hunting. Wild boar and red and fallow deer are the main attractions in the fall, which is the rutting season. The national park takes bids for hunting rights over most of the hunting grounds. The same goes for the farm owners who make their own agreements with hunters and outfitters. For information, contact the Tourist Office in **San Martín de los Andes**.

There are many guided tours, by bus or boat, departing from San Martín de los Andes. There are car rentals, camping sites and fishing, and hunting and mountain climbing guides are readily available. Also recommended is a trip to lakes Huechulafquen and Paimun and the majestic Lanín volcano and the unique monkey puzzle forest. In winter, **Mount Chapelco** (1,980 meters/6,534 feet), only 20 minutes by car from San Martín, is a small, quiet resort for alpine and cross-country skiers.

All facilities are available in San Martín. For hotels, one can choose from **La Cheminee**, **Le Village** or **El Viejo Esquiador**; for restaurants, **El Ciervo** or **El Munich de los Andes** are much frequented. Patagonian Outfitters can see to your travel needs.

There are three roads that link San Martín de los Andes with Bariloche: a paved one, running through the dry steppe, along the Collon Cura River, and two partially paved ones. The middle road (the shortest) runs across the **Córdoba Pass** through narrow valleys with beautiful scenery, especially in the autumn when the slopes turn to rich shades of gold and deep red. This road reaches the paved highway at **Confluencia Traful**. From here, if you take a short turn and go back inland, you come to a trout farm that belongs to the **Estancia La Primavera**. On returning to the paved road that leads to Bariloche, you ride through the **Enchanted Valley**, with its bizarre rock formations.

The third road from San Martín is the famed **Road of the Seven Lakes**. This

ove the
uds at
rro
tedral.

road, almost totally paved, takes you across a spectacular region of lakes and forests and approaches Bariloche from the northern shore of Lake Nahuel Huapi. In summer, all-day tours make the trip from Bariloche to San Martín, combining both the Córdoba Pass and the Road of the Seven Lakes.

Switzerland in Argentina: Bariloche, situated in the middle of **Nahuel Haupi National Park,** is the real center of the Northern Lake District.

Buses, trains and planes arrive daily from all over the country and from Chile, across the Puyehue Pass.

Bariloche has a very strong Central European influence; most of the first settlers were of Swiss, German or Northern Italian origin. These people gave the city its European style, with Swiss chalets, ceramics, chocolates and neat shop windows.

However, something tells you that you are not in Europe; boats are seldom seen on the huge Nahuel Huapi lake, the roads are swallowed in the wilderness as soon as they leave the city and at night, there are no lights on the opposite shore of the lake.

The best way to begin your tour of Bariloche is by visiting the **Patagonia Museum** in the Civic Center. This building and the Llao Llao Hotel were designed by Bustillo, and give Bariloche a distinctive architectural personality. The museum offers displays on the geological origins of the region and of local wildlife. It also has a stunning collection of Indian artifacts.

There are many excursions to choose from in the Bariloche area: half-day tours of the **Small Circuit**, Catedral Ski Center and **Mount Otto**, and whole-day tours by bus or boat to San Martín de los Andes, **Mount Tronador**, **Victoria Island** and **Puerto Blest**. Two recommended trips are to Mount Tronador, the highest peak in the park (3,554 meters/ 11,728 feet) with its impressive vista of glaciers, and to Victoria Island and the *arrayán* (myrtle) forest on the Quetrihué Peninsula. The story goes that a visiting group of Walt Disney's advisors were so impressed by the amazing

The Llao Llao Hotel, on Lake Nahuel Huapi.

white and cinammon colored trees in this forest that they used them as the basis for the scenery in the film *Bambi*.

The range of activities in the Nahuel Huapi National Park includes windsurfing, rafting, mountain climbing, fishing, hunting, horseback riding and skiing. Major facilities are available for all these sports. The **Club Andino** will provide you with any information you need that is related to mountain climbing, including trail guides and details on mountain lodges (where kitchens and food are available).

Those looking for a wild and woolly Patagonian experience should try a horseback trek with Carol Jones, granddaughter of Texas pioneer Jared Jones, who runs her dude-ranching operation out of the **Estancia Nahuel Huapi**, which Jared founded on the shores of the lake in 1889. A ride can be arranged for a morning or an entire week and will take one through breathtaking terrain in the foothills of the Andes. For more information, contact the Jones family at the ranch (tel: 0944-26508).

Regional buys: Chocolates, jams, ceramics and sweaters are among the most important local products. The large chocolate industry has remained in the hands of Italian families and a visit to some of the downtown factories is worthwhile. So is a visit to the ceramics factory, where you can watch the artisans at work. Sweaters are for sale everywhere, and a recommended shop is **Arbol**, on the main street. On the same street is **Tito Testone**, where you can buy jewelry and handicrafts.

The **Catedral Ski Center**, 17 km (11 miles) from Bariloche, is one of the largest in the southern hemisphere. The base of the lifts is at 1,050 meters (3,465 feet) above sea level, and a cable-car and chair-lifts take you up to a height of 2010 meters (6,633 feet). The view from the slopes is absolutely superb. The ski runs range in difficulty from novice to expert, and cover more than 25 km (15 miles). The ski season starts at the end of June and continues through September. Ski rentals, ski schools, restaurants, hotels and lodges are available.

ounter-
ture
nmunity
El Blosón.

Bariloche has a large variety of hotels, ranging from small, cozy inns to first class luxury hotels. **La Pastorella, El Candil**, the **Edelweiss** and the exclusive **El Casco** are some of the choices.

Restaurants offer a variety of fare, from fondue and trout, to venison and wild boar. Try **Casita Suiza, Kandahar**, and **El Viejo Munich**, a meeting place for locals.

For an authentic taste of a regional barbecue, don't miss the **Viejo Boliche**, 18 km (11 miles) from Bariloche. The restaurant is located in an old shed which the Jones family used as a general store at the beginning of the century.

Hippie refuge: El Bolsón is a small town 130 km (80 miles) south of Bariloche, situated in a narrow valley with its own microclimate. Beer hops and all sorts of berries are grown on small farms. The hippies of the 1960s chose El Bolsón as their sanctuary. Nowadays, there are just a few of these idealists left, leading peaceful lives on farms perched in the mountains.

The serene **Lago Puelo National Park** (237 sq. km/92 sq. miles) is an angler's paradise and its mountains covered with ancient forests of deciduous beech trees and cypresses are a delight for wanderers and mountain climbers. The **Amancay Inn** and the **Don Diego Restaurant** offer food and lodging.

The gringo outlaws: Farther south, on the road to Esquel, you come across the beautiful **Cholila Valley**. According to some historians, this place was chosen by Butch Cassidy and the Sundance Kid as a temporary shelter while they were on the run from Pinkerton's agents. A letter sent by them to Matilda Davis in Utah, dated August 10, 1902, was posted at Cholila. After their famous holdup of the Río Gallegos Bank, in 1905, they were again on the run, until they were finally killed by the Bolivian police. Other members of the gang who stayed on in this region were ambushed and killed, years later, by the Argentine constabulary.

Welsh tea: From Cholila, the road going south splits in two. Route 40 turns slightly to the east, through the large

Left, graveyard. Below, a Welsh Bibl

THE WELSH IN PATAGONIA

A Welshman traveling in Patagonia's Chubut Valley may well have a sense of *déjà vu*. On the streets of Trelew he will overhear Welsh spoken, in slightly archaic utterances, by elderly ladies, while in the Andean foothills around Trevelin he can converse in Welsh with a rancher who drinks *mate,* rides like a gaucho and whose other languages are Spanish and English.

Patagonia is partly pampas, largely desert and unrelentingly wind-blown, with only small areas of fertile soil and little discovered mineral wealth. Why would anyone leave the lush valleys and green hills of Wales to settle in such a place? The Welsh came, between 1865 and 1914, partly to escape conditions in Wales which they deemed culturally oppressive, partly because of the promise – later discovered to be exaggerated – of exciting economic opportunities, and largely to be able to pursue their religious traditions in their own language. The disruptions of the 19th century industrial revolution uprooted many Welsh agricultural workers; the cost of delivering produce to market became exorbitant because of turnpike fees, grazing land was enclosed and landless laborers were exploited. Increasing domination of public life by arrogant English officials further upset the Welsh. Thus alienated in his own land, the Welshman left.

Equally powerful was the effect on the Welsh people of the religious revivals of the period, which precipitated a pietistic religiosity that lasted into the post-World War I period. For many, the worldliness of modern life made impossible the quiet spirituality of earlier times, and they saw their escape in distant, unpopulated areas of the world then opening up. Some had already tried Canada and the United States and were frustrated by the tides of other European nationalities which threatened the purity of their communities. They responded when Argentina offered cheap land to immigrants who would settle and develop its vast spaces before an aggressive Chile pre-empted them. From the United States and from Wales they came in small ships on hazardous voyages to Puerto Madryn, and settled in the Chubut Valley.

Although the hardships of those gritty pioneers are more than a century behind their descendants, the pioneer tradition is proudly remembered. Some remain in agriculture, many are in trade and commerce. Although it is mainly the older generation that still speaks Welsh, descendants will proudly show you their chapels and cemeteries (very much as in Wales), take you for Welsh tea in one of the area's many tea houses, and reminisce about their forebears and the difficulties they overcame. They speak of the devastating floods of the Chubut which almost demolished the community at the turn of the century, the scouts who went on Indian trails to the Andean foothills to settle in the Cwm Hyfrwd (the Gorgeous Valley), the loneliness of the prairies in the long cold winters, and the incessant winds, and the lack of capital which made all undertakings a matter of backbreaking labor.

Unfortunately, change comes rapidly; old ways mutate and are overtaken by technology. The Welsh language is losing its hold and will not long be spoken in Patagonia. But traditions remain, and the Patagonian Welsh still hold Eisteddfods to compete in song and verse, they revere the tradition of the chapel even when they do not attend, and they take enormous pride in their links with Wales. ■

Welsh farmer proud of his crop.

Leleque Ranch, along the narrow gauge railway, until it reaches Esquel. The other route to Esquel takes one right into **Los Alerces National Park**. This park covers 2,630 sq. km (1,012 sq. miles) and has a landscape similar to the others of the region, though it is less spoiled by towns and people. The tourists who visit the park during the summer stay at camping sites and fishermen's lodges around **Lake Futalaufquen**, such as the **Quimei Quipan Inn** and the **Futalaufquen Hotel**. One tour you should not miss is the all-day boat excursion to Lake Menéndez, with the outstanding view of **Cerro Torrecillas** (2,200 meters/7,260 feet) and its glaciers. Be sure to see the huge *Fitzroya* trees (related to the American redwood), which are over 2,000 years old.

As you get closer to Trevelin and Esquel you begin to leave behind the Northern Lake District. This area is strongly influenced by Welsh culture, as a sizeable community of Welsh people settled here in 1888 after a long trek from the Atlantic Coast along the Chubut Valley.

Trevelin, 40 km (25 miles) east of the national park, is a small village of Welsh origin. The name in Welsh means "town of the mill." The old mill has recently been converted into a museum which houses all sorts of implements that belonged to the first Welsh settlers, together with old photographs and a Welsh Bible. As in all the Welsh communities of Patagonia, you can enjoy a typical tea with Welsh cookies and cakes here. There is also a barbecue restaurant, El Quincho, which serves excellent food.

Narrow gauge adventure: Esquel, 23 km (14 miles) northeast of Trevelin, is also an offshoot of the Welsh Chubut colony. The town, with 25,000 inhabitants, lies to the east of the Andes, on the border of the Patagonian desert. The railway station is the most southerly point of the Argentine railway network. The narrow gauge railway (0.75 meters/ 2.48 feet), connects Esquel with **Ingeniero Jacobacci** to the north. There is no better way to get acquainted with Patagonia and its people than by a trip on this quaint little train which is pulled by an old-fashioned steam locomotive.

In its remote location, on the edge of the desert, Esquel has the feel of a town in the old American West. One is as likely to see people riding on horseback here as in cars. Sometimes the rider will be a gaucho dandy, all dressed up with broad-brimmed hat, kerchief, and *bombachas* (baggy pleated pants). Several times a year, a rural fair is held in Esquel. People come from miles around to trade livestock and supplies. January is your best bet for catching this colorful spectacle.

In town, several stores are well-stocked with riding tackle and ranch equipment. Ornate stirrups and hand-tooled saddles sit next to braided rawhide ropes and cast iron cookware. At **El Vasco** you can outfit yourself with a typical gaucho wardrobe. This was once goose-hunting country, but they have since become a protected species.

In winter, Esquel turns into a ski resort, with **La Hoya Ski Center** only 17 km (11 miles) away. Compared with Bariloche and Catedral, this ski area is

considerably smaller and cozier. All rental facilities are available. For accommodations, try the **Tehuelche Hotel** or **Los Troncos Inn**. The **Tour d'Argent** is one of the best restaurants in this part of Patagonia.

The beautiful valley: Between the Atlantic Coast and Esquel lies the **Chubut Valley**. Only the lower valley, covering an area of 50 sq. km (19 sq. miles) is irrigated, while the rest is parched.

The Welsh used this valley, which they called **Cwm hyfrwd** (Beautiful Valley), to reach the Esquel/Trevelin area. In her book *Dringo'r Andes* (*Climbing the Andes*), Eluned Morgan describes this route in a very romantic way.

Halfway down the valley, the river cuts through the plateau, forming an impressive canyon with red and white ravines named the **Altars** and **Martyrs valleys**. The latter refers to an ambush set by the Indians in 1883, where a group of young Welshmen was wiped out. The lone survivor, John Evans, managed to escape, thanks to his horse, Malacara, which leapt over the steep ravine. The graves of these unfortunate people, who are vividly described in Morgan's book, can still be seen alongside the road.

Before coming to the lower valley, you will reach the **F. Ameghino Dam** and its artificial lake. They are nestled in a narrow rocky gorge and form an impressive sight.

The lower Chubut Valley was the site of the first settlement established by the Welsh. The towns of Dolavon, Gaiman, Trelew and Rawson developed here, and today they are surrounded by intensively cultivated lands.

Gaiman has an interesting museum similar to the one in Trevelin. The *Eisteddfod*, the Welsh Arts Festival, which features singing and reciting, is held here every August. The river meets the sea close to **Rawson**, the provincial capital city. Coming back from an excursion to Punta Tombo, in the afternoon, drive by the small fishermen's port at Rawson to watch the men as they unload their day's catch, and lazy sea lions grab whatever falls overboard.

Oil pumps the Patagonia South.

274

Trelew is the most important city in the lower valley. Its Welsh ambience has faded, giving way to a modern industrial city. The airport of Trelew is the gateway by which to enter the wildlife-rich Valdés Peninsula area.

Penguin highways: **Puerto Madryn**, on the Atlantic Coast, 65 km (40 miles) north of Trelew, was founded by Parry Madryn in 1865 and is now a center for those visiting the Valdés Peninsula and Punta Tombo. In Madryn, one can stay at the **Tolosa Hotel** or the **Peninsula Valdés Hotel**, which has a wonderful view over the Atlantic. Good seafood can be found at **La Caleta**, and the **Club Náutico**. For information on excursions, car rentals and guides, ask at **Receptivo Puerto Madryn**, right beside the Peninsula Valdés Hotel.

There are two main areas to visit from Puerto Madryn: Punta Tombo and the Valdés Peninsula. **Punta Tombo**, 165 km (102 miles) south of Madryn (108 km/67 miles of which is dirt road), is the largest rookery of Magellanic penguins in the world. The penguins arrive in September and stay until March. In this rookery you can literally walk among thousands of these comic birds as they come and go along well-defined "penguin highways" that link their nests with the sea across the tourist path; and see them fish near the coast for their meals. On your way back to Madryn, don't forget to stop by Rawson's port and the Gaiman Museum.

More wildlife: The **Valdés Peninsula** is one of the most important wildlife reserves in Argentina. It is the breeding ground for southern right whales, elephant seals and sea lions. Guanacos, rheas and maras can be seen loping along the road. The peninsula itself – there's an interpretive center at the entrance – is a large wasteland, with the lowest point on the South American continent, 40 meters (132 feet) below sea level. Years ago, the salt pits of the peninsula produced great quantities of salt which were shipped out from Puerto Madryn.

The **Estancia La Adela** belongs to one family, is spread out over 100,000

hectares (247,000 acres) and has 60,000 sheep. The shearing sheds are close to the elephant seal colony in Caleta Valdés. Some 40,000 elephant seals are found along a 200-km (125-mile) stretch of coastline, the outer edge of the Valdés Peninsula – the only such colony accessible by land outside Antarctica. Most of the beach is protected but tourists have a chance to observe the wildlife at **Punta Norte** and **Caleta Valdés**, where two reserves have been established. About 10,000 elephant seal pups are born each year from late August to early November.

Puerto Pirámides, 95 km (59 miles) from Puerto Madryn, has camping sites, hotels and restaurants. Scuba diving is a popular sport in this area, along with water skiing and surfing. The real attraction is the growing population of southern right whales. In the 19th century there were more than 700 whalers in these waters. An international protection treaty was signed in 1935, but since then the recovery of the mammals has been very slow. The present population

is now 2,000, attracting some 50,000 whale-watchers a year.

The whales come to breed near these shores in early winter and stay until mid-December. October is a good month to observe them because the weather is milder than in winter, but it is also the time of year when most people come. Whalewatching is concentrated on mother and calf pairs and is organized by a few, authorized, experienced boat drivers from Puerto Pirámides. At the same time, you can observe the sea lions and cormorant colonies at the foot of the pyramid-shaped cliff that gives this location its name.

On the small side road out of the peninsula stands a monument dedicated to the first Spanish settlement here, which only lasted from 1774 to 1810, when the settlers were forced to flee from the native warriors. In front of this monument there is a sea bird reserve, the **Isla de los Pájaros**.

Oil country: Four hundred and forty kilometers (270 miles) south of Trelew is Patagonia's major city, **Comodoro Rivadavia**, with a population exceeding 100,000. The local airport has daily flights connecting the Patagonian cities.

In 1907, while a desperate search for drinking water was under way, oil was discovered here. Since then, this has become one of the most important oil-producing regions in the country. Today, Comodoro Rivadavia is a typical Patagonian city, with flat roofs, tall buildings, fisheries, textile factories and the ever present Patagonian wind.

The town witnessed the immigration of Boers from the Transvaal and the Orange State in South Africa, who left their homeland in search of a new place to live after the Boer War. The first ones arrived in 1903, under the leadership of Conrad Visser and Martin Venter. Although some returned to South Africa, there are still many of their descendants living in the region.

Colonia Sarmiento, a fertile valley, lies 190 km (118 miles) west of Comodoro Rivadavia. Heading south from the valley for 30 km (19 miles), one reaches the **José Ormachea Petrified Forest** which has remains more than a million

Left, an itinerant sheep shearer plying his trade. Rig up close a the Perito Moreno Glacier.

years old. This forest, like several others in Patagonia, tells us much of the geological past of this land, which a long time ago was covered in trees.

Santa Cruz: The **Provincia de Santa Cruz** is the second largest in Argentina but with the smallest population per square kilometer. Like the rest of Patagonia, it is divided, for the tourist, into the east, or coastal region, and west, the plains at the edge of the mountains. Most of Santa Cruz is a dry grassland or semi-desert, with high *mesetas* interspersed with protected valleys and covered with large sheep *estancias*.

In the mid 1990s, 32 *estancias* in Santa Cruz were opened for tourists. They have a wide range of facilities: some offer a room or two in the family home, where everything from the dining room to bathrooms are shared. Others have built separate *cabañas* or cabins and a few have reformed the *estancia*'s "big house" into elegant rooms for guests. Nearly all offer rooms with meals, demonstrations, or a share in the farm work, riding, hiking, fishing, excursions, etc. Most are open October to April, and are only accessible by car. The provincial tourist office in Río Gallegos has published a booklet on these farms.

The Coast: Route 3, nearly all paved, follows the coast of Golfo San Jorge to the oil town of **Caleta Olivia**, with its huge central statue of an oil worker, then climbs inland. After 86 km (53 miles), Ruta 281 leads off for 126 km (78 miles) to the town of **Puerto Deseado**, named after Cavendish's flagship, the *Desire*. Virtually unknown for many years, Puerto Deseado is beginning to develop as a tourist center. It is the home base for a number of ships which fish in the western South Atlantic. There are sea lion colonies, an island covered with birds, where you might see penguins and the unusual Guanay cormorant, and where spectacular black and white Commerson's dolphins play with boats in the estuary just outside the town.

Back on Route 3, the next important stop is a pristine natural wonder, the **Monumento Natural Bosques Petrificados**, just 80 km (50 miles) to the west of the highway. This enormous petrified

forest occupies over 10,000 hectares (247,000 acres). At the edges of canyons and *mesas*, the stone-hard trunks of 150 million-year-old *Araucaria* trees stick out of the ground. Some trunks are 30 m (100 feet) long and a meter (a yard) thick, among the largest in the world. A visit to this natural monument is for a day only; it closes at sundown.

Farther south is the picturesque little port of **Puerto San Julián**, also awakening to tourism, with several hotels and a small museum. Both Magellan (in 1520) and Drake (1578) overwintered here and hanged mutineers on the eastern shore. Nothing remains there except a small plaque.

Not far to the south is the progressive little town of **Piedra Buena**, on the Río Santa Cruz, which was followed upstream by Fitzroy, Moreno and other early explorers. Its main attraction is the tiny shack on Isla Pavón, once occupied by Luis Piedra Buena, an Argentine naval hero. Downstream (29 km/18 miles) is the sleepy town of **Puerto Santa Cruz**, with its port, Punta Quilla,

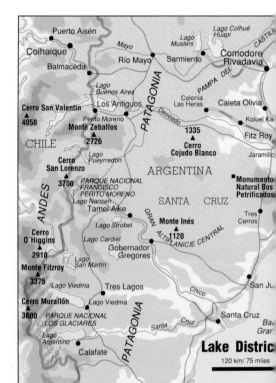

the home base for the ships that service the offshore oil rigs.

The capital of the province is **Río Gallegos**, a sprawling city of 65,000 on the south bank of the Río Gallegos, which has the third-highest tides in the world, at 16 meters (53 ft). At low tide, ships are high and dry on mud flats.

Río Gallegos might seem at first glance one of the least attractive places in the world, but her people are very friendly. There are two museums and signs designate historical spots. The enormous Swift meat packing plant is abandoned, but the train yards, with several old engines, still receive coal from Río Turbio, on the opposite side of the province.

Río Gallegos is a stepping-off point for planes to Tierra del Fuego, and to the lovely scenic areas of Calafate, Punta Arenas and Parque Nacional Torres del Paine in Chile. There are hotels, restaurants, tourist agencies, car rentals, and several bus and airline companies.

Moving southwest of Río Gallegos, Route 3 enters Chile near a series of rims of long-extinct volcanoes. One of these, Laguna Azul, is a geological reserve 3 km (1½ miles) off the main highway near the border post.

Eleven kilometers (6 miles) southwest of Río Gallegos, Route 1 runs southward over open plains to Estancia Cóndor, one of the larger farms, and El Monte Dinero, which has a separate guest house for visitors. From there you can visit **Cabo Vírgenes** (129 km/80 miles from Río Gallegos) and Punta Dungeness (on the border with Chile) at the northeast mouth of the Strait of Magellan. Here you can see Argentina's second largest penguin colony, some 300,000 birds, visit the lighthouse and perhaps watch dolphins just offshore. Near the cliffs are the meagre remains of Ciudad Nombre de Jesús, founded by Sarmiento de Gamboa in 1584.

Sheep: The first governor of Santa Cruz, Carlos Moyano, could find no one to settle in this far, desolate land. In desperation, he invited young couples from the Malvinas to try their hand "on the coast," and the first sheep farmers were English and Scottish shepherds,

soon to be followed by people from many other nations, mainly in central Europe, who remained behind after the 1890s gold rush.

The sheep are shorn once a year, in spring. Farm work intensifies from October to April, with lamb marking, shearing, dipping, and moving the animals to the summer camps. In the fall they are moved back to the winter camps and the wool around the eyes is shorn.

Shearing is usually done by a *comparsa*, a group of professionals who travel from farm to farm, moving south with the season. However, each farm has its own shepherds and *peones* (unskilled workmen) who stay year round, tending fences and animals.

The sheep in southern Patagonia are mainly corriedale, although some merinos have been brought from Australia. Two new breeds which are hardy for this region have been developed on estancias Cóndor and Monte Dinero. The recent low wool prices and the ash from the explosion of the Hudson volcano in 1990 forced many *estancias* to fold. People just locked the gates and went away. The heavy snows of the winter of 1995 caused further devastation.

The West: Western Santa Cruz is spectacular but desolate. Starting again from the top, the northwestern-most town is **Perito Moreno**, a dusty place with little to offer. From here, a paved road leads 57 km (35 miles) west to the small neat town of **Los Antiguos**, on the shore of Lago Buenos Aires (called Lago General Carreras in Chile). There are small farms which produce milk, honey, strawberries and vegetables. Tourist facilities include a hotel, bungalows and a camping site. Three km (1.5 miles) to the west, you can cross the Chilean border to the town of Chile Chico and other scenic areas near the Río Baker.

The only way south is on the **Route 40**, a name that fires the imagination – like Patagonia or Cape Horn – of those who are familiar with this part of the world. It is not a road to be taken lightly. Everyone who has done it is full of admiration for the rugged beauty of the country and are proud they have survived it. Route 40 is not even accurately detailed on most maps, including those of the prestigious Instituto Geográfico Militar. The best one is the ACA (Automóvil Club Argentino) map of the Province of Santa Cruz.

Southern Route 40 is a gravel road – rocky and dusty when dry, muddy when wet. Places marked on the map may have one shack or may not exist at all. You must carry extra fuel and/or go out of your way at several places to get more. No fuel is available on the highway itself. Sometimes small towns, or even larger ones, such as Calafate, run out of gasoline and you may have to wait several days until a fuel truck comes. In southwestern Patagonia there are gas stations only at Perito Moreno, Bajo Caracoles, Tres Lagos, El Calafate and Río Turbio.

If you take any secondary roads, remember that there is no fuel available. You also need to carry spare tires, some food and probably your bed. There are few places to buy food or even a Coca Cola outside the larger towns.

South of Perito Moreno, a must is a visit to **Cueva de las Manos**, a national historical monument located in a beautiful canyon 56 km (35 miles) off Route 40 from just north of Bajo Caracoles. Indian cave paintings are found all over Santa Cruz, but those at Cueva de las Manos (Cave of the Painted Hands) are the most spectacular. The walls here are covered by thousand-year-old paintings of hands and animals, principally guanacos. This is one of the hidden secrets of Patagonia that only the most adventurous manage to enjoy.

Numerous lakes straddle the border between Argentina and Chile. Route 40 lies in the semi-desert well to the east of the mountains. Any excursions to the lakes to the west, such as Lago Ghio, Pueyrredón, Belgrano, San Martín and others, must be made on side roads; there are no circuits, you must come back out on the same road. The road to Lago Pueyrredón leaves from Bajo Caracoles. Near the lake, Complejo Lagos del Furioso accomodates 38 visitors.

The next major stop is **Parque Nacional Perito Moreno** (not to be confused with the town of the same name),

72 kms (45 miles) to the west of Route 40. In the distance is Monte San Lorenzo (or Cochrane), at 3,706m (12,150 feet) the highest peak in Santa Cruz. Within the park you can visit lakes Belgrano and Burmeister. Near the latter is a strange rock formation, the Casa de Piedra, with more cave paintings.

At Tres Lagos, Route 31 leads northwest to **Lago San Martín** (called O'Higgins in Chile). Estancia La Maipú is situated on the south shore. Also at Tres Lagos, Route 40 turns to the west, to the end of **Lago Viedma**, with its glacier coming down off the Campo de Hielo Patagónico Austral. A good dirt road leads 89 km (55 miles) northwest toward **Monte Fitz Roy** (3,405 metres/ 11,166 feet), Cerro Torre and others, among the world's most spectacular peaks. In good weather Fitz Roy can be seen from far away. These peaks attract climbers from all over the world, who describe their experiences in the park register at the northern entrance to Parque Nacional Los Glaciares.

A tiny village, **El Chaltén** (meaning blue mountain, the Indian name for Fitz Roy) nestles in a hidden bowl at the foot of the mountain. This is an enchanted place well worth a visit. The only lodgings are two small inns, some bungalows and basic camp sites, some of which have been so overused as to warrant closing. There are two or three very small stores, no fuel and no telephones. Rustic Estancia La Quinta is nearby. El Chaltén shuts down from April to October. In summer there are two daily buses from El Calafate, 219 km (136 miles) to the south.

Calafate is the main town of the southern lake district, 313 km (194 miles) from Río Gallegos. Halfway there is La Esperanza, a truck stop; nearby is Estancia Chali-Aike which takes paying guests. Most of the drive is past *estancias* over the *meseta central*, coming to a high lookout at Cuesta de Miguez, where the whole of Lago Argentino, the mountains and glaciers beyond and even Mount Fitz Roy can be seen.

El Calafate, a town of about 3,200, nestles at the base of cliffs on the south

shore of beautiful **Lago Argentino**. This is the jumping off point for the surrounding area. Accomodations range from camp sites and a youth hostel to elegant hotels. There are several tourist agencies and a number of good restaurants. Large tour groups do the circuit – Buenos Aires, Puerto Madryn, Calafate, Ushuaia, Buenos Aires – every week.

Parque Nacional Los Glaciares is one of the most spectacular in Argentina. The southern Patagonian ice cap, some 400 km (248 miles) long, spills over into innumerable glaciers, which end on high cliffs or wend their way down to fjords. A number of excursions leave from Calafate. The park entrance is 51 km (32 miles) west of town on the south shore of Península Magallanes. Just beyond, near elegant Hostería Los Notros, you can cross Brazo Rico in a boat for a guided climb on **Glaciar Perito Moreno**, the most famous in the region. A few kilometers farther on, the road ends at the *Pasarelas*, a series of walkways and verandas down a steep cliff which faces the glacier head on, one of the most magnificent sights imaginable, especially on a sunny day.

All of the glaciers are gradually retreating, but Moreno occasionally advances across the narrow stretch of lake at its front, cutting it off. The water then rises in Brazos Rico and Sur until the pressure builds and there's a tremendous collapse of part of the glacial wall. Old water levels can be seen around these lakes. Hiking too near the glacial front is prohibited because of the danger from waves caused by falling ice.

The second major trip from Calafate is a visit to the **Upsala Glacier**, at the far northwest end of Lago Argentino. Boats leave every morning from Punta Bandera, 40 km (25 miles) west of Calafate. In early spring, they cannot get near Upsala because of the large field of icebergs, so they may also visit Spegazzini and other glaciers. Some trips stop for a short walk through the forest to Onelli glacier. On the way back, stop at Estancia Alice, on the road to Calafate. *Asados* (barbecues) and tea are available, and shearing demonstrations are held in season. You may also see black-necked swans and other birds.

Estancias open to the public near Calafate include **La Cristina** which belonged to the pioneering Masters family, situated at the end of a fjord near Upsala Glacier; **Estancia Río Bote** has campgrounds along the Río Santa Cruz. The most elegant of all is **Alta Vista**, five-star and exclusive, overlooking Lago Argentino. Nearby is **Estancia Anita**, not open to the public, but picturesque with its poplar-lined drive and huge shearing shed; many striking workmen died here in the 1920s.

It is only a short distance across the Sierra Los Baguales from Parque Nacional Los Glaciares, Argentina, to Parque Nacional Torres del Paine, in Chile. From some spots near Calafate, the Paine mountains can be seen. But there is no road through. Instead, you must backtrack as far as Esperanza, in the middle of Santa Cruz (at least that section is paved) and then take Route 40 again west and south to enter Chile either at Cancha Carrera or farther south at Río Turbio. You can also fly back to Río Gallegos and fly on to Punta Arenas, where it is still a seven-hour drive north to the Paine National Park.

Río Turbio is a coal-mining town of about 7,800, with a rail line that runs to the port of Río Gallegos. A neighboring village, **28 de Noviembre**, has a population of 3,300.

Route 40 then makes a winding loop across the bottom of the province and goes back north to meet Route 3 just west of Río Gallegos. It is considered the longest road in Argentina.

In the Provincia de Santa Cruz, the major airlines stop only at Río Gallegos. Smaller airlines, LADE, Kaikén, El Pinguino and LAPA fly to the various towns, especially Calafate. Some towns have an Aeroclub which will take visitors up for local photographic flights. Several bus companies operate on Route 3 from Buenos Aires to Río Gallegos and from Gallegos there are daily buses to Calafate and Punta Arenas. There are no bus lines to Tierra del Fuego; most people move across the Strait of Magellan by plane or by private car via the ferry at the First Narrows, within Chilean territory.

Right, a climber contemplate Mt Fitz Roy.

memories of stories of Drake, Cook, and Darwin, or the arduous, careful surveys of Fitzroy and King. One book, *Uttermost Part of the Earth* by E. Lucas Bridges, towers above the others as one of the world's great adventure stories. Bridges, the third white child born in Tierra del Fuego, tells how his father, Thomas Bridges, began the Anglican Mission in Ushuaia (1869), explored unknown areas, worked with and taught the Yahgans and finally settled the first farm, now over 100 years old. The missionaries were followed by a coast guards station, gold miners, sheep farmers, small merchants, oil workers and all those needed to make up a modern town, the most recent being electronics factory workers. In one short century Tierra del Fuego has gone from near-naked natives to tourists arriving on planes or passenger liners.

Across the strait: Politically, Tierra del Fuego is split between Chile (to the west and south) and Argentina (north and east). The Argentine section is part of the new Provincia de Tierra del Fuego,

Antártida e Islas del Atlántico Sur, with its capital in the town of Ushuaia. The rough triangle that is Argentina's part of the Isla Grande covers some 21,340 square kms (8,300 sq. miles, about the size of the state of Connecticut, USA), with 240 km (150 miles) of land border with Chile to the west.

There are three towns: Ushuaia (founded 1869) on the Beagle Channel, Río Grande (founded 1893) on the northern plains, and Tolhuin (founded 1972) on the eastern edge of Lago Fagnano in the center of the Territory. One main road, Route 3, joins Estancia Cullen near the northern tip at Cabo Espíritu Santo at the eastern mouth of the Strait of Magellan, to Ushuaia, and ends, as the last stretch of the Panamerican Highway, at Lapataia, on the southwestern border with Chile.

Visitors arrive by several means. Aerolíneas Argentinas, Austral and smaller airlines provide daily flights from Buenos Aires and other areas. Tourist ships visit Ushuaia briefly as part of longer cruises between Río de Janeiro, Buenos

sheep
ation near
o Grande.

Aires and the west coast of South America. Ushuaia, like Punta Arenas in Chile, is a jumping off point for a number of ships to Antarctica.

Visitors coming by land must cross the Strait of Magellan by ferry, either at the First Narrows (a 20–30 minute barge crossing) or between Punta Arenas and Porvenir (a two- to three-hour crossing). There are no regular bus lines between Río Gallegos and Río Grande (charter services may be available), but there are two lines between Río Grande and Ushuaia. Make airline and hotel reservations well in advance. Campsites are available at several localities.

Gold, fossils and sheep: Many visitors find the northern plains of Tierra del Fuego rather barren, but there is much to do and see. Those arriving by road must enter from Chile at **Bahía San Sebastián**, where there is border control, a small *hostería* (reservations with the Argentine Automobile Club, ACA), restaurant and fuel. Enormous mud flats, periodically covered by 11-meter (36-foot) tides, extend along the west of the

bay. This is an important feeding area for thousands of small birds which escape the northern-hemisphere winter here; the entire coast is part of the Hemispheric Shorebird Reserve network.

This is sheep farming and oil country, where wells dot the grasslands and rolling hills. The eastern Strait of Magellan, in Chile, is dotted with oil platforms. Oil roads wander in all directions, while sheep, cattle, guanacos and wild geese graze among them.

In winter, guanacos can be seen along any of the secondary roads. The best way to see them in summer is to drive north along the bay from the San Sebastián border post. A 45-minute drive will take you to the base of the stony, super-barren **Península Páramo**, but family groups of guanacos will be seen on the salt flats long before that. The base of the Páramo was once the main site of the gold rush (1887–98). Julius Popper set up his mining operation here and became the dictator of the northern plains. Today, nothing remains of his buildings, dredges or cemetery.

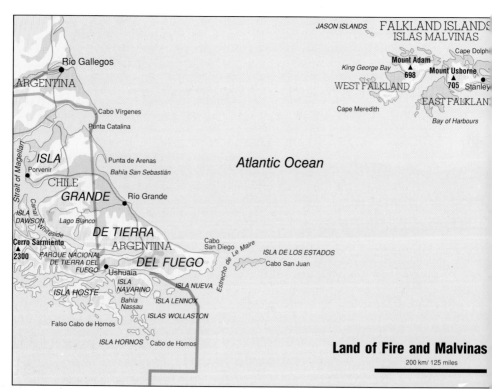

Land of Fire and Malvinas

200 km/ 125 miles

Cliffs along the coast near Cabo Espíritu Santo and the roads near San Sebastián yield both marine and forest fossils, attesting to bygone eras. Sandstone hills farther south are littered with fossil shells and crabs.

The plains may look yellow or brown and appear to have little life, but this is Tierra del Fuego's best sheep land. If you stop to look and listen, you will discover many birds; a short walk may reveal hidden wildflowers. The wind is constant – don't open two opposite doors of a car at the same time, especially if you have papers on the seat.

Going southeast toward Río Grande, **Estancia Sara**, Tierra del Fuego's second largest sheep station, looks like a small town. In the old days, the *estancias* were essentially towns; each had its workshops, gardens, bakery, club and library for the workmen. Before the days of oil, sheep farming was the main industry of northern Fuegia. Thousands of sheep, mainly Corriedale, covered the plains. The *cabañas* of the larger farms produced (and still do) world-class, prize-winning pedigree sheep. *Estancias* such as Sara once had 75 employees; low wool prices, higher wages and difficulty in finding good workmen has reduced that to 15.

Route 3 follows the coastline southeastward. On a sunny day, the cold southwestern South Atlantic beaches may appear almost tropical. In the distance looms **Cabo Domingo**, a picnic and fossil hunting site.

Just south of it is the **Escuela Agrotécnica Salesiana** which functions on the site of the Salesian Mission to the Ona Indians, established in 1897. It is now a national monument. The original church and several other buildings have been restored; there is a small museum of artifacts and mounted birds.

Río Grande: The town of **Río Grande** (population about 45,000) is the center of the sheep and oil region, as well as home of a number of companies producing television sets, radios, synthetics and other products, part of a special 1972 law designed to bring development and more residents to this far reach

e ravages
a beaver
m.

of the republic. This produced a boom-town atmosphere in the 1980s.

Río Grande sprawls over the flat northern coast of the river. The wide, wind-blown streets overlook the waters of the South Atlantic. The Río Grande river has silted up, allowing for little shipping. A wide bridge crosses it to the **Freezer**, a modern meat-packing plant on its southeast coast. Lambs from this freezer were once considered choice in Europe, but various difficulties have kept recent production low.

Río Grande has a number of hotels and *hosterías* (about 750 beds). There are many restaurants, coffee shops and *rotiserías* which offer carry-out food. There is a new cultural center, a number of video clubs, but no movie theatre. The new municipal **Museo de Ciencias Naturales e Historia**, on Calle Elcano near the sea, is well worth a visit.

This is Tierra del Fuego's trout-fishing center. Trout (rainbow, brook, and brown) and land-locked Atlantic salmon which have gone back to the sea, were introduced in the 1930s, and reach record sizes. Until recently fishing was open in all areas, permission being needed only to cross *estancia* land. Now access to this land can be gained only with guides and there is a charge. Fishing is still free if you walk along the river bank from a main road. The Club de Pesca John Goodall, Dal Tours and several other individuals organize fishing excursions. The Río Grande is ideal for sea-run brown trout. Best fishing times are January to March.

Route 3 runs out the opposite side of Río Grande from the bridge, circling southwest to cross another bridge and head toward Ushuaia. Near the airport, just west of town, Route C leads westward to **Estancia María Behety**, a picturesque village with an enormous shearing shed (room for 40 shearers), which is reported to be the world's largest. This local road then wanders northwest and west near the Chilean border. Some sections of this road are paved with fossils; the black sections can become a quagmire.

Back on Route 3, **Estancia José Menéndez** can be seen in the distance on the south side of the Río Grande. It is a picturesque, old-style *estancia* set in grassy, rolling hills, and was the first farm in northern Tierra del Fuego. The original farm, like others that were once extremely large, has been divided up into five smaller *estancias*. It should be noted that the Spanish word *estancia* is translated into English as farm, not ranch (*rancho* = decrepit shack).

Forest and mountain: Near Estancia José Menéndez, Routes B, D, E and F branch off, each winding west or southwest into the mountains, each offering varied scenery of steep hills, plains, forest, *vegas* (damp meadows) and *estancias*. All are fascinating to explore, if you have time and a vehicle.

The gravel **Route B** leads westward, roughly parallel to the Río Grande, passing the farms Cauchicol, Despedida, Aurelia, San José and San Justo, near the Chilean border. The *vega* lands are full of sheep and cattle, the rivers with trout. Kau-tapen ("fishing-house" in Ona) on Estancia La Retranca and San José are exclusive fishing lodges.

Routes D and **E** parallel each other goung southwest from Route B and José Menéndez toward the mountains. Although very picturesque, there are no particular tourist facilities.

Route F winds almost south into the heart of Tierra del Fuego, up and down the steep glacial moraines to reach Lagos Yéhuin and Chepelmesh. There it joins **Route H**, which runs eastward from the Yéhuin over the hills to meet Route 3 near Estancia Indiana. There are several sawmills in the area and among the hills to the south. **Lago Yéhuin**, favored for camping, and the Río Claro to the west are good fishing areas being developed for tourism. A former sawmill has been converted into the **Parador Yawen** with rooms and restaurant. There is also a small hostel by Lago Yéhuin and two companies have camping facilities for fishing tours.

South of Río Grande: Driving to Ushuaia along Route 3 is an education in ecology, for one goes from the flat sea coast through hilly, grassy plains and *vegas*, from low bush land on to scrubby deciduous forest (*ñire* or "low beech");

then turning inland, the road climbs to healthier deciduous forest (*lenga* or "high beech"); up the mountain slopes nearly to the treeline, and then down on the south side of the mountains to thick forest interspersed with evergreen beech (*coihue* or *guindo*) and valleys filled with sphagnum swamps. Route 3 is paved from San Sebastián to near Tolhuin. All other roads are gravel.

Shortly after entering the northern forests, **Route A** runs eastward over high hills and grassy valleys to Cabo San Pablo, another favorite picnic spot. This road continues for some distance beyond San Pablo, but it is not always in good condition. The eastern point of Tierra del Fuego is a mostly unused wilderness of forest, swamp and mountain and can be reached only on foot, horseback or helicopter.

Meandering southward, Route 3 follows the valley of the Río Ewan, gradually rising to a divide which separates the waters running into the South Atlantic from those of the Lago Fagnano or Kami, which flow westward into Chile

to empty via the Río Azopardo into Seno Almirantazgo (Admiralty Sound).

The small town of **Tólhuin** (population 460) lies just north of the 100-km (62-mile) long Lago Fagnano. The word Tólhuin is the Ona name for a nearby heart-shaped hill, and the village is in the heart of the island. Panadería La Unión is reputed to have the best bread in Tierra del Fuego. On the beach of the lake beyond Tólhuin (take the back road out of town) there are fishing facilities, a place for barbecues and the remains of an old police station.

The **Hostería Kaikén** (Upland Goose Hostel) at the southeastern head of the lake is a stopping place for fuel, lunch or tea, and a magnificent view toward mountains in Chile. Colors of the lake change greatly with the weather.

To the southeast of the *hostería* rises Heuhupen, a lone mountain reported to have a resident witch. The area is now full of logging roads for the plywood factory just north of Tólhuin and partly covered by beaver dams.

Route 3 then follows the south shore

glacial
lley along
e Beagle
nannel.

of Lago Fagnano. The south coast of the lake has several small bays, formed when the land dropped during a 1949 earthquake. The highway turns inland past burnt-over forest and sawmills to wind up the mountains at **Paso Garibaldi.** Although sawmills here were once prosperous, pine imported from Chile is cheaper and generally used for construction. In the valley just north of the pass lies Laguna Escondida, with the Hostería Petrel just 4 km (2½ miles) off Route 3, almost hidden at its southern edge. This is a tranquil place to stay.

Be sure to stop at the lookout on Paso Garibaldi to look north over Laguna Escondida and Lago Fagnano. Climbers will find this a fascinating area.

The Beagle Channel: South of the pass, the road curves downward to Rancho Hambre (Hunger Shack) and the Tierra Mayor Valley. Route 3 winds westward through this valley and then southward through that of the Río Olivia to the Beagle Channel and Ushuaia.

A branch road, **Route J**, turns sharply left at the bottom of the mountain to meander 50 kms (30 miles) through the Lasifashaj River valley to reach the Beagle Channel at Bahía Brown. Puerto Williams, Chile, can be seen across the channel. The beach is lined with Yahgan shell middens, the circular mussel heaps that once surrounded their low shelters.

The road continues over hills above the Beagle Channel to **Estancia Harberton**, the oldest farm in Argentine Tierra del Fuego, founded by the Reverend Thomas Bridges in 1886. Open to the public from October to April, the farm offers a guided walking tour of the establishment, Tierra del Fuego's oldest nature reserve (a small wood) with native trees, Yahgan kitchen middens and a model wigwam. One can have tea in the original farmhouse overlooking the bay. You can also visit Harberton by catamaran from Ushuaia (two ships daily in summer), but traveling this way the stay at the farm is short.

Route J, the Ruta del Atlántico, winds eastward along the channel for 30 km (18 miles) of spectacular views and hair-raising turns to finally reach **Estancia**

Traps and boats used to catch crabs, on the shores of the Beagle Channel.

Moat. The whole of this area, Harberton and Moat, are ideal for birds – steamer ducks, cormorants, oyster catchers, perhaps an eagle or condor.

From Bahía Brown, a rather precarious road runs westward along the coast past several small farms of squatters and a fish hatchery to end at Estancia Remolino, built in the 1890s by the Lawrence family, but now almost abandoned.

Back on Route 3, the **Valle Tierra Mayor** is a winter sports center, with five lodges (Haruwen, Las Cotorras, Tierra Mayor, Valle de los Huskies, Altos del Valle) for cross-country skiing, snowmobiles and dog sleds in winter. They also offer food and hiking activities in summer. Las Cotorras offers typical Fuegian *asados* (roast lamb, beef or chicken) year round. The Tierra Mayor lodge serves fondue and hosts cross-country skiing competitions on the spaghnum swamps of the valley floor. It is admirably placed for views the length of the valley between the Sorondo and Alvear mountain ranges.

West of the Tierra Mayor valley lies the Valle Carbajal, between high mountains with views westward toward Chile. To the north is the Paso Beban, a long disused hiking trail. The road follows the Río Olivia along the west side of the beautiful **Monte Olivia**, where peat is harvested from swamps in the valley for sale in Buenos Aires. At last, the **Beagle Channel** appears in the distance.

At the mouth of the Río Olivia a rustic hiking trail follows the coast eastward to Estancia Túnel and eventually all the way to Harberton and points east. On the west shore of the river is the local government fish hatchery.

Route 3 turns westward on a new paved road above the city of Ushuaia, or you can follow the older gravel road along the coast.

Bright lights: The city of **Ushuaia** (population about 35,000) sits in a picturesque bowl on the southern side of the mountains, overlooking Ushuaia Bay, the Beagle Channel, and Navarin and Hoste Islands (both in Chile) to the south. To the east rise the spectacular, pointed Monte Olivia and the Cinco Hermanos (Five Brothers). Ushuaia is

the home of a large Naval Base, government offices, stores for imported goods; it is a base for one or two farms, sawmills, a crab fishery and a growing offshore fishing industry. It hosts several television and radio assembly plants which are gradually being phased out.

A simple triangular monument near the airfield marks the site of the **Anglican Mission** (1869–1907). Thomas and Mary Bridges (1870) and John and Clara Lawrence (1873) became the archipelago's first non-indigenous permanent residents. The official founding of the town was the establishment of a sub-prefecture (coast guard) in 1884.

Ushuaia's **prison** (1902–47) is now within the Naval Base. The octopus-shaped jail is open to the public and contains a new naval museum. Houses with decorative cornices built by prisoners are still scattered in the older part of town. A train once took inmates to fell trees in the outlying forests along the same route plied by the diminutive steam-powered Ferrocarril Austral Fueguino trains that today treat tourists to a four-hour excursion through Tierra del Fuego National Park.

A walk through the town's steep streets reveals a strange variety of architecture. The early wooden houses covered with corrugated iron (to help prevent fires) with their prisoner-produced gingerbread decorations have a somewhat Russian flavor. They are intermingled with modern concrete structures, imported Swedish prefabs, and hundreds of small, wooden shanties. Land is difficult to obtain in the small area hemmed in by mountain and sea; new houses climb the mountain sides; many people live in poor conditions. Nevertheless, building and improvements are going on everywhere.

Ushuaia is much more geared to the tourist than Río Grande. There are a number of hotels (about 1,500 beds), including two large ones on the mountain behind the town. The **municipal tourist bureau** on Avenida San Martín offers information and folders.

The restaurants of Ushuaia feature sea food, *róbalo* (mullet) and *centolla* (southern king crab) from the Beagle

Channel. The *centolla* has been greatly overfished and rarely reaches the size it once did. Those who prefer *asado* (lamb, mutton or beef roasted over an open fire) can try **Tolkeyen** or **Las Cotorras**, both outside of Ushuaia.

Stores in Ushuaia focus on imported items (sweaters, jackets and china from Europe; cigarettes and whisky; radios) which pay only half the import duty of the rest of the country. There is little that is native to Tierra del Fuego. There are three bookstores which feature books on the Fuegian area; these can also be bought at the museum.

Be sure to visit the **Museo del Fin del Mundo**, which houses Indian relics, ships' figureheads, and an attractive collection of local birds. Active research, especially of the eastern tip of the island, Península Mitre, is carried on from this museum.

The world's southernmost research center, **CADIC** (Centro Austral de Investigaciones Científicas), in modern buildings at the southwest corner of the inner bay, is usually not open to the general public, but visiting scientists are welcomed. Investigators there are studying the marine life, geology, glacialogy, climate, flora, hydrology, social history, anthropology and archeology of Tierra del Fuego.

A winding road climbs behind the town to the slopes of the **Montes Martial**, past two large hotels to a chair lift which goes up to the valley at the foot of the small, hanging Martial Glacier. In winter the lift takes you to ski slopes; in summer the glacial hollow at the top of the lift is an ideal place to hike and see Andean flowers, such as the chocolate-scented *Nassauvia*, or even the rare mountain seed snipe. Part way down the road, a cross-country ski track leads over the rise to Ushuaia's first ski slope, a steep cutting on the forested mountainside to the northwest of town.

National park: A 20-minute drive west of Ushuaia brings you to the **Parque Nacional Tierra del Fuego**. The mountains are steeper and nearer the coast than at Ushuaia and points east. Near the park entrance, a road drops down to the

Early morning over Ushuaia.

300

INSIGHT GUIDES
Travel Tips

FOR THOSE
WITH MORE THAN
A PASSING INTEREST
IN TIME...

Before you put your name down for a Patek Philippe watch *fig. 1*, there are a few basic things you might like to know, without knowing exactly whom to ask. In addressing such issues as accuracy, reliability and value for money, we would like to demonstrate why the watch we will make for you will be quite unlike any other watch currently produced.

"Punctuality", Louis XVIII was fond of saying, "is the politeness of kings."

We believe that in the matter of punctuality, we can rise to the occasion by making you a mechanical timepiece that will keep its rendezvous with the Gregorian calendar at the end of every century, omitting the leap-years in 2100, 2200 and 2300 and recording them in 2000 and 2400 *fig. 2*. Nevertheless, such a watch does need the occasional adjustment. Every 3333 years and 122 days you should remember to set it forward one day to the true time of the celestial clock. We suspect, however, that you are simply content to observe the politeness of kings. Be assured, therefore, that when you order your watch, we will be exploring for you the physical—if not the metaphysical—limits of precision.

Does everything have to depend on how much?

Consider, if you will, the motives of collectors who set record prices at auction to acquire a Patek Philippe. They may be paying for rarity, for looks or for micromechanical ingenuity. But we believe that behind each $500,000-plus

bid is the conviction that a Patek Philippe, even if 50 years old or older, can be expected to work perfectly for future generations.

In case your ambitions to own a Patek Philippe are somewhat discouraged by the scale of the sacrifice involved, may we hasten to point out that the watch we will make for you today will certainly be a technical improvement on the Pateks bought at auction? In keeping with our tradition of inventing new mechanical solutions for greater reliability and better time-keeping, we will bring to your watch innovations *fig. 3* inconceivable to our watchmakers who created the supreme wristwatches of 50 years ago *fig. 4*. At the same time, we will of course do our utmost to avoid placing undue strain on your financial resources.

Can it really be mine?

May we turn your thoughts to the day you take delivery of your watch? Sealed within its case is your watchmaker's tribute to the mysterious process of time. He has decorated each wheel with a chamfer carved into its hub and polished into a shining circle. Delicate ribbing flows over the plates and bridges of gold and rare alloys. Millimetric surfaces are bevelled and burnished to exactitudes measured in microns. Rubies are transformed into jewels that triumph over friction. And after many months—or even years—of work, your watchmaker stamps a small badge into the mainbridge of your watch. The Geneva Seal—the highest possible attestation of fine watchmaking *fig. 5*.

Looks that speak of inner grace *fig. 6*

When you order your watch, you will doubt like its outward appearance to reflect the harmony and elegance of the movement within. You may therefore find it helpful to know that we are uniquely able to cater for any special decorative needs you might like to express. For example, our engravers will delight in conjuring a subtle play of light and shadow on the gold case-back of one of our rare pocket-watches *fig. 7*. If you bring us your favourite picture, our enamellers will reproduce it in a brilliant miniature of hair-breadth detail *fig. 8*. The perfect execution of a double hobnail pattern on the bezel of a wristwatch is the pride of our casemakers and the satisfaction of our designers, while our chainsmiths will weave for you a rich brocade in gold *figs. 9 & 10*. May we also recommend the artistry of our goldsmiths and the experience of our lapidaries in the selection and setting of the finest gemstones? *figs. 11 & 12*.

How to enjoy your watch before you own it.

As you will appreciate, the very nature of our watches imposes a limit on the number we can make available. (The four Calibre 89 time-pieces we are now making will take up to nine years to complete). We cannot therefore promise instant gratification, but while you look forward to the day on which you take delivery of your Patek Philippe *fig. 13*, you will have the pleasure of reflecting that time is a universal and everlasting commodity freely available to be enjoyed by all.

Should you require information on any particular Patek Philippe watch, or even on watchmaking in general, we would be delighted to reply to your letter of enquiry. And if you se

Women's shoes:

American	5
European	36
British	4

Men's shirts:

Canadian	15
European	38

Men's shoes:

American	9½
British	9
European	43

Business Hours

onday through Friday, the business
urs are from 9am to 7pm, and the
nking hours are from 10am to 4pm.
some parts of the country, the
ores open from 9am to 1pm and
m 4pm to 7pm.

Media

veral newspapers are available. The
cal papers are *La Nación*, *Clarín*,
mbito Financiero and *Página 12*. The
glish paper is the *Herald*. There are
wspaper and magazine stands
roughout the city, where these and
me foreign papers, as well as many
ernational magazines, may be found
th delay.
There are five stations, and cable
is also available. Most of the pro-
ams are brought in from the US and
me from Europe.
The radio stations carry a variety of
ograms. The BBC is on from 5pm to
out 12.30am.

Postal Services

e main Post Office is located on
rmiento 189, and operates Monday
Friday from 9am to 7.30pm Other
all post offices are located through-
t the city. The hotel is the best
urce for stamps and any other
eded information.

Telecoms

Telegram & Fax

legrams can be sent from any Post
ffice in town or they can be dictated
the ENCOTEL telephonogram system.
e phones to use are 33-9221/35
r domestic telegrams and 33-9251/
for international telegrams. Fax fa-

cilities are available at most of the
larger hotels. Alternatively, the follow-
ing ENTEL offices have facilities:
San Martín: San Martín 332, Monday
to Friday 8am to 8pm.
Ezeiza Airport: Daily 9am to 10pm.
Once: Located at the train station,
Monday to Friday 9am to 7.30pm
Republica: Corrientes 707, 24-hour
service.
Catedral: Peru 1, Monday to Friday 7am
to 10pm and Saturday 7am to 1pm.

Telephone

Using the telephone in Buenos Aires is
an unforgettable experience. The user
must indeed be armed with courage,
but most of all lots of patience. The
system here is by no means up to par.
It is being extended and improved at
the moment, so lots of telephone numbers are being changed without warning. Most of the tourists will probably
be using the phones in their hotel
rooms. For those who venture out and
want to try a pay phone, please make
sure you follow this advice: some of
the public phones are yellow-greenish
pear-shaped domes located on the
streets, in public buildings, bus termi-
nals, and in some bars and restaurants, and the others are orange boxes
and located in most *confiterias* and
restaurants.
Before using the apparatus, a token
or *ficha* must be bought from any
KIOSCO (cigarette and candy stand visible throughout the city) or from the
cashiers at restaurants or bars. These
cospeles are good, generally, for a two-
minute phone call – but this depends
on the time of day the call is made.
Long-distance calls can be placed
through the international operator from
the hotel room or at any office of
ENTEL. Calls to Europe are very expensive. A minute can cost around US$5.

Tourist Information

Local and national tourist information
can be obtained from the various tourist offices in the city. The following is a
list of the most important ones:
Argentine Chamber of Tourism,
Tucumán 1610, 3rd and 6th floor, Buenos Aires. Tel: 40-5108 ext. 13.
National Direction of Tourism (for information), Santa Fé 883, P.B., Buenos Aires. Tel: 312-2232/5550, fax:
313-6834.

Direction of Tourism for Buenos Aires,
Sarmiento 1551, 4th floor, Buenos
Aires. Tel: 46-1251.
Perhaps easiest to find are the several tourist information centers along
Florida, a pedestrian boulevard. Here
in these booths, the traveler can obtain maps of the city and a bilingual
(Spanish and English) tourist information newspaper called *The Buenos
Aires Herald*. It offers complete listings
of what is happening in the city, as well
as other useful information. *Where*, a
booklet giving a complete list of shopping, dining and entertainment, can be
obtained in most hotels.
The provinces of Argentina have offices in Buenos Aires. Pamphlets
about special events, attractions, lists
of hotels, restaurants, etc., are readily
available. The following is a list of
these offices with their telephone numbers. All are located in the central part
of town.

Provincial Tourist Offices in Buenos Aires

Buenos Aires, Ave. Callao 237. Tel:
40-7045.
Catamarca, Cordoba 2080. Tel: 46-
6891/94.
Chaco, Ave. Callao 322, 1st floor. Tel:
45-0961/3045.
Chubut, Paraguay 876. Tel: 312-
2262/2340/4333.
Córdoba, Ave. Callao 332. Tel: 394-
7432/7418.
Entre Ríos, Pte Perón 451, 4th floor.
Formosa, H. Yrigoyen 1429. Tel: 37-
1479/3699.
Jujuy, Ave. Santa Fe 967. Tel: 396-
1295/3174.
Mendoza, Ave. Callao 445. Tel: 40-
6683, 46-1105.
Misiones, Ave. Santa Fe 989. Tel: 393-
1615/1812/1343/1714.
Neuquén, Pte. Perón 687. Tel: 49-
6385; 46-9265.
La Pampa, Suipacha 346. Tel: 35-
0511/6797.
Río Negro, Tucumán 1920. Tel: 45-
9931/7920/2128.
La Rioja, Ave. Callao 745. Tel: 44-
1662/1339, 41-4524.
Salta, Maipu 663. Tel: 392-5773/6019.
San Juan, Maipú 331. Tel: 456-384.
San Luis, Azcuenaga 1083. Tel: 83-
3641.
Santa Cruz, Ave. Córdoba 1345, 14th
floor. Tel: 42-0381/0916-42-1169/
1116.

Santa Fé, 25 de Mayo 358, P.B. Tel: 312-4620/0394/5160.
Santiago Del Estero, Florida 274. Tel: 46-9398/9417.
Tierra Del Fuego, Sarmiento 747, 5th floor. Tel: 40-1995/1881/1791.
Tucumán, Bme. Mitre 836, 1st floor. Tel: 40-2214.

Getting Around

From the Airport

Eeiza International Airport is 35 km (22 miles) out of downtown Buenos Aires. A taxi into the center costs from US$45 to US$65. It's more reliable, however, to take a remise or organized car service directly to your hotel – buy a ticket from the remise desk in the airport foyer. The cheapest option is to go by the airport bus, cenita Leon (approximately US$14) that runs regularly to the center, then take a short taxi ride to your hotel.

Public Transport

Buses

The buses ('colectivos') are a good way to get around Buenos Aires, a very large city. They are one of the means of mass transportation and are usually prompt and very inexpensive. However, try not to get one during the rush hour, as the queues are very long. Bus stops are located throughout the city. The number and destination is clearly marked. Long distance travel on buses is also available. A very large and modern bus terminal is located in **Retiro**. Information on their destinations can be obtained at the terminal from the different companies.

Trains

The future of the antiquated railway lines from Buenos Aires to Bahía Blanca, Bariloche, Tucumán and Córdoba is uncertain. Even the famous "train in the sky" service from Salta to the Chilean border is possibly going to be closed. Information: Ferrocarriles Argentinos, Maipu 88, Tel: 331 3280.

Underground

The subway system, better known as the **SUBTE**, is the fastest and definitely the cheapest way to get around town. The rides are quick, taking no more than 25 minutes, and the waiting is about three to five minutes. The art work that can be observed at some of the stations is quite unique and has an interesting background. Many of these painted tiles were baked by artisans in Spain and France at the beginning of the century and around the 1930s.

Taxis

These can be easily recognized: black with a yellow roof, and are readily available 24 hours a day. The meter registers a number that will correspond to the amount of the fare appearing on a list. These must be shown to the passenger by law. A bit of advice: be careful when paying and make sure the correct bill is given; quick exchanges of bills have been known to take place, especially with the tourist who doesn't know the language or the currency. A small tip is usually given.

Private Transport

Remises are private automobiles, with a driver, that can be rented by the hour, excursion, day or any other time period. They are more expensive than taxis, and a list of these can be located in the telephone directory or at the information desks of the hotels.

Car Rental

Rental of automobiles may be done at the airport upon arrival. The following are some of the better-known car rental agencies:
Avis, Suipacha 268, 7th floor. Tel: 45-1943.
Belgrano Star, Ciudad de la Paz 2508, Belgrano. Tel: 781-5802.
Fast Rent, Uruguay 328, 1st floor. Tel: 40-0220.
Hertz, Esmeralda 985. Tel: 312-6832.
Liprandi, Esmeralda 1065. Tel: 311-6832.
Nacional Car Rental, Esmeralda 1084. Tel: 312-4318/311-3583.
Rent A Car, M.T. de Alvear 678. Tel: 311-0247.
Serra Lima, Córdoba 3100. Tel: 821-6611/84.

Domestic Air Travel

Traveling by air in Argentina is done by the local airlines – Austral, Aerolíneas Argentinas and Lade. **Jorge Newbery Airport**, also known as **El Aeroparque** is used for national traffic.

Tourists wishing to visit several cities can take up a special package offered by Aerolíneas Argentinas called *Visit Argentina*. This is a booklet of 4, 6 or 8 coupons, each of which allows a segment of travel within Argentina. For example, one segment might be Buenos Aires to Rio Gallegos one way, another might be Buenos Aires to Mendoza; apart from Buenos Aires, a city can only be visited once.

The *Visit Argentina* booklets can only be bought in conjunction with an international air ticket, and is fully refundable if not used. There is no set time limit on using the coupons, although they are only valid for as long as the international ticket on which they are bought.

The price is US$450 for 4 coupons and US$120 for each additional coupon – which works out rather economically, since distances in Argentina are huge and flying is expensive. A return ticket to Ushuaia, for example, costs US$500.

Ferries

Traveling to Uruguay on the Ferry is a pleasant trip, inexpensive and entertaining. The well known companies are: **Ferrytur** located on Florida 780 Tel: 394-2103/5336/5431; **Aliscafo** located on Av. Córdoba 787, Tel: 393-4691/2473/0969/2672; **Tamul** located on Lavalle 388, Tel: 393-2306/1533, 362-8237. Other companies can be contacted through a travel agent.

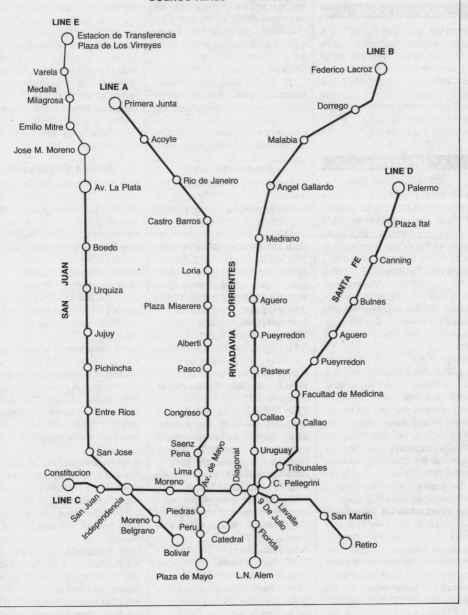

BUENOS AIRES — THE SUBWAY

Where to Stay

Choosing a Hotel

Due to the "economic miracle" hotel prices have risen dramatically, especially in the capital. The going rate for a double room in an inexpensive middle class hotel is around US$150 a night, inclusive of tax. It is better to check out the really inexpensive hotels before you book. Following is a brief list including price ranges.

Buenos Aires

Hotels $200 and Over

Alvear Palace Hotel, Avenida Alvear 1891. Tel: 804-4031, fax: 804-9246. BA' most elegant hotel in the city's most chic neighborhood. French decor, excellent restaurant and tearoom, boutiques, health club, business center.

Ceasar Park, Posadas 1232. Tel: 814-5150, fax: 814-5148. Modern, large luxury hotel in the Recoleta. Lobby piano bar, three restaurants including elegant buffet, health club with pool, business center. Popular with business set.

Claridge Hotel, Tucumán 535. Tel: 314-7700, fax: 314-8022. Very British, old-fashioned, centrally located. Health club with pool, penthouse suites with gardens, pleasant bar.

Crowne Plaza Panamericano, Carlos Pellegrini 525. Tel: 348-5000, fax: 348-5250. Located on 9 de Julio in the shadow of the Obelisco, renovated modern 18-floor tower, health club with pool, popular with conventions/conferences, excellent restaurant.

Hotel Inter-Continental, Moreno 809. Tel: 340-7100, fax: 340-7199. Four blocks from Plaza de Mayo in Monserrat, modern 19-story hotel, restaurant/bar, health club and indoor pool. Popular with business people.

Libertador Kempinsky, Avenida Córdoba 690. Tel: 322-2095, fax: 322-9703. In the heart of the microcenter, bar and pool on the top floor, restaurant, popular with European business set and tourists.

Marriot Plaza Hotel, Florida 1005. Tel: 318-3000, fax: 318-3008. Newly renovated, elegant hotel on Plaza San Martín, favorite with visiting heads of state and royalty. English/French decor, famous restaurant Plaza Grill, health club, outdoor pool.

Park Hyatt, Posadas 1082. Tel: 326-1234; fax: 326-3736. Near the French Embassy and the Recoleta, fairly new, large modern hotel in French style, two restaurants, lounge, health club and outdoor pool, popular with business set and visiting rock stars.

Sheraton Buenos Aires, San Martín 1225. Tel: 318-9000; fax: 318-9353. Located in Retiro, 24-stories highrise towers commanding magnificent view of the river and port area. Rooftop bar, international restaurants, tennis courts and pool, favorite with business set.

Hotels $100–$200

Carsson Hotel. Viamonte 650. Tel/fax: 393-0029. One block from Florida, faded elegance but charming, quiet, English style bar, most affordable of group.

Gran Hotel Colón, Carlos Pellegrini 507. Tel: 325-0717, fax: 325-4567. Across from Teatro Colón on 9 de Julio, modern but cozy, luxury suites available with patio, rooftop outdoor pool, restaurant, lots of tourists.

Gran Hotel Dorá, Maipú 963. Tel/fax: 312-7391. Where Argentine author Borges took his afternoon tea, around the corner from Plaza San Martín, antique but tasteful, good service.

Hotel Bisonte/Hotel Bisonte Palace, Paraguay 1207. Tel: 816-3941, fax: 816-5775. M.T. Alvear 902. Tel: 328-4751; fax: 328-6476. Two branches with same ownership, highly recommended, pleasant, modern, conference rooms available, bar.

Hotel Continental, Diagonal R. Sáenz Peña 725. Tel: 326-1700, fax: 322-1421. Managed by the Marriot chain, located between Plaza de Mayo and the Obelisco, classic French-style building, café 24 hours.

Hotel Crillon, Santa Fé 796. Tel: 312-8181, fax: 312-9955. French-style antique building refurbished, very modern inside, many services for the business traveler, 24 hour room service, located on Plaza San Martín.

Hotel Park Plaza, Parera 183. Tel: 815-5028, fax: 815-4522. On a quiet side street in the Recoleta, elegant classic European style, 8 floors – each one dedicated to a famous painter.

Hotel Plaza Francia, E. Schiaffino 2189. Tel/fax: 804-9631. Classic brick-colored building, located in the Recoleta near the Fine Arts Museum, quiet, good breakfast served in rooms, highly recommended.

Hotel Recoleta Plaza, Posadas 1557. Tel: 804-3471, fax: 804-3476. Attractive small French-style hotel in Recoleta, restaurant and room service.

Lafayette Hotel, Reconquista 546. Tel/fax: 393-9081. Conveniently located in microcentro, recently remodeled with English-style decor, restaurant and room service.

Lancaster Hotel, Avenida Córdoba. Tel/fax: 311-3021. Very European, fancy lobby, pretty sunlit rooms, nice bar/tearoom.

Hotels $100 and under

Gran Hotel Hispano, Avenida de Mayo 861. Tel: 345-2020. One block from Plaza de Mayo and close to San Telmo, renovated antique building, popular with European budget travelers.

Gran Hotel Orly, Paraguay 474. Tel/fax: 312-5344. Basic, inexpensive accommodations, good location.

Hotel Diplomat, San Martín 918. Tel: 312-6124, fax: 311-2708. Around the corner from the Plaza Hotel and Plaza San Martín, 1970s-style decor, good service.

Hotel Embajador, Carlos Pellegrini 1185. Tel/fax: 326-5306. Good location at 9 de Julio and Santa Fe, modern, large rooms, cafe.

Hotel Impala, Libertad 1215. Tel/fax: 812-5696. Two blocks from shopping street Santa Fe and very near to Recoleta, modern, basic accommodation, café.

Hotel Phoenix, San Martín 780. Tel: 312-4323, fax: 311-2845. Best of the group with 4 star service, old world charm, beautiful turn of the century building with antique iron elevator and glass cupolas, next door to Galerías Pacífico.

Hotel Promenade, M.T. Alvear 444. Tel: 312-5681, fax: 311-5761. Clean, 70s modernish decor, basic accommodations, dark rooms.

Hotel San Antonio, Paraguay 372. Tel: 312-5381. Charming, small, with air of old-fashioned European pension, good value.

Hotel Waldorf, Paraguay 450. Tel:

12-2071; fax: 312-2079. Close to Iorida and Santa Fe shopping streets, modern, comfortable, bar, larger rooms and suites.

Aparthotels and Suites

For longer visits, a good alternative is an aparthotel or suite hotel which give you the services of a hotel with the convenience of a furnished apartment, including a kitchenette. Per night prices range from $100 for a studio to $333 for a 3-room apartment. Corporate and longer-stay discounts are offered.

Feir's Park All-Suites Hotel, Esmeralda 1366. Tel: 327-1900; fax: 327-1935. One block from Libertador in elegant neighborhood, room service, pool, healthclub, business center, option of connecting suites.

Plaza San Martín Suites, Suipacha 1092. Tel: 328-4740, fax: 328-9385. Between Plaza San Martín and 9 de Julio, newly built and modern, health club, room service.

Suipacha y Arroyo Apart Hotel, Suipacha 1359. Tel: 325-8200; fax: 325-1886. In upscale neighborhood near Libertador and 9 de Julio, good service, healthclub and outdoor pool, patio and garden, parking garage.

Torre Cristóforo Colombo Suites, Oro 2747. Tel: 777-9622; fax: 775-9911. In Palermo two blocks from US embassy, tall modern tower, excellent service, rooftop bar, restaurant, healthclub, outdoor pool.

Ulises Recoleta, Ayacucho 2016. Tel: 304-4571, fax: 806-0838. Across from the Alvear Palace in the Recoleta, European style, classic building with only 25 apartments, antique furnishings, warm atmosphere.

In the Sierra of Córdoba

Gran Hotel La Cumbre, La Cumbre, Tel: (0548) 51469. Traditional family hotel.

El Ciervo de Oro, Hipólito Yrigoyen 995, Tel/Fax: (0547) 22498. A lovely small lodge-type hotel right on the lake. Great food.

Ushuaia

Cabo de Hornos, San Martín y Rosas, Tel: (0901) 22313. Pleasant.

Del Glaciar, Camino Glaciar Martial, Tel: (0901) 30636, Fax: 30638. New 4 Star hotel above the city.

Hostería Mustapic, Piedrabuena 230,

Tel: (0901) 21718. One of the few inexpensive hotels.

Calafate (Lago Argentina)

Posada Los Alamos, Moyano y Bustillo, Tel: (0902) 91144, Fax: 91186. Very comfortable, good cuisine.

La Loma, B. Roca/15 de Febrero, Tel: (0902) 91016. Inexpensive and cosy.

Mar Del Plata

Mar Del Plata, Gran Hotel Provincial. Tel: (023) 95949, Fax: 915894. Mar del Plata. The oldest and most traditional of hotels, still considered a grand hotel. Large number of rooms are available and a very good restaurant.

San Miguel de Tucumán

Caesar Park, Posadas 1232, Tel: (01) 814 5150, Fax: 8145148. First class hotel, furniture in country house style.

Claridge, Tucumán 535, Tel: (01) 314 7700, Fax 3148022, centrally located, classical palace with comfort and style. Well known for its excellent restaurant.

Críllon, Santa Fe 796, Tel: (01) 312 8181, Fax: 312 9955. Spotless city hotel, higher price range.

Deauville, Talcahuano 1253, Tel/Fax: (01) 812 1560. Inexpensive, close to the Recoleta entertainment district.

Hotel de las Américas, Libertad 1020, Tel: (01) 393 3432, Fax: 393 0418. Clean, good location, mid price range.

El Lapacho, Reservations through Swiss Hotel Metropol. Situated 86 km from Miguel de Tucumán.

Libertador Kempinski, Córdoba 680, Tel: (01) 322 2095, Fax: 322 9703. Newly renovated, fitness club in the Penthouse.

Park Hyatt, Posadas 1088, Tel: (01) 326 1234, Fax: 326 3032, deluxe, converted city villa.

Sheraton Hotel & Towers, San Martin 1225-1275, Tel: (01) 318 9000, Fax 318 9346. Well regarded for years, high-rise building commanding magnificent view of the harbor and Rio de la Plata from the roof of the top bar. A favourite of travelling business people.

Swiss Hotel Metropol, 24 de Septiembre 524, Tel: (081) 311180, Fax: (081) 310379.

Uruguay, Tacuari 83, Tel: 334 2788. Simple, inexpensive and clean.

Youth hostel (Albergue Juvenil), Brasil

675, Tel: (01) 362 9133. Old building in San Telmo, friendly atmosphere, no age limit.

For hotels in the Provinces, go to the addresses already listed for the Province Houses where representatives can give you a complete listing of hotels, motels, campsites and student quarters, including prices and availability. Some will make a reservation, but usually you'll have to do this yourself or contact a travel agency. Prices vary from season to season, so it's best to check upon arrival, unless you come at peak season, when reservations are recommended. Summer vacations start about December 15th and end as late as March 15th. Winter vacations start about July 5th and end mid August. Schools have two weeks' winter break, but the Provinces have different schedules in order to prevent overcrowding in the ski resorts.

Outside Buenos Aires

Puerto Iguazú

Internacional Iguazú, reservations Tel: (01) 311 4259, Fax: 312 0488. 5-star complex with casino, pool and golf course.

Las Orquídeas, Ruta 12, at km 5, Tel: (0757) 20 472. Comfortable and inexpensive, outside the city in a great location.

Portezuelo, Avenida del Turista 1, Tel: (087) 310 05, Fax: 310 510. Good service.

Provincial, Caseros 786, Tel: (087) 218 400, Fax: 218 993. Huge rooms, pool, completely renovated in 1991.

Hotel Salta, Buenos Aires 1, Tel: (087) 211 011, Fax: 310740. Best hotel in town. In the main square.

Jujuy

Hotel Termas de Reyes, Tel: 0382; telex: 66130 NASAT. Located about 12 miles (19 km) from the city, offers thermal baths in all rooms, good facilities and heated pool.

Mendoza

Hotel Aconcagua, San Lorenzo St 545, Tel: (061) 243321. A few blocks from the main shopping area, very modern architecture, pool and air-conditioned rooms.

Plaza Hotel, Chile 1124. Tel: (061) 23-3000. A more traditional hotel, located in front of a beautiful plaza, with lovely antique furnishings.

Hostería Puente del Inca, Ruta 7, Las Heras, Tel: (061) 380 480, Fax: 380477. Secluded inn 2718 metres (8,918 ft) above sea level. Aconcagua massif in sight.

Bariloche

Edelweiss Hotel, Av. San Martín 232, Tel/Fax: (0944) 261 65. A large hotel with sauna, fitness rooms and a good restaurant.

Llao Llao Resort Hotel, Reservations Tel/Fax : (01) 311 3432/33. Reopened in 1993. One of the best located hotels in Argentina, approximately 18 miles out of town on the shores of Lago Nahuel Huapí.

Eating Out

What to Eat

A person could eat out every day of year and still not savor the cuisine of all the restaurants of Buenos Aires. Dining out here is a delightful experience. Food, wine and service are excellent, for the most part. A complete listing of all restaurants in the city would be impossible. A recommended gourmet guide is the *Guide to Good Eating in Buenos Aires*, published by the English-language *Buenos Aires Herald*.

Argentina is well known for its beef, and most tourists will prefer this to other types of food (*see page 154*). The typical meal will be *empanadas* (meat pastries, although the filling will vary according to the region), *chorizos* or *morcillas* (pork, blood sausages), an assortment of *achuras* (sweetbreads) of course, this is only the appetizer. For the main course, a good *bife de chorizo*, or *tira de asado*, or *lomo* are the most popular choices, accompanied by various types of salads. To finish off, one might choose a nice flan (custard), topped with *dulce de leche* and some whipped cream. Don't think of calories, just enjoy.

Buenos Aires

Dining out is a favorite pastime of porteños, but the menu is not the only attraction. Restaurants are a place to socialize, to see and be seen, and share a bottle of wine until the wee hours of the morning. Nevertheless, porteños take eating seriously. A list of recommended eateries follows, but don't be afraid to try any clean, well-lit place that catches your fancy. There are hundreds of good restaurants in the city, where the food is almost universally fresh and well-prepared in a simple Southern European style.

Restaurants in Buenos Aires open for lunch at noon, and for dinner around 8pm. But no one dines out in the evening before 9pm, with restaurants really coming alive between 10pm and 11pm. Weekends, restaurants stay busy much after midnight. Price categories are for two people, with house wine:

Inexpensive: $40 or less
Moderate: $40 - $80
Expensive: $80 or more.

Regional Argentine

El Ceíbal, Güemes 3402. Tel: 823-5807; Cabildo 1421, Tel: 3402. Great place to try specialties from Northern Argentina, including locro (corn chowder), humitas (tamales) and empanadas. Inexpensive.

Italian and Mediterranean

Bice, Davila 192. Tel: 315-6216. The original is in Milan, with ten more around the world, the BA version in Puerto Madero, a very posh Northern Italian eatery, with modern twists on traditional pasta. Moderate.

Fellini, Paraná 1209. Tel: 811-2222. Trendy and lively restaurant overlooking beautiful plaza, interesting fresh and imported Italian pastas, gourmet pizzas, and specialty salads. Moderate.

Filo, San Martín 975. Tel: 311-0312. Eclectic, arty decor, bar in front and upbeat music, serves unusual pizzas, fresh pastas and salads. Inexpensive.

Piola, Libertad 1078. Tel: 1078. Just off Santa Fe, similar in style, atmosphere, and menu to Filo, but smaller and cozier. Inexpensive.

Restaurant Como, Juncal 2019. Tel: 806-9664. Stylish and colorful Barrio Norte favorite, mediterranean menu

including innovative chicken and fish and grilled beef. Moderate.

Teatriz, Riobamba 1220. Tel: 81 1915. Casual, warm atmosphere with a touch of elegance, also in Barri Norte, mediterrean menu with interesing pasta, chicken and fish, and wonderful desserts. Moderate.

International and French

Au Bec Fin, Vicente Lopez 1825. Te 801-6894. Classic French cooking in splendid restored mansion, a Buenos Aires institution, dinner onl Reservations. Expensive.

Catalinas, Reconquista 875. Tel: 313 0182. Country French decor an innovative menu (rabbit with figs, fis with hazelnuts, grilled baby eels) including lots of seafood choices Reservations. Expensive.

Cholila, Davila 102. Tel: 315-6200 New restaurant run by Argentina's hot test chef, Frances Mallman, in BAs most happening spot, Puerto Madero A truly international and innovative menu, including wonderful dishes from all over the world but distinctl Argentine. Great portside patio Moderate.

El Gato Dumas, Junin 1745. Tel: 804 5828. Offerings from the idiosyncrati master chef Gato Dumas include "ec static double chicken breasts" and "perfumes of crayfish and chicken." Reservations. Expensive.

Le Trianon, Avenida Del Libertado 1902. Tel: 806-6058. A charming intimate restaurant located in the pal ace garden of the Ornamental Art Mu seum, featuring a truly gourmet French menu and a simple, elegant atmos phere. Reservations. Expensive.

Lola, Ortíz 1805. Tel: 802-3023. Nouvelle and original cuisine, including rabbit, lamb, and duck dishes, in at tractive atmosphere. Reservations Expensive.

Mora X, Vicente Lopez 2152. Tel: 803 0261. Menu created by the same culinary director of Au Bec Fin, with a loft/gallery atmosphere heightened by mural size paintings and tall ceilings, features informal French cooking and grilled meats. Moderate.

International Cuisine

Broccolino, Esmeralda 776, Tel: 322 7652. Very popular trattoria.
El Aljibe (Hotel Sheraton), San Martín 1225, Tel: 311 6311. French haute

...isine. An exciting menu. Expensive.

Pulpo, Tucumán 400, Tel: 311 282. Popular fish restaurant in the ...nter.

...ato Dumas, Junín 1745, Tel: 806 ...301. Gourmet meeting-point in the ...ecoleta area.

...ver Green, vegetarian restaurant ...hain with inexpensive lunch buffets, ...cations include Tucumán 666 and ...armiento 1728.

...os Inmortales, Av. Corrientes 1369, ...el: 373 5303 (branches in Lavalle ...44 and Junín 1727). The best pizza ...Buenos Aires.

Parillas (Steakhouses)

...hiquilín, Montevideo 321, Tel: 373 163. Italian Pasta and Argentinean ...sado.

Mirasol, Davila 202. Tel: 315-6277. ...pscale parrilla in posh Puerto ...ladero, elegant atmosphere, reserva...ons. Expensive.

...l Palacio de la Papa Frita, Lavalle ...35. Inexpensive and popular.

...a Cátedra, Cerviño 4699. Tel: 777-...601. In the heart of the pleasant ...alermo district, nice atmosphere, ...rilled beef but also interesting inter...ational cuisine and fresh salads. ...Moderate.

...a Chacra, Avenida Córdoba, Tel: 322 409. Huge portions.

...a Estancia, Lavalle 941, Tel: 326 ...330. Classic Asado-Restaurant in the ...eart of the city.

...a Veda, Florida 1. Tel: 331-6442. ...asement floor, dark wood panelling, ...xcellent steak poivre, tango dinner ...how most evenings. Reservations. ...xpensive.

...os Años Locos, Av. Costanera R. ...Dbligado. Tel: 783-5126. The most ...opular of the riverfront parrillas. Mod...erate.

...Río Alba, Cerviño 4499. Tel: 773-...5748. Also in Palermo, popular restau...ant famous for brochettes and enor...mous filet mignon steaks. Moderate.

There are lots of trendy steak res...aurants along Avenida Costanera (at ...the Rio de la Plata), for example Los ...Años or El Rancho Inn.

Pizza

...Los Inmortales, Corrientes 1369, ...Lavalle 746, Callao 1165. Small chain ...of legendary BA pizzerias where the ...decor is dedicated to the life and times ...of tango stars and the pizza is consist-

ently good, try the classic napolitana, covered with tomatoes and garlic. Inexpensive.

Pizzería Guerrín, Corrientes 1372. Typical porteña pizzeria in the heart of the Corrientes theater district, with a mind-boggling selection of toppings. Inexpensive.

El Cuartito, Talcahuano and Paraguay. The closest BA comes to a sports bar, with clippings and photos covering the walls, soccer on the television, delicious pizzas and cold beer. Inexpensive.

Popular Eateries

Barbaro, Tres Sargentos 415. Tel: 311-6856. Literally a BA landmark, a charming, old world version of the hole-in-the-wall bar, a great place for a simple midday meal or for music, beer and bar food in the evening. Inexpensive.

Chiquilín, Sarmiento 1599. Tel: 373-5163. One block from Corrientes, with the quintessential BA-restaurant atmosphere, serving very reasonable pasta and beef specialties. Fills up quickly on weekends. Inexpensive.

El Trapiche, Paraguay 5099. Tel: 772-7343. Typical neighborhood restaurant in Palermo, with cured hams, tins of olive oil and bottles of wine decking the walls and ceiling. Great grilled beef, homemade pastas and seafood. Inexpensive.

La Casa de Esteban de Luca, Defensa and Carlos Calvo. In the heart of San Telmo, restored colonial-era home of the Argentine "poet of the revolution", popular Sunday lunch after the San Telmo fair. Inexpensive.

Pippo, Montevideo 345. No frills but great atmosphere and unbeatable prices. Try a bife de chorizo (T-bone steak), or a bowl of vermicelli mixto (pasta noodles with pesto and bolognaise sauce), washed down with the house red and seltzer. Inexpensive.

Restaurant Dora, L.N. Alem 1016. Tel: 311-2891. An upscale version of a popular eatery with rave reviews on the enormous steaks and simple seafood dishes, a downtown "don't miss". Moderate.

Rodi Bar, Vicente Lopez 1900. Tel: 801-5230. Cozy, neighborhood restaurant nestled amongst the famous gourmets of the Recoleta, featuring simple homemade food. Inexpensive.

Spanish

El Globo, H. Yrigoyen 1199. Tel: 381-3926. One block from Avenida de Mayo, near Congreso, try their paella or puchero (seafood stew). Moderate.

Pedemonte, Avenida de Mayo 676. Tel: 331-7179. A favorite with BA politicians, turn-of-the-century decor, featuring Spanish cuisine, pastas and grilled beef. Reservations. Expensive.

Plaza Mayor, Venezuela 1389. Tel: 383-0788. Spanish seafood dishes are the house specialty, situated amongst the mini independent-theater district, popular with younger crowd and open latenite. Moderate.

Tasca Tancat, Paraguay 645. Tel: 312-5442. Squeeze in at the long, antique wooden bar and enjoy Spanish style squid, delicious potato omelettes, grilled mushrooms, and creamy custard for dessert, all to soft jazz and warm lights. Closed weekends. Inexpensive.

Vegetarian

Yin Yang, Paraguay 858. Tel: 311-7798; Echeverría 2444. Tel: 788-4368. A delicious respite from Argentine beef, featuring fresh salads, soups, homemade wheat bread, brown rice and stir-fried veggies, and various other meatless treats. Inexpensive.

Confiterías (Cafés)

Café La Paz, Corrientes 1599, Tel: 465542. Popular with students and intellectuals, open until late.

Confitería del Molino, Rivadavia 1801.

Confitería Ideal, Suipacha 384.

El Rosedal, Caseros 2822.

Florida Garden, Florida and Paraguay.

Ideal, Suipacha 384, Tel: 3260521. Smart stylish meeting point for the elderly.

La Biela, Avenida Quintana 600, Tel: 804 0449. At the heart of the Recoleta scene, very well-known.

La Giralda, 1449 Corrientes.

Las Violetas, Rivadavia 1801.

Richmond, Florida 468.

St James, Córdoba and Maip.

Steinhauser Cafe, Avenida Cabildo 1924.

Tortoni, Avenida de Mayo 829, Tel: 342 4328. 140 years old, billiards, live jazz, poetry readings, decaying grandeur.

Attractions

The Argentine people are extremely culture orientated. European trends are watched carefully, but Argentines maintain their own traditions. Thus, a wide range of activities are available. Museums, galleries, theaters, bookstores and several libraries are among the places to be visited. Be sure not to miss any of the ones listed below while in Buenos Aires.

Museums

Museo Nacional De Arte Decorativo, Avenida del Libertador 1902, Tel: 801 5988. Ornamental art paintings, earthenware and sculptures from the 15th century to the present day, displayed in a beautiful baroque-style setting. Open Wednesday–Monday 3–7pm.

Museo De Bellas Artes, Avenida del Libertador 1473, Tel: 803 8817. Paintings from different periods but mainly 19th century. Many Argentine painters as well as famous works by Van Gogh, Picasso, Manet, Rodin, Renoir etc. Open Tuesday–Sunday 9am–12.45pm and 3–6.45pm.

Museo De Motivos Populares Argentinos José Hernández, Avenida Libertador 2373, Tel: 8027294. Houses the most complete collection of folkloric art in the country. Many gaucho artifacts, earthenware, silverware and musical instruments. Open Monday–Friday 8am–7pm, weekend 3–7pm.

Museo Municipal De Arte Moderno, San Juan 350 and Avenida Corrientes 1530, 9th floor, Tel: 469426. Wonderful collection of works by Matisse, Utrillo, Dali, Picasso etc. Open Monday–Friday 10am-8pm, weekend 12–8pm.

Museo De La Ciudad, Alsina 412, Tel: 331 9855. A museum about the city's history. Worth visiting. Open Monday–Friday 11am–7pm, Sunday 3-7pm.

Art Galleries

Art is greatly appreciated in this country. Many lovely art galleries can be found as you walk around the city. Three well known galleries are: **Galeria Ruth Benzacar**, Florida 1000. **Galeria Praxis**, Arenales 1311. **Galeria Palatina**, Arroyo 821. But, if you have the time to browse, take the side streets and you might run into some exquisite old houses containing interesting exhibits.

Theaters

Teatro Colón, tickets available from the box office located on Libertad Street 621. Tel: 382-0554. Information by phone: 374-8611. Most of the renowned performers of the world are well acquainted with this magnificent theater. The building is Italian Renaissance style with French and Greek influence. It holds 3,500 people, with about 1,000 standing. The acoustics are considered to be nearly perfect. Opera is one of the favorite programs for the season. In 1987, Luciano Pavarotti performed *La Boheme* here and tickets were sold out well in advance. Ballets are another favorite, performed by greats such as Nureyev, Godunov and the Bolshoi Ballet. The local company is very good and many of its members go on to become international figures. The Colon also has a magnificent museum, where all of the theater's history and its mementos are stored. It is an enlightening experience to have a guided visit of the theater and the museum. Call 382-6632 to make an appointment.

San Martín Theatre, offers a variety of plays and musicals. Check the local paper for performances.

The theater season in Buenos Aires usually opens in March, with a variety of plays. The Argentines like to go to see a good play and are highly critical. There is always something worthwhile seeing. Check the local paper or with the hotel for the current and best ones available. Recitals and concerts are promoted by the Secretary of Culture in an effort to bring culture to the people. The public responds enthusiastically by attending all events. Open-air concerts are very popular on hot summer evenings and are held in any one of the numerous parks in the city.

Movies

Going to the movies is a popular for of entertainment. Recent national ar international films are shown, som times in the original version. Listing appear in any of the local papers.

Nightlife

The nightlife in Buenos Aires is quite bit more active than in most major ci ies of the world. People walk carefre in the late hours of the night. Crim although rising, is still not a major co cern. The center part of town, on Cal Florida and Lavalle, at midnight mig appear to most as midday.

Movies are open past 11pm an there are some restaurants in the ci that never close.

Discos, nightclubs, cabarets an bars can be found in most of the cit Hear the latest hits from around th world and dance into the morning a "Cemento," located on Estado Unidos 700, or for a more forma crowd, dance at "Le Club," o Quintana 111, or at "Hippopotamus," Junin 1787.

Other possibilities include:
Bailanta Terremondo, Thames 2425
Contramano, Rodriguez Pena 1082.
Mau Mau, Arroyo 866.
Morocco, Hipólito Yrigoyem 851.
New York City, Av. Alvarez Thomas 1391.
Pacha, Costamesa Norte.
Snob, Ayachcho 2038.

For the very young crowd, there are new discos opening up every day. Ice skating has become the latest form o entertainment for young and old alike. You'll be able to find ice skating rinks all over Buenos Aires and in most of the major cities of the provinces.

The Argentines, as a whole, enjoy staying up late. Restaurants in Buenos Aires open up as early as 8pm, but in the provinces many don't open until 9pm The big cities of the interior, like Cordoba, Mendoza, Bariloche, Salta, etc., that attract many tourists, also have a lively nightlife. The theater shows are not as varied as in Buenos Aires, but a little bit of everything is available. A good tango show will be found almost everywhere, but the best shows are in Buenos Aires.

Tango Shows

Good tango shows are everywhere but the best are in Buenos Aires. Reservations are highly recommended.

Bar Sur, Estados Chuidos, Tel: 362 6086

Casa Rosada, Chile 318, Tel 361 8222

El Viejo Almacén, Av. Independencia/corner Balcarce, Tel: 362 3602

Cano 14, Talcahuano 975, Tel: 393 4626

El Castillo, Pedro de Mendoza 1455, Tel: 28 52 70

Michelangelo, Balcarce 433, Tel: 331 5392.

There are typical local cafés (confiterias), serving wonderful expresso, tea, soft drinks and alcoholic drinks throughout Argentina. A few, especially in Buenos Aires, are highly recommended. See *Eating Out* page 315 for other traditional places.

Festivals

A number of colorful annual festivals take place around Argentina.

Mendoza

Festival de la Vendimia. The grape harvest festival is held here, in the center of Argentina's wine country, every March. Three days of festivities culminate with an extravaganza of lights, music and dancing, held in an amphitheater set in the Andean foothills.

Córdoba

This central town has several festivals each year. The most important is the Cosquin, a celebration of international folkloric music and dancing. Check with a travel agent for the dates.

Villa General Belgrano

This small village near Córdoba hosts at least two festivals a year: the Alpine Chocolate Festival in winter, and an Oktoberfest (Fiesta de la Cerveza).

San Antonio De Areco

In November this town, 70 miles (115 km) from Buenos Aires, celebrates Tradition Week, when gauchos show off their skills in rodeo events. The town also has a gaucho museum (R. Guiraldes) and, on weekends, the local artisans sell their wares around the town plaza.

Shopping

A few words of advice before mentioning some fine places to go shopping; there are two main streets for good shopping. The most known and the most "touristy" is Florida. Anything the average tourist might want to buy can be found here. The next main street is Avenida Santa Fe. Many shopping galleries are located on either side of the avenue, and once again nice things are available. The exclusive part of town, with the most expensive boutiques, is located in the Recoleta area, along Ave. Alvear, Quintana, Ayacucho and some little side streets. The antique stores in this area are exquisite – and so are the prices! But, more on antiques a little later on.

The fine jewelry stores are located at the beginning Florida and on Ave. Alvear. Also, Stern is located in the lobby of the Sheraton Hotel.

The garment district is known as Once, and is accessible by taxi.

Buenos Aires also has quite a number of factory outlets, where good quality is available, there is a larger selection and best of all – the price is right. People who live here are well acquainted with these and will shop here rather than in stores. The only inconvenience is that they're usually located far from downtown.

Antiques

The best known area of Buenos Aires for antiques is San Telmo. It's one of the most historic barrios (neighborhoods) of Buenos Aires. Every Sunday the San Telmo Fair takes place. The plaza is surrounded by stalls which sell quite an array of objects, from new to old, ordinary to odd, and that can be very cheap or outrageously expensive. Only the trained eye can find the bargains. The rest just think they have found a unique piece, when, in fact, they have only purchased a copy. So, beware! Around the plaza, there are many reputable antique stores. Prices are high, but some beautiful pieces can still be found.

Auction houses are very popular and good buys can be obtained. Some of these are:

Roldán y Cia, Rodriguez Peña 1673. Tel: 30-3733.

Naon y Cia, Guido 1785. Tel: 41-1685.

Banco de la Ciudad, Esmeralda 660. Tel: 392-6684.

Small antique shops can be found throughout the city. The prices are negotiable. Along Rivadavia avenue, around the 4000 block, quite a number of these shops are located. As these stores are not known to many, the prices and the attention are good. Also, along Libertador Avenue, towards Martinez and the San Isidro area, there are a number of shops with some very worthwhile pieces. It just takes time and a little knowledge on the subject.

La Baulera, located on Av. Monroe 2753, has quite a different assortment of collectibles, and the owners will try to help find that unique piece. Other listings of shops can be obtained either from your hotel or from your copy of the *Buenos Aires Herald*.

Artisan Fairs take place on the weekends in different parts of the city. Some of these are:

Plaza Francia – near the Recoleta area on Sunday.

Plaza Manuel Belgrano – Juramento 2200 every Sunday.

Plaza Mitre – San Isidro on Sunday.

Tigre – Puerto de Los Frutos every Saturday and Sunday.

Furriers

Pieles Chic (5th generation furrier, excellent furs and very competitive prices).

Hipolito Yrigoyen, 1428-Vicente Lopez. Tel: 795-3836/8836.

Pieles Wendall (Ted Lapidus Representative), Av. Córdoba 2762. Tel: 86-7220.

Dennis Furs (YSL Representative), M.T. de Alvear 628. Tel: 312-7411.

Jewellers

Koltai Joyeria (Antique quality jewelry), Esmeralda 616. Tel: 392-4052/5716.

Ricciardi, Florida 1001. Tel: 312-3082.

Antoniazzi-Chiappe, Av. Alvear 1895. Tel: 41-6137.

Stern Jewellers, Sheraton Hotel.

Lovasi Joyeria, Rodriguez Pena 419. Tel: 46-5131.

Leather Goods

Coalpe (handbags), Mexico 3325. Tel: 97-4620.

Colicuer (handbags), Tte. Gral. Perón 1615, lst floor. Tel: 35-7463.

Maximilian Klein (handbags), Humberto Primo 3435. Tel: 93-0511.
Viel (handbags and shoes), Viel 1550. Tel: 922-2359.
La Mia Scarpa (custom made shoes), Thames 1617. Tel: 72-6702.
Belt Factory, Fco. Acuña de Figueroa 454. Tel: 87-3172.
Kerquelen (custom made and quick service), Santander 747. Tel: 922-2801.
Le Fauve (latest leather fashions [jackets, skirts, dress pants] & competitive prices with personalized attention), Sarandi 1226. Tel: 27-7326. Arenales 1315. Tel: 44-8844.
Casa Vuriloche, Uruquay 318. Tel: 40-9673.

Regional Handicrafts
Artesanías Argentina, Montevideo 1386,
Tuyunti, Florida 971, Tel: 542 8651
Artisan Fairs take place at the weekends in different parts of the city. Some of these are:
Plaza Francia - near to the Recoleta area on Sunday
Plaza Manuel Belgrano - Juramento 2200 on Sunday
Plaza Mitre - San Isidro on Sunday
Tigre - Puerto de los Frutos every Saturday and Sunday

Sweaters
YSL, Catilan, Obligado 4422 (at the 4400 block of Cabildo). Tel: 70-3991.

Sport & Leisure

Outdoor Pursuits

A complete description of sports activities, both for spectators and participants, can be found in the Sports Chapter of this book. A few recommendations are listed below:

Duck Hunting
Duck and partridge hunting, on a very large *estancia* nestled in the marshlands of Santo Fe Province, about 800 km from Buenos Aires. Very comfortable accommodations for groups of up to 6. Contact: Condor Special Safaris, Adriana Maguirre, Ave, Las Heras 3790, 5th floor, Buenos Aires, 1425 Argentina, tel: (54) (1) 801-4742, or Salty Salztman, P.O. Box 648, Manchester, Vermont 05254, USA., tel: (802) 362-1876, telex: 495-0637.

Tren a las Nubes: The "Train to the Clouds" is an all-day excursion from the N.W. town of Salta. It gets its name from the dizzying heights reached at the top stretch of the journey. The train runs on Saturday, October–April. The scenery is spectacular. Information can be obtained in Salta, or from the central Ferrocarriles office in Buenos Aires.

Estancia Getaway
Visitors to Buenos Aires have the chance to get away from the buzz of the city, in the small town of San Antonio de Areco, just 71 miles (115 km) away. In this peaceful location, with beautiful scenery, the Aldao family has converted the Estancia La Bamba into a country inn, with all the facilities to make a stay both comfortable and memorable. For more information, contact 392-0394/9707 or a travel agency in Buenos Aires.

FALABELLA HORSES
A visit to the Estancia El Peludo will provide an interesting side trip from Buenos Aires. Located 40 miles (65 km) from town, this ranch raises the unique and famous miniature Falabell Horses (named for their breeder). Some of these horses are owned by such international figures as the Kennedy family, the Carters, and Jua Carlos of Spain. Those interested i visiting the estancia, and perhaps buy ing a horse, can contact Mrs Falabell at 44-5050/1404.

Fly Fishing
Spend a secluded vacation fishing fo trout in the clear lakes and streams c the Andes. Accommodations, equip ment and guides provided. Contact Caleufu River SRL, M. Moreno 1185 (8370) San Martín de Los Andes Neuquen, Argentina, tel: (0944) 7199 telex: COSMA CALEUFU or for similar fa cilities: Cosmopolitan Travel, L. Alem 986, 7th floor, Buenos Aires 100l, A gentina, tel: 311-7880/6695/2478, 6684, telex: 9199 CASSA AR.

OTHER FISHING
Chascomus is a small city beside a lake, about 78 miles (125 km) south of Buenos Aires. It is accessible by ca or train. The lake has brackish wate fishing, and the main catches are pejerrey (a type of catfish) and a ver aggressive fish called the tararira Equipment is available for rent at the local fishing club.

Argentina is famous for its fishing and the trout fishing here is consid ered to be among the best in the world. One can fish along the coast, ir the streams up in the Andes, or in the countless lakes and rivers in between. Ask a travel agent for more details, and reservations.

Horse Racing
The two main tracks in Buenos Aires are the Jockey Club Track, in San Isidro, and the Palermo Track, in Palermo. Races run about four times a week. Smaller tracks are located in most of the major Argentine cities.

Horseback Trekking
Spend from half a day to a week riding under the open skies of the Andean foothills, near the town of Bariloche. Similar to dude ranching operations in the US, but more rugged, with camping beneath the stars. Contact: Carol Jones, Estancia Nahuel Huapi, (8401) Nahuel Huapi, Neuquen, Argentina, or

Ians Schulz, Polvani Tours, Quaglia
68, (8400) Bariloche, Argentina, tel:
0944) 23286, telex: 80772 POLVA AR.

Pato

This uniquely Argentine sport is some-
mes played for public audiences on
ne *estancias* around Buenos Aires.
ontact a travel agent for information.

Polo

the best place to see polo in Buenos
ires is at the centrally located
alermo field. The most important
hampionship is usually held here in
November. Tickets can be purchased
t the box office.

Skiing

he main ski resorts in Argentina are:
he Cerro Catedral Complex, located
ear Bariloche. Valle de las Leñas, in
ne south of Mendoza Province. Los
enitentes, a small resort near the
own of Mendoza.

There are also a number of small
acilities located throughout the south-
rn provinces, including one in Tierra
lel Fuego, and another near Esquel.
Contact a travel agent for details and
eservations. Package tours are avail-
ble, and tend to keep down the costs
f a ski vacation.

Trekking

rekking in the Andes, including an
ight day trip, through spectacular scen-
ry, to the foot of Aconcaqua. Contact:
ernando Grajales, Optar Tours,
Mendoza, Hosteria Puente del Inca,
el: 061 380-480, Prov. Mendoza, Ar-
entina.

he traditional Atlantic seaside resorts
lo not fit the European idea of a
estful beach holiday. Pinamar, Villa
Gesell and Mar de la Plata are be-
ieged by millions of Porteños during
he hot summer months and the huge
hotel complexes are completely
ooked. It is party time everywhere
nd discos and bars are packed until
sunrise. In wintertime, however, these
holiday resorts are transformed into
host towns. Quiet, undeveloped
beaches are only to be found further
south near Bahía Blanca.

Further Reading

General

The Whispering Land; The Drunken
Forest by Gerald Durrell.
Los Parques Nacionales de la Ar-
gentina by F. Erize. Buenos Aires:
Incafo, 1981.

History

The Afro-Argentines of Buenos
Aires: 1800-1900 by George Reid An-
drews. Madison: Univ. of Wisconsin
Press, 1980.
The Voyage of the Beagle by Charles
Darwin. USA: Bantam Books, 1972.
The Battle for the Falklands by Max
Hastings and Simon Jenkins. New
York: W.W. Norton and Co., 1983.
Twenty-Four Years in the Argentine
Republic by Anthony King. Reprint of
1846 edition.
Two Thousand Miles' Ride Through
the Argentine Provinces by William
Mac Cann. Reprint of 1853 edition.
Perón: A Biography by Joseph Page.
New York: Random House, 1983.
The Little School: Tales of Disap-
pearance and Survival in Argentina by
Alicia Partnoy. New York: Cleis Press,
1986.
The Speeches of Juan Domingo
Perón by Juan Perón. Gordon Press.
Argentina: A City and a Nation by
James R Scobie. New York: Oxford
Univ. Press, 1964. The best general in-
troduction to the country's history and
geography.
Gauchos and the Vanishing Frontier
by Richard W. Slatta. Lincoln: Univ. of
Nebraska Press, 1983.
Tschiffely's Ride by A. A. Tschiffely.
New York: Simon and Schuster, 1933.

Patagonia & Tierra Del Fuego Travel

The Uttermost Part of the Earth by E.
Lucas Bridges. New York: Dutton, 1949.
In Patagonia by Bruce Chatwin. New
York: Summit Books, 1977
A Description of Patagonia and the
Adjoining Parts of South America by P.T.
Falkner. Reprint of 1935 edition.
Tierra del Fuego by R. Natalie P.

Goodall. Buenos Aires: Ediciones
Shanamaiim, 1979.
Far Away and Long Ago; Birds of La
Plata; Idle Days in Patagonia by W.H.
Hudson. London: Everyman's Library,
1984.
Tales of the Pampas by W.H. Hud-
son. Berkeley: Creative Arts Book Co.,
1979.
La Colonización Galesa en el Valle
del Chubut by B.M. Ruiz. Buenos Aires:
Ed. Galerna, 1977.
Tierra del Fuego, the fatal
Lodestone by Eric Shipton.

Culture

Currents in the Contemporary Argen-
tine Novel by David Foster. Univ. of
Missouri Press, 1975.
The fictional writings of Jorge Luis
Borges, Ernesto Sábato and Julio
Córtazan all give an insight into Argen-
tina's cosmopolitan culture.
Note: The Suggested Reading list was
compiled by Philip Benson.

Other Insight Guides

Other Insight Guides highlight destina-
tions in this region and titles include
South America, Buenos Aires, Brazil,
Peru, Chile, Ecuador and Venezuela.

Insight Guide: South America unlocks
the secrets of 10 countries on this fascinating continent.
From the rainforests to Rio de Janeiro, Insight Guide: Brazil captures
the natural beauty, the joy and sponta-
neity of this South American Giant.

Adorama 184
Fiora Bemporad 36/37, 38, 41,
42R, 44, 45, 46, 47, 48, 49,
51L&R, 53, 55, 56/57, 58, 60,
61, 62, 63, 65, 76/77, 80, 81,
85L&R, 92L&R, 98, 145, 150,
158, 159, 168, 242, 260
Gabriel Bendersky 266
Biografia de la Pampa 2
Don Boroughs 79, 89, 169, 201,
206, 267, 286/87
Marcelo Brodsky/Focus 9, 162,
183, 261
Roberto Bunge/PW 14/15, 16/
17, 82R, 106, 167, 175, 182,
185L&R, 199, 212, 214, 223,
232, 233, 240, 245, 247, 248,
249
Gustavo Calligaris/Focus 20/21,
186
Marcelo Canevari 99
Carlos Carrio/PW 109,
Maria Cassinelli/Focus 24, 110,
180, 273
Roberto Cinti/PW 12/13, 22, 25,
26, 27, 34, 117, 118, 119, 122,
123, 126, 208, 211, 213, 215,
222, 224, 225, 228, 229, 230,
236/37, 262, 265, 269, 270L&R,
272, 293, 295, 300, 303
Pablo Rafael Cottescu 100, 113,
252/53, 258, 268, 274
Mauricio Dolinsky/Focus 209
Arturo Encinas/Focus 86. 87,
111,
Carlos Fadigati/Focus 84, 101,
231, 238/39
Sindo Fariña/Focus 112, 153
Domingo Galussio 301
Glyn Genin 10/11, 202/03
Eduardo Gil 1, 66/67, 70, 72, 73,
74, 75, 90, 93, 94/94, 132/33,
143, 152R, 160, 161, 173, 244
Carlos Goldin/Focus 271
German Gonzalez/Le Fauve 83

Rae Goodall 288, 291, 297
R.N. Goodall 284/85
Thomas Goodall 290, 292, 302
Rex Gowar 108
Joseph Hooper 254/55
Migone Izquierdo/Focus 176
Marcos Joly/Focus 102, 103, 210,
235
Federico B. Kirbus 121, 234
Eduardo Lerke/Focus 52, 107, 157,
178/79
Hans Lindner/Focus 171
Luis Martin/Focus 33
Julio Menajovsky/Focus 18
Arlette Neyens 31, 82L, 125, 136/
37, 138
Alex Ocampo/PW 39, 68, 69, 104/
05, 144, 146L&R, 147, 151, 152L,
155, 156, 163, 164, 165, 166,
170, 172, 177, 188/89, 190, 193,
195, 196, 197, 198
Carlos A. Passera/Ph 23, 114/15,
116, 120, 127, 275, 276, 277,
298, 304
Javier Pierini/Focus 187
Rudolfo Rüst/Focus 130/31
Alfredo Sanchez/Focus 78, 204/05
Jorge Schulte 28/29, 30, 32, 35,
96, 128/29, 142, 216/17, 218/19,
226, 227
Topham Picturepoint 279, 281
Uniphoto Pictor Cover
David Welna 88

Maps Berndtson & Berndtson

Visual Consultant V. Barl

Index